FORCE-FREE GUNDOG TRAINING: THE FUNDAMENTALS FOR SUCCESS

Try -

JO LAURENS

Leslie McDevitt
OBAT Training

ISBN 978-1-5272-4650-8

Front cover image by Craig Koshyk
Book design by Adam Silverman

Visit dogworks.org.uk and galodygundogs.com

Three Corners Publishing

The main category of the publication — 1. Nonfiction / Sport / Hunting & Shooting — 2. Nonfiction / Animal Science / Behavior — 3. Nonfiction / Pets / Dogs / Training — 4. Nonfiction / Sport/ Hunting & Fishing — 5. Nonfiction / Sports & Recreation / Hunting

For Slate —

who showed me the way

(24.10.04 - 1.6.18)

ACKNOWLEDGEMENTS

I could not have written this book without the help and support of my husband, Adam Silverman. Adam, at times when I 'forgot' about the book for months, you urged me to press on with it. You have given up many hours of your time to help co-ordinate and commission illustrations. When the project seemed doomed, you spent so much time researching publishing. You enabled things to seem manageable when I felt swamped by so many tasks. For all this — thank you so much.

Huge thanks go to Pippa Mattinson, who has supported me in many ways over the years. Thanks, Pippa, for writing the foreword to this book. Thanks also for your own considerable contributions to the field of force-free gundog training. A big thanks especially for your vision, which resulted in the Gundog Club.

A massive thanks to Craig Koshyk for the useful feedback on an early draft and also for the stunning cover photo. Craig, your photos truly capture the beauty and athleticism of working gundogs and the world needs to see more of your work. Thank you for allowing me to use one of your photos on the cover.

A huge thanks to my agent, St John Donald, for going above and beyond.

Thanks to the many proofreaders and feedback-givers for all your thoughts and suggestions. There were too many to mention by name, but you do know who you are.

Thanks to my gundog students over the years, who have taught me what I need to teach them. You have enabled me to work with far more dogs than I could ever own, in a lifetime.

And thanks to my own dogs for continuously putting up with the latest reworked version of 'me' and where I'm at — and for revealing the flaws in my training!

TABLE OF CONTENTS

FOREWORD

BY PIPPA MATTINSON

Behind the scenes in the world of dog training, an important movement has been quietly taking place. Dog trainers are changing over to force-free training methods. In many dog sports and disciplines this change is almost complete and dog training methods are overwhelmingly positive. Within the working gundog community the pace of this transition has been slower until now.

The gundog community has been one of the last dog training disciplines to adopt modern dog training methods. The working environment for gundogs is a demanding one. There are challenges to overcome when teaching gundogs without the use of any force. But one by one, the barriers to force-free gundog training have been dismantled by dedicated and passionate force-free trainers. Jo Laurens is one of these trainers and has been at the forefront of this movement which now sees force-free gundogs not only working in the shooting field, but succeeding in competition too. Jo is an accredited instructor with The Gundog Club which made the switch to force-free training in 2018 and diligently advances her own skills and knowledge by competing and adding to her many professional qualifications.

Traditional dog training is a craft that has been handed down from one generation to the next. It has always had to rely on some degree of force or intimidation to prevent dogs misbehaving. And like any craft, some people have more aptitude for it than others. Force-free dog training is very different. It is firmly rooted in behavioural science and relies on principles that can be applied across all the very different behaviours and actions that you want your gundog to carry out. Anyone can apply these principles and Jo explains them with great clarity in this book. No aptitude or special skills are needed on your part. You don't need to have some kind of magical 'dog sense' just a willingness to learn and practice.

Jo is passionate about changing the way we treat our gundogs without judging those who come from traditional dog training backgrounds. If you have made mistakes with your dogs in the past that's okay. This book focuses on the future. Once you have learned the basic principles of force-free training, you'll be able to apply them to every aspect of your dog's behaviour. Jo leads you through this process in easy steps, and at the end of this book you will be able to strike out on your own.

This is a very individual book. Never afraid to learn from others, Jo thinks outside the box and incorporates successful dog training methodologies and techniques from around the world. You'll find traditional British retriever training principles with a modern force-free twist, sitting side by side with advanced American style retriever drills. She has the rare ability to take any traditional gundog training method and figure out to achieve the same outcome without the use of force. Jo Laurens is a talented writer and her book is much needed. It dispels many myths about the pros and cons of force-free dog training and deserves a space on every gundog owner's bookshelf. Above all, it will help you to raise a happy, confident, well trained dog.

August 2019

• • • • •

INTRODUCTION

There is no one way to train a gundog using force-free methods. In fact, force-free trainers may strongly disagree about the details: As I've been writing this book, I have often found myself thinking 'that's not what so-and-so would do' or 'I know this person would disagree with me on that'. Which is all to say: This book can't convey to you *the* force-free approach — because there isn't one. There are many. This is not a definitive text. And I don't have all the answers. This is just *my* approach to things.

I have tried to write the book I wish I had found when I was stumbling around in the dark, trying to figure things out and immersing myself in all I could. Fortunately for me, I had a friend stumbling around in the dark with me — also competing with his dog. The lengthy emails we sent between each other — trying to figure out how to train certain things, and why something wasn't working — were formative for me and incredibly helpful. The dark became... well, slightly less dark. Or maybe we stumbled less.

This sense of community and support is crucial. Being the lone force-free gundog person in your training class, or on your shoot, can feel very isolating. And isolation leads to exclusion and withdrawal. And — we need you! There is now a strong force-free community online and on social media. If you are reading this book and find yourself alone in your desire to train your dog without force, I hope you will find us.

All force-free trainers share a commitment to the tenets of training without the use of positive punishment or aversives. This book is built on that shared belief and ethical position. The book is not going to attempt to persuade trainers who currently use aversives to stop doing so. It does not devote much space to illustrating the drawbacks and pitfalls of positive punishment or aversives.

The book began as a series of handouts, which I wrote for my own gundog students. It evolved into a book when I started to fill in the gaps between the handouts. I realised that students needed things, which I had previously taken for granted, spelt out in detail. I'm very grateful to those who learn with me, for the opportunity to discover what they need me to teach.

I am also deeply grateful to others I've learnt from — they have been many and varied. I've picked up training ideas from other countries, from force-free trainers in other dog sports, and from traditional gundog trainers. I've tried to credit specific trainers who have influenced me — and to point you towards their own original work — but I apologise in advance if I've overlooked anyone. This was not intentional.

I am British, but I have a lot of family in America and I am very influenced by US training methods. This book comes from a British perspective, but I hope the principles are useful to gundog folk who want to train without the use of force — wherever they may live.

People who are interested in force-free gundog training may include:

- traditional handlers with existing gundog experience who are thinking about 'crossing over' to force-free methods or who want to reduce their use of force

- traditional handlers who would like to explore learning theory and to pick up new training ideas — wherever they come from

- force-free handlers who don't know much about gundog training but would like to apply their existing knowledge to gundog work as a sport

- force-free handlers who are already somewhere on their gundog training journey and are feeling stuck or looking for help

- pet dog owners who don't know much about gundog training or force-free methods but who want to train their dog as a gundog without the use of force — or have been advised to do so, to retain good control over their dog

My original intention when beginning this book, was to include all levels of training — right up to the 'finished' or 'fully-trained' dog. (Such a dog does not exist — but these phrases serve a purpose, as they denote a high level of training.) However, it soon became apparent that I would only be able to include what I define as 'basics' in this book. And that more advanced training — such as lining, handling, steadiness to flush, training on live game, blind retrieves, advanced water work, pointing and more besides — would need to wait for the next book.

A note: Throughout the book, I have used the word 'criteria' as both singular and plural. The word is commonly used in this way by dog trainers today and I have followed this usage.

• • • • •

HOW TO USE THIS BOOK

SECTION 1: FUNDAMENTALS This section is thematic with a focus on central tenets of force-free gundog training, on which the remainder of the book is based. The areas covered in this section are *fundamentals* which should always be kept in mind whilst training. I would really encourage you to read this section in detail.

SECTION 2: BEHIND THE SCENES This section takes you behind the scenes of successful force-free gundog training. What are we doing the rest of the time, when we are not training? This is just as important as the actual training itself, since dogs are learning all the time. What is the rest of the dog's life, like? How do we use food? How can we control motivators to enable us to raise a dog that can train around high distractions at a later time? What equipment do we need? What about your dog's interactions with other dogs?

SECTION 3: BASICS This section covers the training of specific foundation behaviours. These basic behaviours are largely the same for all subgroups of gundog — although sometimes the emphasis is slightly different. When these differences matter, I've pointed them out.

I debated whether to cover very commonly-trained behaviours (like sit) in this book, or whether I should just 'take it as read' that dogs can already respond to some cues. In the end, I realised that the way these behaviours are trained from the beginning is part of what contributes to success later, when they become more advanced (i.e. sit-to-lush). And that what may at first appear simple (sit), can develop into a more complex behaviour. So I decided to include this material.

If you are starting with an older dog, just follow along the same steps as you would with a puppy.

SECTION 1

FUNDAMENTALS

1.1

A BIT ABOUT TERMINOLOGY

Here are the terms you should understand to get the most out of this book. The book will still make sense without such an understanding, but you are going to be a better communicator with other trainers and handlers if we are using the same language.

This list is not intended to be exhaustive.

AROUSAL: When a dog's excited interest in something reaches the point where it is difficult for her to respond quickly and consistently to simple cues, we could say that the dog is over-aroused. With gundogs, high arousal commonly occurs around game — sight, sound or scent of it. High arousal levels are correlated with an increased heart rate, increased rate of respiration, and dilated pupils. If the dog is on a lead, she may be right at the end of it, staring outwards, or standing up on her back legs — or running frantically back and forth. She may refuse food, or she may snatch it with a hard mouth and eat it without even looking at you. A dog in a state of high arousal may be unable to control herself. She may be physically unable to respond to cues. I understand this as the dog not being in her 'thinking brain'. Positive punishment is typically ineffective at these times, because the dog's behaviour is not under her voluntary control.

Obviously some degree of excited interest, directed towards game, is desirable in a gundog. *Optimal* arousal is associated with speed, style, and drive — all valuable qualities. But when over-arousal leads to unwanted behaviours or an inability to respond to handlers, it is necessary to find ways to reduce arousal levels — to get dogs back into their thinking brains.

When working with over-arousal in gundogs, a lot can be learnt from the field of dog reactivity. Work with reactive or fearful dogs is similarly aimed at helping dogs reduce their arousal levels around various stimuli — typically people and other dogs. I discuss this subject further in Section 3.5, Focus and engagement. I would especially recommend deeply investigating Leslie McDevitt's training system called Control Unleashed — and Grisha Stewart's Behaviour Adjustment Training (BAT) — to achieve more cross-fertilisation with another field of force-free training which has a lot to offer gundog work.

CUE: A cue is the force-free equivalent of a command in traditional training. It is the word or hand signal or body movement or sound (a cue can really be anything the dog can discriminate) which signals to the dog that a reinforcement is available, *if* the dog performs the behaviour. The word 'sit' is a cue. The 'sit' whistle is a cue. The 'sit' hand signal is a cue.

Why not call these things commands? If we are 'commanding' the dog to perform behaviours, when the dog fails to perform the required response, she can then be understood as 'disobeying' us. Conceiving of your dog as disobeying a command predisposes many handlers to use aversives: That 'bad', 'disobedient' dog! Instead, conceiving of the dog as failing to understand our cue — as *our training itself* being inadequate — typically leads to a very different emotional response in us. And, so, a very different approach to training.

ENGAGEMENT: A 'disengaged' dog, is a dog which is not offering us attention or focus; a dog which does not respond to our words or movements; and, in short, a dog which has fallen out of relationship with us. An 'engaged' dog is the opposite: A dog which offers us attention or focus; a dog which is responsive to our words and actions; and a dog which remains connected to us, sometimes despite considerable distance and distraction.

Although engagement is closely associated with the concept of attention or focus from the dog, it is not the same thing. It is possible for a dog to be very engaged with us, whilst not actually looking at us. (During retriever heelwork, for example — when a dog must look ahead, to mark — and yet must not move even one step out of heel position.)

Engagement reflects an invisible connection between handler and dog, a connection which is a product of the relationship between them. The driving force for that connection — the desire for it — is located *in the dog*: The dog *wants* to remain in relationship with the handler. The dog *wants* to receive cues and reinforcers from the handler. The dog is almost pushing the handler, in a 'let's-do-training' way. Engagement is not about the handler cajoling or begging the dog to respond.

For a more detailed account of engagement and for steps on how to develop and foster it, see Denise Fenzi and Deb Jones' excellent book *Focus and Engage*.

ENVIRONMENTAL REINFORCER: Reinforcers (rewards) are not only on our person (treats and toys) but also occur naturally in the environment. I often ask my students to tell me what their dogs find reinforcing. They say 'treats' 'toys' 'petting' 'tug... and then get stuck. If those were the only reinforcers that existed for their dogs, these people would not be at a dog training class. They would have perfect control over their dogs! The main reason dog owners find themselves at a dog training class, is because dogs find *other things in the environment* reinforcing. And these environmental reinforcers are frequently more reinforcing to dogs than anything the handler can (comfortably, hygienically and easily!) put in their pocket to use themselves. They include:

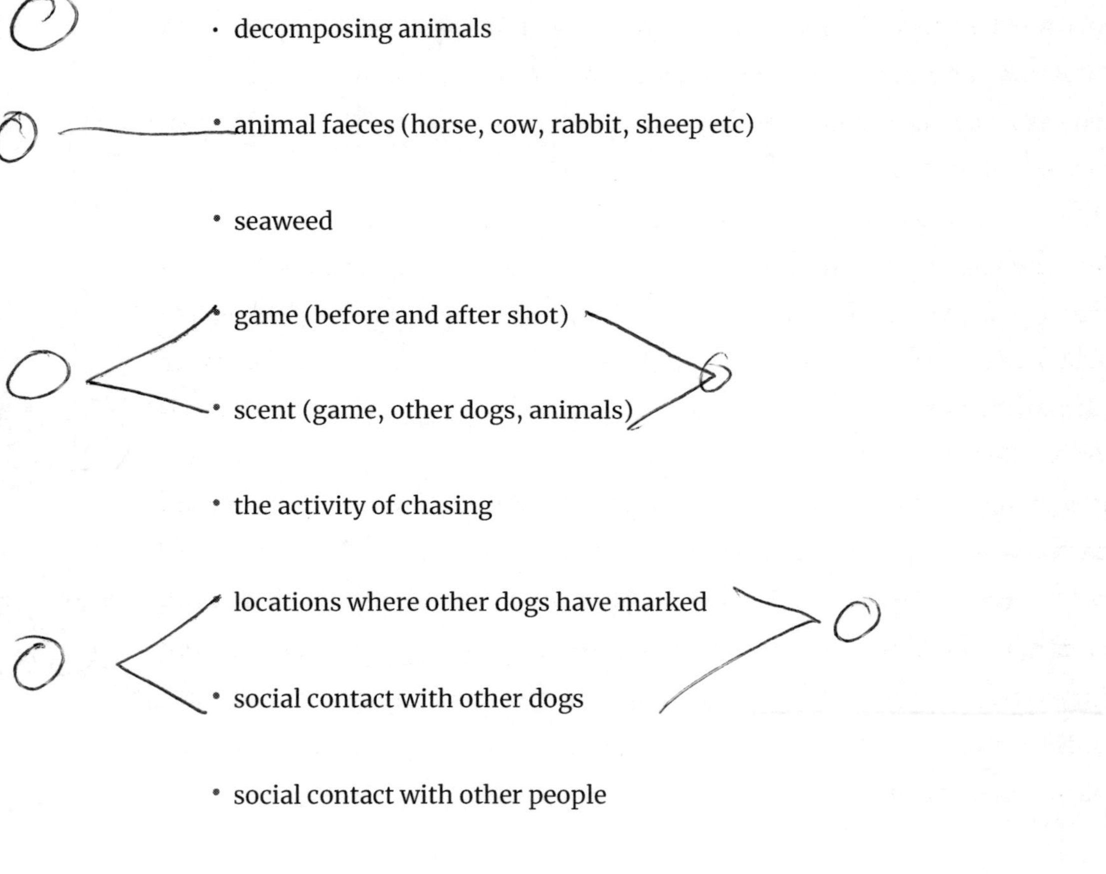

- decomposing animals
- animal faeces (horse, cow, rabbit, sheep etc)
- seaweed
- game (before and after shot)
- scent (game, other dogs, animals)
- the activity of chasing
- locations where other dogs have marked
- social contact with other dogs
- social contact with other people
- left over BBQ remains

Since the reinforcer is not on your person, it is likely that you are going to have imperfect control over it — and over the dog's access to it. You may not even be aware of it (scent) unless it explodes from cover (game) or until it is being eaten (animal faeces)! Environmental reinforcers are a huge reason gundog training is so challenging — and also why prevention is so important. Environmental reinforcers can provide dogs with opportunities to 'self-reinforce' on behaviours we really don't like — such as when a dog has a fun chase on a rabbit after being unsteady.

But, equally, environmental reinforcers can be powerful reinforcers for trainers to *allow* dogs access to, when they want to reinforce a behaviour: The dog which is steady gets the retrieve. The dog which sits to the whistle gets to hunt on. A good gundog trainer understands how to use environmental reinforcers — even though they are not on the handler's person. And a good gundog trainer also understands how to prevent the dog's free access to these reinforcers — that is, how to *control* the dog's access to them.

Lastly, it should be noted that not everything a dog finds distracting or interesting in the environment, is an environmental reinforcer: Dogs can also be distractible when they are anxious. This can result in hyper-observant behaviour (directed towards a perceived threat) and a dog which finds it hard to focus on her handler in the presence of that stimulus. This book is not going to address how to work with dogs which are preoccupied or lack focus because they are fearful. If you believe your dog is fearful of something animate in the environment (people, other dogs, livestock, traffic), then those stimuli will not function as environmental reinforcers for your dog — and your goal should be to reduce your dog's fear. I would highly recommend you check out Grisha Stewart's approach called Behaviour Adjustment Training (BAT) and also Leslie McDevitt's system, Control Unleashed.

FORCE-FREE: This is not a perfect term. You might object to it. But it is very hard to find a suitable term to describe the sort of training covered in this book. To call this training '*reward-based*' seems to leave some room for positive punishment. To call it '*clicker training*' makes the clicker sound more central than it is. (The clicker is fantastic for early foundational behaviours, but by the time you get to advanced stages of training you might not be using it much at all. There are also so-called balanced handlers who use clickers *and* aversives.) '*Positive* training' leaves room for positive punishment — which is just as positive (scientifically speaking) as positive reinforcement(!). Using 'positive' in this way also confuses learning theory's use of the word (as additive), with the common understanding of the word as 'yay — happy — dog enjoying herself'.

Emily Larlham grapples with these difficulties and has coined the term 'progressive reinforcement' which she defines as 'rewarding desired behaviours and excluding the intentional use of physical or psychological intimidation'. However, progressive reinforcement comes across as somewhat technical to those without knowledge of learning theory.

So, through a process of elimination, I come back to 'force-free'. The force we are free from, here, is force *to make the dog perform a behaviour* — for example: forcing a sit, forcing a retrieve via force-fetch, or forcing a dog to walk at heel. In other words:

- force occurs when the dog is made to *do* something, not where our goal is only to *prevent her* from doing something
- *force involves the application of an aversive by the trainer* — whether it's through positive punishment or negative reinforcement.

To me, the distinction between force and prevention is very clear — but this subject has become extremely confused in many discussions on social media, where people make the claim that 'there's no such thing as positive-only [force-free] dog training'. These people argue that the use of a leash, or prevention itself, is force. This view reflects a misunderstanding of prevention. After all, we are not using force when we hold a child's hand to cross a road. We are not using force when we keep our dogs indoors overnight, instead of allowing them to roam the neighbourhood. We are not even using force if a child has a tantrum in a store and has to be gently carried out, restrained and screaming. Safety dictates the necessity of prevention — as much for toddlers as for dogs! Misinterpreting prevention as force leads to nonsensical conclusions, taking us on a slippery slope towards the view that 'aversives are ok, because even restraining a dog is an aversive'.

The use of a leash or long-line, attached to a harness and used to prevent a dog from carrying out unwanted behaviours, does not constitute the use of force — since we are neither: 1) making the dog *do* anything (we are stopping the dog from doing something), nor 2) applying an aversive. We are removing the undesirable choice from the menu. There is a difference between using a leash to prevent running in — and deliberately yanking that leash to administer an aversive. (For more on prevention and its key role in force-free training, see Section 1.2, Prevention.)

HABITUATION: Habituation refers to 'getting used to' something — so that the something fails to elicit the response it originally elicited. For example, a young dog, on first entering a rabbit pen, may be over-excited by birds and rabbits flushing everywhere. The dog may leap around and be unable to respond to the handler. But, should the handler find the quietest corner of the pen and just hang around there with the dog, over about 5-10 minutes, the dog may 'habituate' to these conditions and be able to respond.

Another example: When first entering a new field with a dog, the dog is very distracted by the scent, sight and sounds of the new location. The dog finds the environmental reinforcers very appealing. Consequently, the handler finds it difficult to train the dog. Should the handler hang out with the dog for several minutes — on leash, so the dog is not free to discover ever-new stimuli — the dog often then wants to engage with the handler and to work. Over time, the dog becomes able to focus on the handler sooner — until the handler can enter a new environment and have a dog which is engaged immediately.

Habituation deserves to be 'a thing' in force-free gundog training. It is extremely effective and yet goes unrecognised and under-utilised.

HUMAN EMOTIONS: A major cause of canine reactivity ('aggression') is frustration: We've all seen a dog on leash, barking out of frustration whilst she is walked past another dog she wants to reach. Sometimes the frustration is so much that she turns around and bites her own handler. We call this 'redirection': Her emotion was so great that she could not contain it — it had to have an outlet, somewhere, to alleviate her feelings somewhat. Similarly, research shows that rats experience less stress in stressful situations, when they are able to direct their own aggressive response to that stress, onto subordinate rats: Their stress is mitigated, when they have an outlet for it in the shape of another.

Now, think about the gundog handler who has been working for weeks on sit-to-flush. A rabbit gets up and the dog chases the rabbit. This is a pretty stressful and frustrating situation, where weeks of work appear to be wasted. It takes a very self-aware trainer to contain that frustration and stress, in that moment, and not to redirect it onto the dog — through positive punishment — thereby similarly mitigating the handler's own experience of these unpleasant emotions.

When dogs don't behave in the way we want them to behave, it is normal for the handler to experience frustration. After all, our own goals and objectives have been frustrated and denied. How does that sense of frustration make us behave, in that moment?

The administration of positive punishment to dogs is reinforcing for many *handlers*: The dog is doing something the handler considers undesirable, the handler administers positive punishment and the dog stops doing it (temporary suppression of behaviour). *The handler's behaviour of punishing the dog has now been reinforced*, because the unpleasant thing has stopped (negative reinforcement). Science tells us that behaviour which is reinforced will reoccur — therefore, the handler will continue to administer positive punishment to the dog in the future. We, too, are subject to the laws of learning theory!

When positive punishment is used, the dog's undesirable behaviour may stop *in the short term* — leading people to believe that it works — but it will reoccur in the long-term. From the handler's perspective, however, the immediate reinforcement experienced for punishing the dog (the dog's unwanted behaviour stopped), far outweighs the punishment involved when the behaviour reoccurs at some later point: Research shows that immediate and strong reinforcement will always outweigh a delayed punisher which is harder to attach, causally, to the behaviour.

In short, as handlers, we can be so focussed on the smallest of changes in our dog's behaviour that we forget to pay attention to our *own* internal world and to account for that in the training process.

OPERANT CONDITIONING: Through operant conditioning, a dog makes an association between a particular behaviour and a consequence. There is so much more to dog training than simply analysing behaviour using the 'four quadrants'. Still, it's important to have a basic knowledge of them because they are part of the history and development of force-free training:

- ***Reinforcement (or reinforcer):*** Anything which makes a behaviour *more* likely to occur. Giving a dog a treat for sitting, makes sitting more likely to occur. So the treat is a reinforcement/reinforcer. Tip for remembering: We reinforce walls or buildings to make them stronger. So, reinforcement involves making a behaviour stronger.

- ***Punishment (or punisher):*** Anything which makes a behaviour *less* likely to occur. Jerking a lead when a dog pulls, makes pulling less likely to occur. So jerking the lead functions as a punishment/punisher. It makes the behaviour weaker.

- ***Positive:*** The *addition* of something. Think of the plus symbol '+' in mathematics. Positive in this context does *not* mean upbeat, happy, reward-based, '*yay*!' force-free, forward-looking or optimistic. It simply means adding something (+).

- ***Negative:*** The *removal* of something. Think of the minus symbol '-'. Negative in this context does not mean 'down on someone' bad, nasty, disapproving, pessimistic, or backwards. It simply means 'removing something' (-).

The four terms above (reinforcement, punishment, positive, negative) give us the following four combinations:

- ***Positive reinforcement:*** The *addition* of something (positive) which makes a behaviour *more likely* to occur (reinforcement). Some examples of positive reinforcement include:

    - giving the dog a treat when she sits. Here, sitting has been reinforced (made stronger) through the addition of a treat (positive).

    - calling the dog back and having a game of tug. Here, the recall has been reinforced through the addition of a game of tug (positive).

  Most of the things you probably think of commonly as rewards, will fall into the category of positive reinforcement. It's what most folk mean when they talk about rewards or reinforcement. A trainer might think: '*Good girl, for coming back when you were called! Here's a treat.*'

- ***Positive punishment:*** The *addition* of something (positive) which makes a behaviour *less likely* to occur (punishment). Some examples of positive punishment include:

- a lead jerk to stop a dog pulling. Here, pulling has been punished (made weaker) through the addition of a lead jerk (positive).

- a scruff shake for a dog which ran in. Here, running in has been punished (made weaker), through the addition of a scruff shake.

Most of the things you probably think of as being punishment, will fall into the category of *positive* punishment. It's commonly what most folk mean when they talk about punishment. A trainer might think: *'No! Don't try to chase the rabbit, here's a lead jerk because you did.'*

You can see how *positive* reinforcement and *positive* punishment both involve *adding* something, whether it be treats, toys or something which reinforces behaviour... or lead jerks, scruff shakes or something which punishes behaviour.

- ***Negative punishment:*** The *removal* of something (negative) which makes a behaviour *less* likely to occur (punishment). You might think that force-free trainers don't use punishment, but that's not entirely right.

Force-free trainers don't use *positive* punishment. But we do use *negative* punishment. For example:

- a dog doing a stay, stands up when a treat is on the way to the dog's mouth. The treat is returned to the pouch — the dog 'loses' it. We can say that standing up has been punished by the loss of the treat.

- a dog tries to pull on the lead. The handler stops walking. The dog loses forwards movement and access to new ground. So, pulling on the lead has been punished.

Negative punishment involves the dog losing something she wanted.

Tip: If 'too bad, Fido — you lose!' is something you could say to the dog, then you are likely using negative punishment. A trainer might think: '*You jumped up on me. Too bad, you lose my attention — I'm turning my back on you.*'

- ***Negative reinforcement:*** The *removal* of something (negative) which makes a behaviour *more likely* to occur (reinforcement). Here's where the everyday understanding of these words collides with learning theory. Reinforcement sounds like such a pleasant thing, doesn't it? Well, negative reinforcement is actually not very nice. It's what's happening in avoidance training:

    - A trainer pinches a dog's ear (applies an aversive). When a dog puts a dummy in her mouth, the ear pinch is stopped (removed). This reinforces (makes stronger) the behaviour of the dog getting the dummy in her mouth. Because the dog learns to get the dummy in her mouth as quickly as possible to 'turn off' the ear pinch.

Of course, in order to remove the unpleasant or painful thing, you have to apply it in the first place. A trainer might think: '*Sit, and I'll stop the ecollar nick.*'

Finally, under operant conditioning, we must cover the old chestnut, which is:

VARIABLE REINFORCEMENT: This refers to the type of reinforcement ratio at work in casinos, when humans play slot machines. You don't always win when you play a slot machine. In fact, most of the time you lose (or casinos would not make any money!). But sometimes you win. This 'sometimes you win, sometimes you lose' is variable reinforcement in action — and it has been said that variable reinforcement is responsible for a great deal of gambling's addictiveness: The subject always believes that the next reinforcer is imminent, so keeps going.

At first, the dog training world was very excited about variable reinforcement and the received wisdom was that we, too, should implement it — by reinforcing every correct response only during the training phase of a new behaviour and then, once the dog 'knows' the behaviour, moving to a variable reinforcement schedule by *not* reinforcing every correct response but only *some* of them. This, it was reasoned, would surely result in a stronger and more determined behaviour from the dog.

However, this is one of those situations where studies carried out in laboratory conditions don't translate well to real-life scenarios. We will discuss this further in Section 1.4 — Generalisation and distraction management.

Lastly, it would be more academically correct to refer to variable reinforcement as intermittent reinforcement. I continue to use the term variable reinforcement, since it's how most people recognise this reinforcement schedule.

PROOFING (OR GENERALISATION): Just because a dog can sit in the kitchen, doesn't mean she can sit when a bird flushes from under her nose. To achieve the latter, we need to teach the dog that the 'sit' cue means the same thing, *under many different conditions and circumstances.* We call this process 'proofing' — so we speak of 'proofing' the sit against these various environmental conditions. Alternatively, we can also say we are 'generalising' the sit and call this process 'generalisation'. Too often there is a lack of proofing or generalisation which has occurred in training a gundog — resulting in handlers resorting to punishment for what they perceive to be disobedience — when, really, the issue is a lack of generalisation or proofing. There is more information on this, in Section 1.4, Generalisation and distraction management.

SUCTION: This term comes from North American retriever training and refers to the way in which environmental features — such as bodies of water, cover, or sloping terrain — can function to take a dog off a straight line, particularly when running blind retrieves. It's almost as if the environmental feature 'sucks' the dog away from the straight line they were sent on.

Here are some examples of suction in action, so you can get a sense of it:

- A dog is sent on a retrieve across a lake, but veers right — off a straight line — wanting to get out of the water onto a nearby island. The shore had suction for that dog; it pulled her off the straight line.

- A dog is running a drill and is sent for one dummy, but spots another which is closer and so runs in a banana line veering towards the dummy she is not supposed to get. She doesn't actually get the wrong dummy, but her line was affected by her knowledge of the other dummy. The other dummy had suction for that dog; it pulled her off the line.

- A dog is running marked retrieves and does not mark a retrieve very well, beginning to hunt for it too far to the left. The dog had just previously completed a retrieve even further to the left. The location of fall, for the previous retrieve, had suction for that dog; memory of that retrieve affected her behaviour and caused her to look in a different location compared to where she would have looked, without that previous retrieve.

What is behind suction? Sometimes it is simply that the dog does not yet *understand* how to account for, say, sloping terrain or a change in cover — and still maintain the straight line.

But often reinforcers play a part: Either the dog is perceiving a *current* reinforcer (the tempting shore nearby; the dummy they are not supposed to get) — or she is remembering a *past* reinforcer (a previous location of fall on a retrieve; a previous cast which led to a dummy). Or the terrain itself is offering up a more reinforcing route than the straight line, for the dog. (The dog may prefer not to run up a steep hill or through thick cover.)

So, we can say that *suction originates in the dog's perception of current and past reinforcers — and how that perception affects behaviour.*

As suction is about the influence of reinforcers on a dog's behaviour, it is very relevant, as a concept, for force-free gundog training. We're going to pilfer this one...

TRADITIONAL: Sometimes traditional trainers take offence at being called traditional. Perhaps because they hear it as meaning 'old-fashioned'. Or maybe they hear the term used in opposition to 'force-free' — they might hear, in this, an accusation that they are 'hard' on their dogs. They are understandably offended, because many traditional trainers consider themselves to be what most people would describe as 'soft' trainers. They don't understand why force-free trainers are implying they are monsters!

It's important to explain that there is nothing judgemental intended, when I refer to 'traditional' trainers. I simply mean 'the way that things have conventionally been trained, by the majority of trainers, in mainstream gundog training'. It's a factual description, not a judgement.

Even amongst traditional trainers, there is great variation in the type and quantity of aversives used in training. That is how some traditional trainers get a reputation for being heavy-handed, whilst others are known to be softer handlers. Some traditional trainers might consider that they use *no* aversives. In truth, many traditional trainers don't even realise they are using aversives, so here are a few examples of traditional training in the UK:

- pushing a dog's rear down to make her sit
- giving lead corrections for moving out of heel position
- running at a dog in an intimidating manner

- shouting at a dog
- slapping a dog's chin for rolling a dummy or attempting to reclaim it after delivery

If a trainer is doing any of the above, they are not force-free. They are using aversives. They are a traditional trainer, for the purposes of how we are using that term.

There are many aspects of traditional training which don't involve the use of aversives. Most dogs love to retrieve. Therefore, any time there is a retrieve involved in an exercise, traditional trainers are using positive reinforcement. Any time they deny the dog a retrieve (because they weren't steady, for example), they are using negative punishment. Many gundogs love to hunt. Any time they are allowed to hunt on, after a successful stop whistle, that is positive reinforcement. So, by no means is traditional training only about aversives.

As force-free trainers, we love these aspects of traditional training and we aim to make as much use of them as possible, in force-free work. And of course, many traditional trainers are hugely experienced in reading the land, guessing where the game will be, predicting how a dog will behave, training hunting/quartering and pointing, understanding scenting conditions, and many more aspects of field-craft — all of which, we need. We would be completely lost without traditional training. We don't want to reinvent the wheel — or throw the baby out with the bathwater!

I have learnt a huge amount from traditional trainers and I count many amongst my friends.

1.2

PREVENTION – TO THE POINT OF EXTINCTION

Most traditional gundog trainers resort to positive punishment at certain times in training. Their reasoning goes something like this:

My dog 'knows' these commands. Therefore, she is not disobeying because she does not understand. Instead, this is wilful disobedience. What am I supposed to do? Put a treat on her nose and lure her into a sit when she starts to chase after a rabbit? What else can I do in that situation, but 'correct' her? Anything else is completely ineffective.

Notice the euphemism that is the word 'correct', here. Glossing positive punishment as 'correction' makes it sound innocuous and also implies that the punishment is quite dispassionately administered, without anger or heat: Like a ballet instructor would correct a slightly un-turned out ankle by gently rotating it further. This is far from the reality of what usually happens in gundog work under the guise of correction — which would be more appropriately termed positive punishment...or even abuse.

But how, then, do force-free gundog trainers achieve results? What do we do when Fido starts running after that rabbit — run after her, with a sausage?

With these misconceptions, it's no wonder many think force-free training is ineffective.

THE 'POSITIVE-IS-PERMISSIVE' MYTH

It's time to dispel a myth. It's the myth which says that force-free trainers are permissive 'cookie shovers'. A 'cookie shover' is a trainer who just feeds their dog, regardless of the dog's behaviour. It's the same myth which says that, if a dog does something which force-free trainers don't like, the trainer just watches the dog get the reinforcer (the chase on the bunny, for example). Those who see force-free training in this way, can't imagine any other options: *Since force-free trainers don't 'correct' the dog, they must just let the dog have what she wants, right?*

But using force-free methods and letting your dog do whatever she wants, are not the same thing. It's not a case of 'Fido, could you possibly sit? Oh, never mind, don't worry.' That would be permissive. And effective force-free trainers are not permissive.

In force-free training, we are concerned with *controlling the dog's access to reinforcers*. If you control the reinforcers, you will control the dog.

You might have heard the phrase 'money is power'. Money is reinforcement for humans. The reason that having money results in power is because people will do what you ask, to earn your money. The same goes for dogs: If you have control over what they want, they will do what you ask, to earn your reinforcers. (Ethically, this can create difficulties — for humans and dogs — but that is beyond the scope of this book.)

Control is not force. Control is a dog falling over herself to do what *you* want, because *you* have what *she* wants.

CONTROLLING ACCESS TO ENVIRONMENTAL REINFORCERS

Reinforcers, for dogs, are not just treats and toys in our pockets. In the dog's mind, there are only things out there in the world, that she wants. Whether that's a decomposing rabbit, play with another dog, dummies you haven't cast her towards, or cow dung.

We see these things as distractions. The dog sees these things as reinforcers. *A distraction is just a reinforcer which you don't want the dog to get.*

But how does the dog know she is not supposed to try to get it?

Most people put nothing in place to prevent the dog from accessing the 'wrong' reinforcers. And so she accesses them more and more, having learnt what fun this is.

The world is a feast of these environmental reinforcers, to a dog.

There is a well-known child-development experiment where a child is left alone in a room with a chocolate cake and told not to touch it. Almost all the children do eat the cake, to the point that the experiment is about whether they lie about having done this or not. If a human toddler finds it difficult to resist accessing a reinforcer when it is available, you can assume that your gundog will also try to have her cake and eat it. Moreover, when she goes out for a walk, she's in an environment where there's not just one 'cake' on offer, but a dozen or more. You are walking through a landscape of cakes, expecting her to focus on yours!

Force-free trainers need to be excellent at knowing the following:

- Where, at any moment in time, are the reinforcers for the dog?
- What behaviour are they likely to reinforce, and is this behaviour desirable?
- Are the reinforcers able to be controlled on your person?
- If not, how can you control the dog's access to these reinforcers so that you can use them to reinforce desirable behaviours?

Experienced trainers look ahead. They anticipate the ways in which dogs will attempt to self-reinforce on environmental reinforcers and they put prevention in place from the first day they bring their new puppy home.

Inexperienced owners don't look ahead. They don't know what environmental reinforcers the dog will try to access, until the dog starts accessing them. By this time, there is a reinforcement history for the unwanted behaviour. Even then, they frequently don't put anything in place to prevent the exact same thing from happening again. And again.

Take the situation of a dog starting to chase a rabbit: If there are no means in place to prevent this happening, the trainer has no alternative but to allow the dog to chase the rabbit or to use positive punishment to inhibit her desire to chase.

With a long-line on, the trainer suddenly has the option of restraining the dog. Now the dog can't get what she wants, even if she doesn't (yet) respond to the handler. What we have doesn't look very impressive — as it's probably a dog flailing around on the end of a long-line — but this step is crucial because we have removed the reinforcer, which is the chasing of the rabbit. The behaviour of chasing now will not be reinforced (made stronger). And we can begin to train an alternative behaviour.

I don't want you to think prevention is only applicable when it comes to preventing a chase on game. A few other examples include:

- reventing 'running in' on retrieves, by holding a training tab
- preventing sniffing and wandering off from heel position, through the use of a leash
- preventing the wrong dummy from being retrieved, by asking an assistant to pick it up before the dog reaches it.

And so on.

This manipulation of environmental reinforcers is crucial: Being the provider of treats and toys is only 50 per cent of force-free training. Prevention is the other 50 per cent.

You can have every tasty treat in your pocket, but if your dog finds game reinforcing and decides to go and chase, all your treats are useless. When reinforcers are in the environment, you can't remove them from the dog — you can't 'magic' them away. But you *can* remove the dog, from them!

And that's what prevention is about.

THE INVISIBILITY OF PREVENTION

Prevention is the rabbit which is not being chased. Prevention is the dead bird which is *not* getting eaten. Prevention is the other dog which is *not* getting played with.

Prevention is the thing we are *not* letting happen. Prevention is about everything which *doesn't* exist — everything which *wasn't allowed* to exist — because we prevented it.

But, encompassing 'everything which wasn't allowed to exist', prevention is pretty invisible.

It's not invisible if you know what to look for: If I see someone's dog trailing a long-line on the beach, I beam a big smile.

But, for most people, prevention goes unrecognised. And that is the main reason people don't perceive its importance: They don't see it, when it is happening.

After all, prevention is not (by itself) going to result in a dog walking backwards whilst juggling fireballs. It is not as sexy as shaping a dog to wink. You're not going to see someone preventing their dog from doing something unwanted, turn to the person next to you, and say 'Wow, did you see that...*prevention* happening?'.

Yet prevention of unwanted behaviours is at least 50 per cent of force-free gundog training, if not more. Prevention is crucial for training a gundog using force-free methods and you should keep it at the forefront of any training you plan.

EXTINCTION – THE DYING OUT OF A BEHAVIOUR

You might have taught your dog the 'leave' behaviour by putting a treat on the floor and covering it with your hand every time the dog makes a move for it. Eventually the dog gives up trying, because she never succeeds. At which point we can say that the behaviour of trying to get the treat '*extinguishes*'. We can then reinforce that alternative response of *not* trying to get the treat.

Extinction means that a behaviour has completely stopped. If a dog is no longer chasing hares, chasing hares has 'extinguished'. The dog has stopped trying to do the thing you don't want her to do. To remember what extinction means, think of dinosaurs dying out — becoming *extinct*.

If you wait for an unwanted behaviour to occur before implementing prevention, the behaviour acquires a reinforcement history: Just one amazing chase on a hare can be so reinforcing that your job of achieving a sit-to-flush is made much harder. The answer to this? Don't wait to see if your dog is going to be a chaser before putting a long-line on. Wait to see that your dog *isn't* one, before taking a long-line off! That way your dog will never acquire a reinforcement history for the unwanted behaviour.

Using our ongoing example of rabbit-chasing, let's look at a couple more important points relating to prevention. Firstly, it's important that you *always* put the long-line on — not just sometimes. If you put it on sometimes, the dog will sometimes still be able to do the unwanted behaviour (chasing). Being able to chase sometimes (and not at other times) causes your dog to get addicted to trying — just in case she's going to be able to chase *this* time. This 'sometimes-it-works, sometimes-it-doesn't-work' situation, prevents extinction from ever being achieved and ensures a perpetual state of 'maybe today?' for the dog.

Remember that only when the dog has stopped trying, can we say that the behaviour has extinguished. If you always put means in place to prevent what you don't want from happening, you will remove the occasional powerful reinforcer — and the behaviour really should extinguish for good. (Especially when coupled with teaching an alternative behaviour which you prefer — like sit!)

Secondly, if you sometimes put a long-line on and sometimes you don't, you will give the dog the opportunity to compare long-line *on* (a dog prevented from chasing) with long-line *off* (a dog free to chase). Once the dog has learnt this meaning, we can say she is '*long-line-wise*'.

Let's compare this to a known problem for US e-collar trainers: US e-collar trainers know the implications of a dog which is '*collar-wise*'. This dog will perform well in training, wearing the e-collar. (Even when the collar isn't used.) But, in competition, when the collar has to be taken off, the dog refuses commands. The dog knows that when the e-collar is off, she is 'safe' and can't be shocked. How has the dog been able to learn this? Through being able to compare e-collar on (shocks) with e-collar off (no shock — ever). It is really hard to recover from this situation and to undo the learned associations. To avoid this scenario, US e-collar trainers will have pups wearing e-collars long before they ever use them. 'Dummy' collars are available, which look exactly like functional e-collars and weigh the same amount — but don't work. The goal is for the dog to think of the e-collar almost like a part of their anatomy, to take it for granted. To forget about it. To grow up with it. Every time the dog is taken out and trained, the e-collar is on, whether it's used or not.

What does this mean for force-free training? A long-line isn't an e-collar. It doesn't work by administering an aversive. But these same principles apply: The dog can learn that when the long-line is off, she is free and can access whatever environmental reinforcers she wants. And when it is on, you prevent her — so she learns there's not much point in trying at these times. Once the dog has learnt the significance of the long-line like this, you can end up with a dog which is perfect when the long-line is on, but ignores you when it's off. And this is very difficult to fix, and will involve things like slowly cutting the line down to blur the difference between line on and line off.

A much better solution is: Always keep the long-line on, until you are not needing to use it — ever.

This is 'prevention, to the point of extinction'.

EXTINCTION BURSTS – A BEHAVIOUR IN DEATH THROES

Imagine how you feel when you put money in a vending machine for a canned drink, and the machine malfunctions and doesn't give you the can. Every other time, in the past, machines have discharged your drink when you have put money in. You press the same button again. Then you press it harder. You jab at it many times, quickly, with your finger. You hit the machine. You kick the machine. You swear at it. You try to sway the machine. Eventually, when none of this works, you give up.

But you didn't just give up and walk away, to begin with. You tried everything you could think of, in increasing desperation. And your final efforts (kicking the machine, swaying the machine) were much more extreme than the first things you tried (like pressing the button again).

All this was your '*extinction burst*' for the behaviour of trying to get a drink from the vending machine.

Similarly, before a dog stops trying to access a reinforcer she has previously been able to access, she will also go through an extinction burst — a phase of *trying even harder*. It's important to know this and to be expecting the extinction burst, when training a dog.

For example, if you have just put a long-line on your dog — and your dog has previously been able to chase game — she will similarly keep trying to chase bunnies and birds for a while. Her attempts might get more desperate, more sustained, and stronger. Do not give up at this point! Extinction is just around the corner, but if you conclude it's 'not working' and give up now, you will only reinforce this new exaggerated behaviour, which will become the new norm.

Going back to the vending machine example, imagine what would have happened if your last and most exaggerated effort (let's say — swaying the machine) worked and your drink came out then. The next time the machine doesn't give you a can, you will probably skip straight to swaying the machine immediately — after all, that's what worked for you, last time. Your most extreme attempt was reinforced.

If you implement prevention and you just see a dog flailing around on a long-line, it doesn't mean it's not working and you should give up and let the dog have the reinforcer anyway. If you do that, at this point, you will only reinforce that even more increased struggle — and that will become the behaviour. (Just like your swaying of the vending machine.) You will inadvertently train your dog to do the unwanted behaviour — with even more intensity!

Instead, when you implement prevention — and the dog's attempts to get the reinforcer appear to be intensifying — don't feel despondent, but have a little cheer to yourself: This is an excellent sign that extinction is in progress.

It's not possible to state how long an extinction burst will last before you achieve extinction. Moreover, we don't just want to achieve extinction on one particular occasion or repetition (rep): Our ultimate goal is to see the dog not even attempt the undesired behaviour when the opportunity next presents itself, on an unexpected and fresh rep. This is the difference between a dog leaping around on a long-line after a rabbit and eventually giving up — and a dog seeing a rabbit bolt and making no attempt to chase in the first place. For all dogs, extinction will happen even faster if you also teach another incompatible behaviour for your dog to carry out at that tempting moment (ie — sit or stand).

If a dog has previously learnt that it is possible to access environmental reinforcers freely and at will, the length of time you need to implement prevention in order to achieve extinction, is going to be considerable — because there is a reinforcement history for the unwanted behaviour. Extinction of a behaviour takes longer when there has been a history of fantastic reinforcement for that behaviour. On the other hand, the extinction burst will be over a lot faster for a dog whose handler has implemented prevention from the time they brought the dog home as a young puppy — as there is no reinforcement history for the unwanted behaviour.

Think also about how you *felt*, with the vending machine: You felt frustrated — you were denied something enjoyable which you were used to getting.

Your dog's behaviour is also a result of frustration. Your dog doesn't understand why she can no longer chase the bunny. In desperation and frustration, she tries even harder. This behaviour is not about disobedience or stubbornness or lack of respect. Just as your frustration with the vending machine wasn't about that, either!

• • • • •

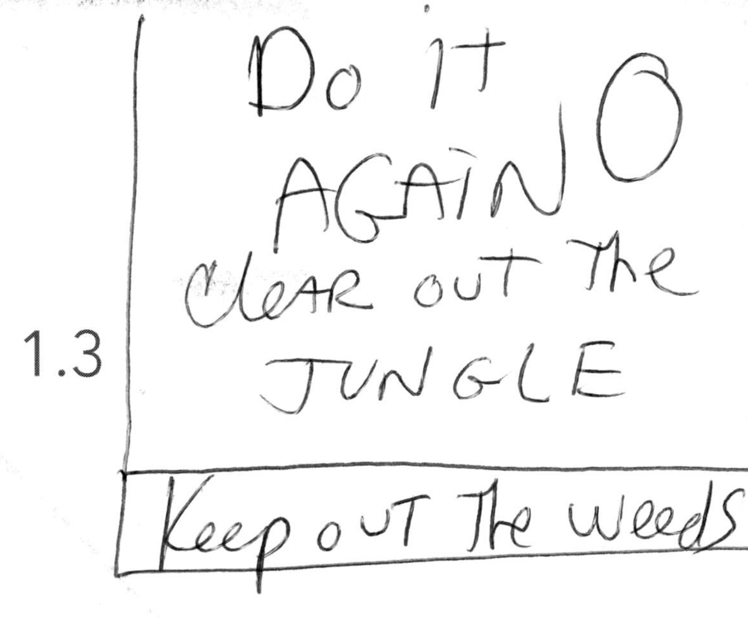

1.3

REPETITION – TO THE POINT OF FLUENCY

When we are training a dog, we are connecting 1) a cue with 2) a behaviour. For example, the word ‘sit’, with the behaviour of ‘put butt on the ground’.

Think of your dog’s brain as a jungle. The more you go over and over the same spot, the more you wear down a path. That path you’ve created is a neural network in the brain; it’s the connection between cue and response (behaviour). If you only go over it a few times, the connection will be very weak and liable to break down at times of stress. We could say that the jungle is quickly going to grow back over your path.

It takes a lot of repetition (of cue > behaviour > click > reinforcement) to attach a cue to a behaviour adequately. Even indoors, with no distractions. Despite this, people often think that their dog 'knows' a behaviour on cue, because she has done it successfully just a few times. Instead, achieving reliability requires us to get those reps in — with calm consistency.

The added difficulty, for gundog work, is that we often need to replace a previously reinforcing behaviour (like chasing) with another (like sitting). That is: The rabbit which is flushing, needs to become the cue to sit — instead of the cue to chase. Attaching a new behaviour (sit) to a cue which is already *repeatedly* associated with a self-reinforcing behaviour is quite challenging and requires many more reps from us. Repetition is working against us here — since it is repetition of the unwanted behaviour and the unwanted connection between cue (rabbit) and response (chase).

We don't have much choice about some cues in gundog work — because they come from the game itself. For example, the behaviour we call 'sit' has the following cues, any one of which means 'sit':

- birds flushing
- ground game flushing
- gunshot
- shot game/dummy falling to the ground
- whistle peep
- 'sit' (word)
- the handler stops walking, during heelwork.

When a bird is flushed and shot, the dog which has been trained to hear this list as 'sit', is hearing 'sit' repeatedly — via different cues: Bird flushes (sit), bird is shot (sit), bird falls (sit), and some handlers may initially give the whistle peep (sit).

We can conceive of some of these listed items as *distractions* — things which the dog must ignore or resist in order to perform the sit behaviour successfully. If we conceive of things in this way, we will be attempting to proof 'against' these distractions. There's nothing wrong with this, as an approach — but it is somewhat oppositional, with us setting ourselves up against the distractions. We will get a much stronger behaviour if, instead, we can conceive of this entire list as *cues* — cues for the behaviour we want: We *need* the rabbit to run, to cue the dog to sit. (Just as much as we also need the word 'sit', to cue the dog to sit.) When the most tempting thing in the world, becomes the cue for self-control, we are onto a winner.

Since we need to attach behaviours (like sit) to many different cues, we then need additional reps: *Each cue requires the same number of reps to attach it reliably to the behaviour of sitting.* And it is far easier to achieve many reps of the word 'sit' or the sit whistle, than it is to achieve reps of rabbits flushing.

This brings us onto the subject of fluency. We can say that a behaviour is 'fluent' when the dog responds instantly to the cue; the time taken for the dog to process that cue is very short. Think about driving a car: You are driving along when the person sitting next to you shouts out 'RIGHT!' You immediately turn right. There is just a fraction of a second between the word 'right' and your behaviour of turning right. You don't continue driving straight, thinking about this word and what it means — mulling it over. You recognise and respond to it instantly.

Now, imagine setting your sat-nav to give instructions in a foreign language. (If you are like me, you might actually have done this for the comedy value.) When the sat-nav says '*tourne à droite*', you don't immediately turn right. You think:

'à droite... à droite' what does that mean again?' — and then you turn right. What were you doing, whilst you were trying to remember what 'à droite' means? You were still driving straight. To an observer, it might have looked as if you weren't responding at all. It might have looked as if you were *ignoring* the sat-nav.

When you are training a dog, you will sometimes find a similar delay in response. A traditional trainer might think a dog is being disobedient when not complying fast enough, and be inclined to punish — after all, the dog does respond eventually, so they know and are deliberately disobeying, right?

Whereas a force-free trainer knows that the dog needs many, many reps to cement together that cue ('sit') with that behaviour (butt on the ground). And, just like you had to think about 'à droite' and, in the meantime, kept driving straight, so, in the same way, your dog is trying to remember what behaviour the cue is associated with — and may continue with whatever she was doing for a few seconds, appearing slow to respond.

In gundog work, it can be difficult to provide your dog with sufficient reps for fluency to result. If you rely entirely on 'natural' encounters with game, it's hard to get the reps in. They will happen one here, one there, and then nothing for a few days. It will take the dog longer to learn, because the environment and context and setting will be so different from one encounter to the next; the dog will be generalising at the same time as learning. Ten encounters in thirty minutes, in one environment, is going to result in faster progress than sporadic unexpected encounters of different game species, in different environments.

If you rely entirely on natural encounters with game, you will also not be prepared for what is about to happen and so you may be taken by surprise, finding yourself not ready to grab the long-line for the sake of prevention.

So, you need to manufacture situations to get enough repetitions in, until you begin to see the dog giving up the old environmental reinforcer and instead playing you, for your reinforcer. How do you manufacture situations which will enable you to gain the reps you need for fluency? You need a set-up which you can control entirely, and a flush you can cause to happen again, and again, and again, and again.

For teaching a dog not to chase at the flush of game, 'bolting rabbits' can be useful. (A dummy on a giant piece of elastic which whizzes past the dog, allowing you to practise sit-to-flush.) 'Flirt-poles' are another idea (rabbit skins tied on the end of horse lunging whips, and moved about on the floor to simulate game being flushed). Bird launchers used with live birds, are fantastic. I have even used fluffy battery-operated children's toys, which jiggle and jump up and down and squeak and move around, for steadiness training!

None of these creative alternatives can replace experience on game itself. But if you do enough of the groundwork using these lesser distractions which are entirely under your control, you will need to do fewer reps with the real thing to achieve results. When you do move onto the real thing, a rabbit pen is indispensable and will enable you to use game whilst also controlling and predicting the encounters.

• • • • •

1.4

GENERALISATION AND DISTRACTION MANAGEMENT

More generalisation is required in gundog work than in almost any other dog sport. The majority of other dog sports specify requirements precisely — from the size of the ring, to the number of paces taken, to jump dimensions. As a result, handlers know what to expect and can train their dogs to deal specifically with these requirements. In gundog work, anything nature can throw at you is possible. Many gundog handlers hugely underestimate just how much generalisation is required for successful training.

Gundog work — involving, as it does, the living world — is almost infinite in its variety. A rabbit can flush quickly, from cover, or slowly, after having had a look around. Away from the dog or towards the dog. Across the dog's line of vision. Through open ground. In and out of grass. Down a rabbit hole. Each of these constitutes a variation on 'a rabbit flushing'. A dog may know 'sit' when a rabbit is running in open cover, from left to right of field of vision. Yet the same dog may not know 'sit' when the rabbit is running from right to left. Or into a rabbit hole. Or after a look around. And then there are baby rabbits. And hares. And then there are different environments, such as a dense wood, marshland, an open field. Different terrains (hilly and flat) and different weather conditions.

Too often, the justification given for punishment is that the dog knows the behaviour; that the dog has been taught it, already, and that somehow her inability to respond is therefore disobedience rather than innocent not-knowing. This line of thinking leads to explanations like 'she's having you on' or 'she's blowing you off'.

What a dog knows and doesn't know is not a black or white thing. A dog may know 'sit' to a bird flushing, yet not when a rabbit flushes. Each time something different is encountered — whether an aspect of the environment or game — a trainer may need to go back to the beginning of training the behaviour again. Progress will be much quicker than the first time it was taught.

In order to help the dog generalise a behaviour, a handler needs to be aware of the distractions which are present in the environment — of their proximity, of the dog's level of interest in them and of previous training around similar distractions. With this information, the handler can judge whether it's even worth asking for a behaviour or whether it's best to withdraw and reduce the intensity of the distractions, by increasing the *distance* from them.

Distance is not the only variable we can manipulate. If a dog does not yet understand that a flush on game, is a 'sit' cue (and still views it as a distraction), the intensity of that distraction will also be reduced when the game removes itself — when it flies or runs off. In other words, as time elapses from the flush, so the degree of distraction is progressively reduced. With a novice dog, you can begin by restraining the dog on a long-line during the flush, without asking for a behaviour. Once you judge that the dog's arousal level has dropped to a point that the dog is able to respond to you, ask for a sit and reinforce. With repetition, you will find that the dog is able to respond earlier — until you do get that sit-to-flush. It doesn't matter how long you wait, because you are all the time preventing the behaviour you don't want (chasing) using the long-line. So there are no reinforcements available, other than your own.

We have discussed, here, two main ways to adjust distraction levels — 1) the dog's distance from the distraction and 2) the time elapsed since the distracting event.

This manipulation of variables — identifying them and controlling distance or duration from them — is often lacking in traditional gundog training. Too often gundogs are subjected to punishment for failing to respond under conditions they have not even been trained for.

A WORD ABOUT VARIABLE REINFORCEMENT (OR 'INTERMITTENT REINFORCEMENT')

When a trainer puts behaviours onto a 'variable reinforcement schedule', it means that the trainer is not reinforcing every correct response that occurs — they are reinforcing only some of the correct responses. I do not recommend using a variable reinforcement schedule.

The original research behind variable reinforcement schedules involved laboratory studies using rats and pigeons. Every correct response was reinforced during the learning phase of a behaviour. Then, once the animal knew the behaviour, it was moved to a variable reinforcement schedule. The research found that behaviours grew stronger when a rat or a pigeon wasn't reinforced for every behaviour — but was only reinforced intermittently, for some of the behaviours.

Pretty soon, this information had filtered through to dog training and dog trainers began to advocate reinforcing dogs for every correct response only during the learning phase of a behaviour and then switching to a variable reinforcement schedule, once the behaviour was trained.

But the problem is that a laboratory is not real life, in all its messiness. In a laboratory, the pigeon or rat is in a white box (a Skinner box), with no confounding variables. That is the whole point of an experiment — to control for all variables. There is nothing in the pigeon or rat's experimental box, except for the lever for the animal to press - which provides reinforcement. There are no competing environmental reinforcers. Everything is accounted for, and conditions are identical for each subject. It is a highly controlled environment. And it is pretty boring for the rat or pigeon, except for the opportunity afforded to perform the behaviour.

We cannot extrapolate any findings from this highly artificial environment to the ever-changing natural environment — with infinite variables: The natural world is not a white box. It is full of competing environmental reinforcers, the majority of which we (as handlers) are completely unaware of (scent, humidity, wind direction). Have we adequately trained heelwork whilst there is the smell of rabbit in the air being propelled towards the dog on a 20mph back wind, with moderate levels of humidity, keeping the scent low and strong, whilst the dog is extremely hungry? Unlike a scientist with her rats and pigeons in a lab, we can never definitively say that we are now finished with the learning phase; that we have trained a behaviour against all the variables the dog will encounter — to the degree that we can now put that behaviour onto a variable reinforcement schedule.

Then there comes the difficulty of scientifically and accurately implementing randomisation — because it is necessary to reduce reinforcers gradually. And, since we don't want things to get predictable, we must also reduce them randomly. Yet, randomisation is extremely hard for humans to calculate. Hence the existence of random number generators! The impracticality of all this is obvious.

We come back to the fact that the real world is not just a white Skinner box, with nothing else for the dog to do, but to keep playing our training game. The real world can always offer a dog other, more accessible, reinforcers. And this presents us with a real difficulty if those other reinforcers are available on a much higher rate of reinforcement than our own: Every time the dog sniffs something interesting, that is reinforcing. Not every fourth sniff, but every single one. And research shows that, in situations where there are competing reinforcement schedules, the highest rate of reinforcement will 'win'. (So says 'matching law' research.)

Many handlers assume that they need to reduce reinforcers during training. And perhaps this says more about human psychology than it does about science. In truth, we need to remain generous and consistent sources of reinforcement for our dogs.

Lastly — and very importantly — for gundog work, we don't even need to think about reducing reinforcers. After all, when we are working a dog or on a shoot, we can easily continue to use food reinforcers. And, unlike many other dog sports — where reinforcers are unavailable whilst the dog is under assessment — reinforcers in gundog work remain available because reinforcers are built into the work itself: Hunting is reinforcing, running is reinforcing, picking game and retrieving it, is reinforcing. Game scent is reinforcing. We have bred these dogs to find these behaviours reinforcing. Whilst we will continue to use food reinforcers whenever possible for behaviours like the recall — behaviours which are not innately reinforcing — for the majority of behaviours, we only need heavy use of food reinforcers for beginner and intermediate dogs — only during the stages of training behaviours out of context of the dog's 'real job'.

The more 'finished' a dog becomes, the more we can utilise those environmental reinforcers — releasing the dog to access them when we choose. The dog transitions effortlessly to these environmental reinforcers, from food reinforcers. Consequently, there simply isn't the need to think too hard about reducing reinforcers in gundog training.

IN SUMMARYS

Using force-free methods to train a gundog successfully requires us to understand certain fundamental principles or core concepts. To be successful, you need to implement:

1. Control over the dog's access to environmental reinforcers
2. Repetition of multiple cues, to the point of fluency
3. Prevention, to the point of extinction

These core concepts are not very obvious or visible. Even if you were to watch someone implementing them perfectly, on the surface you might just see a dog on a long-line, getting clicked and treated.

Yet these concepts are crucial for success.

1.5

BECOME A MAGPIE – DON'T REINVENT THE WHEEL

ON NOT REINVENTING THE 'CLICKER' WHEEL

There are many good general clicker trainers worldwide who can help you achieve basic clicker-trained behaviours, and can also teach you excellent clicker training skills.

Think about the very baby-beginnings of most behaviours you need, for a gun-dog:

- positions (whether sit/stand/down)

- a recall
- heelwork
- focus/attention
- a basic retrieve.

These are not gundog-specific behaviours. They are covered on every good 'pet dog' training course, the world over. All advanced gundog training evolves from these simple and *non-gundog* beginnings.

In a pet dog training class, you will likely be training these behaviours indoors, in a hall — and not out in the field. But that's fine, because you should always start behaviours in less distracting environments, anyway. You can, when you are ready, repeat the training outdoors to proof against a more distracting environment. You will know what to do outside, because you will repeat exactly the same thing you were taught to do indoors.

Moreover, you will understand the use of the clicker as a marker; that each click must result in a reinforcer; how to hold and coordinate clicker, treats and dog leash; and your dog will be used to practising behaviours with the distractions of other dogs and people around. If you have a puppy, you also have the benefits of an intense socialisation experience from attending class. A series of good, general clicker training classes should be the bedrock of any future training you do with your dog. For people starting out, I recommend *Click for Joy* by Melissa C. Alexander.

All gundog training has baby-beginnings indoors. Well-run pet dog classes are never beneath us. Everyone (even the most hardcore gundog trainer) can benefit from attending good clicker training classes and learning more about timing, reinforcers, delivery of these reinforcers, attaching cues to behaviours and working around the types of distractions that might be expected in these situations (like other dogs and people).

ON NOT REINVENTING THE 'TRADITIONAL GUNDOG' WHEEL

Since gundog training involves working with strong environmental reinforcers (such as game) and with innately reinforcing behaviours (such as hunting and retrieving), it can be seen that much of even traditional gundog training actually employs positive reinforcement. As force-free practitioners, we need to be able to identify and isolate these components of traditional training which do not involve aversives — and incorporate them wholeheartedly into force-free training programs. For example, there are some fantastic DVDs from US bird-dog trainers which demonstrate how to use birds to get puppies pointing and steady — in an entirely force-free way. (I highly recommend the US DVD *Perfect Start* by Jon Hann of Perfection Kennels.) Equally, other videos and articles by traditional trainers show the development of retrieving abilities and even early directional work with young retriever puppies — which is entirely force-free. US retriever drills have much to offer the force-free trainer when it comes to handling and directions — using positive reinforcement, instead of force. And many traditional trainers possess considerable knowledge about field-craft, scenting conditions, quartering, where to find game — and much more.

To avoid learning anything about traditional training methods is to lose out on knowledge which traditional trainers have been refining for decades. Reinventing the wheel — or at least, making a force-free wheel from scratch, uncontaminated by knowledge from traditional sources — is going to take a long time, as long as it has taken existing methods to evolve from scratch. If we go that route, force-free gundog work isn't going to look like a reliable way to get results for maybe another hundred years!

There are still very, very few gundog trainers using force-free methods. The force-free gundog trainers writing about — or passing on — what they are doing, is even smaller. If we restrict ourselves further, what is left is very limited. We would be left reinventing the gundog wheel from scratch. To mix metaphors, we would be throwing the baby out with the bathwater.

Besides, if we want to replace traditional training methods with force-free methods, we need to understand what traditional methods are trying to achieve — and why and how they work (if they do). To counter the use of aversives, to equip ourselves with the best arguments against them and to devise replacement techniques for training desired behaviours, we need to know how success is currently achieved in traditional circles. We cannot live in a force-free bubble.

Even using force-free methods, we are still part of the wider gundog community. It's important to understand the discourse used by most of this community, in order to be able to situate ourselves within it — and to feel that we belong to it. Because it's almost impossible to be successful (whatever you define that as), whilst also being isolated.

Being well-connected will see you being invited to shoots or given access to land to train on, or other perks, which you would not otherwise have enjoyed. Negotiating 'disapproval-of-training-methods' with 'not-disrespecting-traditional-handlers-themselves' and yet 'remaining-a-likeable-person-within-a-group' can mean walking a tightrope at times. Your disapproval of traditional methods is likely to be met with more acceptance if it is accompanied by an understanding of the traditional methods used — rather than 'received wisdom' or garbled second-hand accounts of those methods.

When you get out into the field, you will sometimes be working right next to people who use aversives. And it is not always the most effective approach to challenge them directly, at that moment. So, at some point, you *will* end up being exposed to things you would rather cut yourself off from, completely. I'd go so far as to say this is inevitable, currently, if you pick gundog work as your dog sport. If it is important to you to see and know absolutely nothing of aversives in your training, there are many other dog sports where it is possible to do just that. But, before you leave us, keep in mind how influential you could become, in turn, quietly working your own dog in a force-free way.

Finally, you need practical experience — both with your own dogs, but also watching others work their dogs. You can read books about gundog work but — whilst valuable — these are no replacement for first-hand experience. This is necessary to learn what is considered 'excellent work', of a typical nature, for your specific dog, in your country. Only then can you ever have a hope of training your dog towards this. After all, if you don't know what end result you are aiming for, how are you ever going to make progress? It's like trying to make a cake without reading the recipe in advance, and without any photos of the end result! This is not about knowing *training methods*, it's about knowing desirable *end results*. It is not about '*How do I do that?*', it is about '*What do they want to see?*' You can't very well begin to train your dog as a gundog, without knowing the hoped-for end result.

People coming to class tend to expect their trainers to impart all this information to them. But, at class, we are concerned with teaching your dog in a way which suits where they are, at that current moment — not communicating to you the optimal end results, for your breed. Trainers can try to do that, but there is only limited time at class — and it's very difficult to convey this sort of information verbally, anyway. Nothing replaces videos and practical experience.

If you are a force-free handler who is beginning to get involved in the traditional gundog scene, you will experience internal struggles. Many force-free handlers object even to watching footage of dogs scruffed, given leash corrections, receiving e-collar shocks, or having ears pinched or toes hitched. You may well want to turn all this off and avoid it completely. This is understandable. But, for all the above important reasons, I would urge you not to.

So, what should you do?

- Watch video clips on YouTube of gundogs training and competing. Be aware of 1) the subgroup of gundog, and 2) the country they are in. Also be aware that there is a lot of poor-quality material on YouTube, and a lot of dubious sources (which might actually look superficially impressive) — so don't take anything there as necessarily useful!

- Read traditional gundog training books and learn about US e-collar training systems and the stages dogs are put through in training. Look beyond any advice you disagree with. Instead, what is the desired end result? And how can you achieve that, without the use of force?

- Join online forums for your subgroup of gundog. These may be in another country to your own. Be aware that requirements differ from one country to another — both in terms of competition requirements and expectations in the shooting field.

- Join relevant groups on Facebook to learn more from discussions and for networking. Pippa Mattinson has a great Facebook group, Positive Gundogs, specifically for people who are already committed to force-free training. The Gundog Club is force-free and also has a Facebook group called The Gundog Trust — Graded Training Scheme. Come and join us!

- Volunteer to help out with a local club. Clubs are always looking for dummy throwers and helpers, or stewards for tests, and, by helping out, you will learn a lot about what is desirable. You will also make contacts and get to know people — and endear yourself to the club as a helpful person — before you appear with your own dog and your own ideas!

- Ask if you can watch at a field trial or two. Usually you can spectate from the gallery, if you ask in advance.

- Watch as many traditional DVDs and videos, as you can — particularly footage from trials. In the UK, you can purchase these from Paul French. In the US, DVDs are much more readily available — check out gundogsupply.com for equipment, DVDs and books.

- Get involved with your local shoot (if you live in the UK) and start beating — but resist the urge to take your dog with you until you have achieved a good level of control and are well on the way with her training. Meanwhile, observe and learn about the whole situation of a shoot, the different roles people have and the different capacities the dogs work in.

It is very hard to get involved and engaged with a community, in the way I've described here — whilst, at the same time, distancing yourself from that community through not using aversives. It can be especially hard to manage this if you are new to gundog training. If you feel this might be difficult for you, or if you don't feel able to defend the way you want to train when others around you may put pressure on you to do otherwise, wait until you have a solid base in clicker training and have progressed as far as you can there — in terms of what is available where you live — before investigating these sources.

ON NOT REINVENTING THE 'OTHER DOG SPORTS' WHEEL

Most people compartmentalise dog sports. Instead, I would encourage you to think of 'excellent training', generally — regardless of the sport involved. You never know when a skill or a behaviour you have learnt in application to another sport, could help you in gundog training. And force-free gundog training needs this cross-fertilisation.

Other dog sports are light years ahead of gundog training when it comes to having developed effective force-free training solutions. Rather than reinventing the wheel (again), it makes sense to learn as much as possible from top force-free trainers in other dog sports.

For example:

- How do working trials 'send-aways' relate to blind retrieves for gundogs?
- What can you learn from agility or working trials about jumping, and training your gundog to jump 'over' on cue?
- What can you learn from agility about target-training for contacts, and how can this be applied to mat training and directional training for gundogs?
- How do obedience trainers achieve a reliable retrieve, on all kinds of objects, in breeds not known for retrieving ability?
- What can you learn from dogs training in schutzhund or working trials, in terms of their high prey drive for toys and the sleeve, and their ability to switch this on and off when highly aroused? How is this relevant to control in gundog work around game?
- What can you learn from methods like BAT or Control Unleashed — developed to help reactive dogs remain under-threshold near triggers — when it comes to training a gundog to maintain focus and to remain quiet and calm around high distractions and in situations of high arousal?

I have looked into all of the above and taken some elements I've found useful into what I do with gundogs. But I'm sure there is much more to be mined, from other dog sports. I'd encourage you to be creative and to think outside the box, so force-free gundog training can progress by using the discoveries of other dog sports and does not need to reinvent everything from scratch.

When it comes to other sports, the most knowledgeable and skilled trainers are not necessarily those at your nearest local club. Look out for one-off workshops and seminars by top trainers in various dog sports. These trainers will have an excellent understanding of how dogs learn and are likely to use the clicker or a verbal marker rigorously, as well. You will learn things, here, which you can import right back into gundog training. And you can always go along as an observer or spectator, without your dog.

• • • • •

Sometimes you might see someone training their dog and it looks beautiful. The dog is responsive and working with the handler well. You watch them, admiringly. You try to remember what is happening, then go home and attempt it with your own dog. It doesn't seem to work at all. You don't understand why; whether it's you, or the method, or your dog. Things are just not working for you like they were working for the other handler you saw. You give up.

When you are looking at successful training, you are seeing only the tip of the iceberg. Underneath all of that – making it possible – are many other factors which the successful trainer has implemented. These things are not visible when you look at a dog and handler. And they are not things you can instantly implement – they take time to get working in your favour. But without them, training may fail.

A successful theatre production has a lot going on behind the scenes which enables everything to operate so slickly. And yet the audience has no idea about any of this. In the same way, successful dog training has a lot behind it which goes unrecognised – but is essential for success.

Let's take a look behind the scenes...

SECTION 2

BEHIND THE SCENES OF SUCCESSFUL TRAINING

2.1

FOOD MOTIVATION

WHAT IS FOOD MOTIVATION AND WHY IS IT IMPORTANT?

Your dog's relationship with food is very important, for training purposes. If your dog values food, you can use food as a reinforcer. (She might also enjoy chasing rabbits, but keeping rabbits in your pocket is a lot harder than keeping a tub of tasty treats!) If your dog doesn't value food, you don't have such easy control over what she wants. So you will find it hard to have control over her, too.

At class, we see some dogs focussed completely on the food in their owner's hand. And we see other dogs turning their heads away and almost saying 'Yuck, get that treat off my nose, I'd rather sniff this other dog's butt!' Obviously the first sort of dog is going to be a lot easier to train.

It's an old adage, but in dog training there is only the stick or the carrot. If we are not using the stick, our carrots had better be really tasty!

WHAT YOUR DOG VALUES IS (MAINLY) LEARNT, NOT GENETIC

I often hear owners telling me that their dog just doesn't like food much, especially outdoors. They say this like it is a fact, a *fait accompli*, an unchangeable 'thing' about their dog. Like she has brown fur or black nails.

Sometimes this is given as a reason for them not being able to use food in training: 'I can't use food rewards — my dog won't eat food outside.'

There *is* a genetic component to food motivation. As anyone knows who has owned a Labrador. Some breeds — and individuals — are naturally more or less motivated by food than others.

However, by far the biggest influence on your dog's attitude towards food is *you*. Fussy dogs are almost entirely created by their owners. All dogs have the potential to be motivated by food, because without food they would die.

If your dog is lacking food motivation, it is because of something you have (or haven't) done. And, even if you believe she *is* food-motivated, ask yourself if you can make her even more food-motivated. *Is she as food-motivated as she is able to be?* Obviously, I am not advocating starving her, but we do want her to urgently need to earn those treats.

The vast majority of dogs I see are not food-motivated enough. And a lack of interest in food makes our task as gundog trainers much harder — because we

need to work in close proximity to competing motivators for our dogs, like game and scent. We need our dog to want what we have, even in the presence of these environmental reinforcers.

Puppyhood is a really important time for establishing the 'right' attitude towards food. It is very possible to take an older dog who lacks food motivation, and turn her into a food-motivated dog. But it is far easier just to raise a puppy in such a way that they value food from the beginning.

Here's how to create a food-motivated dog...

DO NOT 'FREE-FEED'

'Free-feeding' refers to putting down food for the dog to help herself to, whenever she wants. She can graze on it all day. Free-feeding usually begins when a dog doesn't finish all her food, so the owner leaves the food out for her to snack on.

If you worked in a chocolate factory and helped yourself to chocs all day from the conveyor belt, whenever you wanted, would you be that pleased if someone gave you a box of the same chocolates?

Even worse, if someone asked you to *do* something to *earn* the box of chocolates? You probably wouldn't want to. Chocolate isn't a scarce resource for you. It's there always, whenever you want it.

The same goes for dogs: If food is always available, whenever the dog wants it, food is *devalued* for the dog.

So:

- Remove any food left by the dog, immediately. Put the food back in the bag or fridge.
- Do not offer food again until the next meal time.
- Do not 'spice-up' the food by adding tasty stuff to it. You will train the dog to refuse the food because she knows something tastier will be added.
- Do not hand-feed, piece by piece, if a dog is reluctant to eat. Your dog may then not eat unless you continue to do this.
- Do not verbally encourage the dog to eat the food or praise her for eating it. We want the dog to want the food. If you're behaving as if she's doing you a favour by eating, the pressure you put on her will only result in increased avoidance.

Just remove the food. Once the dog realises that food is available at certain times of the day and not at others, she will start to make the most of the times when it is available and to eat it while it's there. She may go a bit hungry for a few days while she figures this out, but she's not going to starve.

If you do this for a few days without seeing much improvement, reduce the amount you are feeding by *half* for at least three days — and see if this makes a difference.

TRAIN WITH MEALS

If you ate a gourmet three-course lunch for free and then I asked you to run up six flights of stairs for a slice of bread and butter, would you? No.

If your dog gets 'free' food several times a day (meaning she doesn't need to *earn* it or do anything to get it), in ample quantities, she is going to be less interested in *working* for food at other times. Why work for something which is available for free, at other times of the day?

Rather than put down a big bowl of free food for your dog, use her meals to train with. You can practise all of your basics inside the house, using your dog's meals — except for the recall, which you should always use the tastiest treats for, even when training indoors. When training, you click, then give your dog a few bits of kibble each time. (We will discuss training with raw food, below.)

If you don't have time to train with a meal, rather than giving it to your dog for free, use a treat dispenser toy — a buster cube, a Kong Wobbler or similar — so she still has to *work* to earn the kibble. If you feed wet or raw food, stuff a Kong with it. Freeze the Kong to make it more challenging.

Think of the 'enrichment' programmes which zoos run for animals in captivity — they scatter food, so the animals can forage for it. Research shows animals prefer to work for their food in this way than to get it 'for free'. Working for food leads to psychological enrichment for your dog, too.

But don't get carried away with the treat dispensers and food toys. Your main goal is to train your dog, so ensure you are doing that with the majority of your dog's meals.

DO NOT OVERFEED

The vast number of dogs I see are over-weight. And also lacking in food motivation. This correlation is very meaningful!

There is a key phrase in dog training which goes: *Deprivation increases motivation.*

This means that the more the dog is deprived of something, the more motivated she is by it. Of course, I am not advocating you starve your dog. But keeping a dog on the hungry-side before training sessions is very beneficial. And certainly avoid piling on the pounds. (Since satiety is the opposite of deprivation.)

Rather than feeding the amount written on the packet or tin, look at your dog and think for yourself whether she is under or overweight — then adjust amounts accordingly. This is especially the case for growing puppies: We don't feed our children by looking at recommended amounts on food packets, and you don't need to feed your puppy that way either.

Puppies grow in spurts, so you may at times need to increase and then decrease the amount you are feeding. Once your puppy begins to approximate adult size, the amount she needs to eat hugely decreases. Don't keep feeding three or even four meals a day, indefinitely. If you notice a lack of interest in meals from your puppy, consider switching to two meals a day, if you are still feeding three. Carrying excess weight in puppyhood is damaging to developing joints and can predispose a dog to hip and joint issues later in life, amongst other health problems.

Your dog should have a visible waist when looked down on from above, and you should be able to identify each rib easily, when you run your hands over her rib cage. There should not be a thick layer of fat between your fingers and her ribs. Most gundog breeds should ideally look lean and fit.

IMPLEMENTING THESE PRINCIPLES WHILST RAW FEEDING

I have come late to the table of raw food (pun intended!). I firmly believe that feeding raw is the healthiest option for your dog. If you are new to feeding raw, I would recommend you start with a complete raw mince — there are many manufacturers making these now.

Feeding raw does present some challenges to the food motivation subject, though:

- With raw food, it is difficult, messy and unhygienic to train with your dog's meals. It's not impossible — you *can* click and offer a spoon of raw mince — but it's not easy. Treat delivery is an important aspect of clicker training: The way in which you deliver the treats (rolled, thrown, near you, on a mat, over an obstacle, on the floor, in the dog's mouth) contributes to the end result — and can make or break a behaviour. For obvious reasons, it is difficult to use the full range of treat deliveries, with raw food. So, people who raw feed and clicker train tend not to use their dog's food for training purposes and instead use additional treats on top of their dog's meals. Whilst this usually works fine once you've established good food motivation, I can't recommend it for puppies (who are still learning about the value of food) or if food motivation needs improving.

- If you feed bones or carcasses, you won't get many reps in, per meal. You *can* say 'sit', click, and feed the dog half a chicken, but you will only get to do a couple of reps per meal. And there will be a long wait in between, whilst the dog crunches away. Doing multiple rapid reps of any behaviour is not going to be possible. And multiple rapid reps are important for developing a fluent response in your dog. Practice makes perfect: *Repetition to the point of fluency.*

- It is commonly accepted that raw food is very tasty for most dogs. So, not only do we have dogs getting food for free, twice a day — but they are getting *delicious* food for free, twice a day. These two factors combined are a double-whammy when it comes to decreasing food motivation in training. You may not notice this lack of motivation in the house with your training treats — a dog can look very responsive in the house, when there's not much else to do. But once you get outside, where environmental reinforcers challenge your own reinforcers for prime position in the dog's reward hi-

erarchy, you start to see how food motivated a dog *really* is — not just how food motivated they are when there's nothing better to do, but how food motivated they are *when there are other options for reinforcement.*

Yet feeding raw is the healthiest option. So — what do we do about this? There is not a perfect solution, but these are my suggestions for feeding raw whilst maintaining food motivation:

- ***Be very careful you are not over-feeding your dog.*** It can be hard to estimate portion size when feeding raw and I've seen many people overfeeding their dogs, especially on raw food. Feeding too much food (of any type) greatly reduces food motivation. It also predisposes your dog to hip dysplasia and other health issues. Keep your dog on the hungry side of things, so she continues to be keen to work for food. This alone will help a lot with maintaining food motivation. One comment people make about complete raw foods is that they can be expensive. So, do yourselves a favour and don't overfeed them — and save money in the process!

- ***Use Ziwipeak*** (an air-dried raw food made in New Zealand) instead of complete raw for a while. Ziwipeak is dry and comes in flakes. You can handle it easily, so it is great to use for training purposes around the house. If (like me!) you want to do a lot of training at home with a young puppy, you might feed *only* Ziwipeak in puppyhood — which is the time of your dog's life when you will need to do most training at home. If you want your puppy to have some raw mince too, use that to stuff Kongs with (and freeze them to last extra-long). Ziwipeak may seem very expensive at first, but it is dense in calories and nutrition, so you won't be feeding very much of it. And again, remember to feed according to your dog's shape rather than the recommendations on the packet!

- ***Try training with the complete raw.*** This is an imperfect solution, but it's worth mentioning. Whilst you won't be able to throw the food on the floor (which is essential for some exercises) and therefore won't be able to train everything in this way, you may be able to train some behaviours. Get a box of latex gloves, squidge a blob of raw mince together and deliver that each time you reinforce. If it works better, you can deliver (after a click) into an empty bowl on the floor for the dog to eat it from. Alternatively, invest in a 'GoToob' — a silicone squeezy tube you can fill with raw mince and squirt out, directly into your dog's mouth. This works best with very smooth minces, so you may need to add some water.

- ***Use your dog's complete raw to stuff Kongs and chew toys*** — rather than giving it to her for free in a bowl. With a puppy, you can use these as part of your crate training or alone training. You can also freeze Kongs stuffed with raw, so they last longer and help with pain during teething. This way, your puppy will still have to work for her food. And then you can use Ziwipeak by itself at meal times, for training.

When training away from the house, or when attending training classes, you can *mix your puppy's dinner of Ziwipeak, with tastier foods* — and shake it all up together. In this way, part of the treats you use at class or away from the house, will comprise your dog's regular dinner — they won't all be extra treats. Obviously don't feed your dog dinner before attending a training class, as she will get a whole load of treats (including her meal) at training.

If you ever notice that your dog is starting to lack food motivation or to be less than enthusiastic about training treats — especially away from the house or in more distracting environments — the first thing to think about is *not* increasing the tastiness of the treats, but ask:

- ***Am I over-feeding my dog?*** Reduce food by at least a third or a half for a couple of days and see if things improve.

- ***Is my dog overweight?*** Be honest. Can you feel every rib? Can you see a clear waist? Does your dog look athletic? If not, reduce food until you like what you see.

If the above measures don't improve things and your dog continues to lack food motivation or to be more interested in other things (dogs, people) for your liking:

- ***Switch to feeding Ziwipeak only (for meals) for a while.*** This will reduce the comparative tastiness of meals and ensure that your training treats retain the 'wow' factor by comparison. Hopefully this will only be a short-term measure whilst your dog learns to value food, which she will maintain even when switched back to fresh raw.

USING FOOD AWAY FROM THE HOUSE

When you train away from the house, the goal is to use nutritious and healthy foods which are also of high value for the dog. Obviously any meats will probably be cooked, but they should not be processed — hotdog sausages/frankfurters, salami and sausages all contain a lot more than just meat, including nitrites and other preservatives, which research shows are potentially carcinogenic.

So, in choosing meat products, think 'pure' meat.

- Look at which joints for roasting are on sale, and buy and roast one. Or roast a whole chicken. Cut the meat up, bag it in portions in freezer bags, and freeze until you need it. This works out to be very economical.

- Look at hearts, kidneys and livers in freezer sections — very cheap!

- Mild cheddar cheese is another popular and healthy training treat.

- A tablespoon of blueberries with each meal is great for your dog. But why add these to meals, when she can work for them as training treats each day? Add them into the treats you take out with you.

- Add in the Ziwipeak you would usually be feeding at the nearest meal time and shake it all up. Ta da! These are your treats for training away from the house.

Any leftover meat scraps from human meals can be saved separately from the other treats, for recalls. Also, pieces of gristle, excess fat, fish skin, prawn heads — things which you would usually throw out — make great recall treats!

RECALLS

For recall treats, you need to pull out all the stops and use amazingly squishy, wet food items kept separately from the above treats. Your recall is *the* most important behaviour, because it can save your dog's life — so we need to pay it well. Many years of running training classes proves to me that these are the most amazing foods to use for recalls:

- paté

- tinned sardines

- smoked mackerel (or any oily fish)

- gourmet wet dog food of a good quality.

If you don't want to touch these messy treats, put them in a ziplock bag or Addis beaker and use a plastic toddler spoon — giving your dog a spoonful each time.

IN CONCLUSION...

Food motivation is sitting quietly in the background of *all* your training — supporting it, or (when lacking) sabotaging it.

What you feed, how you feed, when you feed and how much you feed all influence your dog's attitude towards food. It can take several weeks, or even a month or so, to initiate a new attitude towards food.

Even if you believe your dog is already food-motivated, implement the above advice and you may find a huge increase in her food motivation. It's all relative!

Remember: Control is not force. Control is a dog falling over herself to do what *you* want, because *you* have what *she* wants.

2.2

HOW TO STOP 'WALKING THE DOG'! (AND HOW TO START TRAINING HER!)

The concept of walking the dog each day is so firmly embedded in popular consciousness that it is tricky to introduce this concept. You may even consider it cruel to deprive a dog of a daily walk.

Yet — particularly for hard-running HPRs and spaniels — *not* walking the dog is key to helping a gundog achieve her potential.

'What's wrong with walking the dog?'

We discussed environmental reinforcers, earlier in this book. Environmental reinforcers, are reinforcers in the environment — not on your person. They could be game, scent, other dogs, people, dead animals, BBQ remains and so on.

Before we look at what's *wrong* with a dog walk, we need to define the term. I've had this conversation with people in the past, only to find that we have different understandings and have been talking at cross-purposes — causing a lot of confusion.

When I say 'dog walk', I am referring to what most pet owners would do on a daily basis. On this 'dog walk', a person walks along, with a dog off-leash. The person might be thinking about something, listening to music, texting on their phone or bird watching. Or talking to someone else.

What is the *dog* doing? Usually sniffing stuff. Marking/peeing on things. Eating dead animals. Running up to other dogs and playing with them. In all ways, exploring the environment and learning how infinite is its ability to provide reinforcers: '*Here's some seaweed, which a female dog peed on. Here's a dead crab. Here's a dead bunny to sniff. Here's a pheasant to flush and chase. Here's another dog to play with. Here's some poo to eat, yum.*'

Cut back to the dog's owner, trailing along boringly, usually without any treats — or with some dried kibble or pet-shop-bought junk food.

The dog is learning: '*My owner is boring. The environment is fantastic!*'

With the environment reinforcing the dog like this, the behaviour being reinforced is that of seeking out those environmental reinforcers. Just because the owner is not having anything to do with things here, doesn't mean the dog isn't learning or being trained: The environment is training the dog. But the environment may not be teaching her what the owner wants her to learn!

Dogs need to learn where to look for their reinforcers. They can learn that they are 'out there' in the environment, or they can learn that they are on you — food or toys or other reinforcers. It doesn't take much for a gundog with good working instincts to discover environmental reinforcers. These are often all-too-evident to the dog! But the concept of working for *your* re-inforcement is something which can take the dog some time to understand.

What a dog finds reinforcing is *learned*. Help your dog to learn to look to you for reinforcement and prevent her from learning to look to the environment (with some exceptions, which we'll get to later).

Perhaps 'walking the dog' should be renamed 'training the dog to ignore me'. People might do less of it, then: '*I'm just off out, to train the dog to ignore me. I'll be back for tea, ok?*'

'But my walks aren't like that. My dog focusses on me lots. We are always playing games together.'

In some ways, this is great. You have found a way to manage your dog's interest in environmental reinforcers and to achieve a focussed dog. Well done. You are going to be able to take 'safe' pet walks with your dog. But is she going to be successful as a *working* dog?

I believe that, if we want to have a top-notch *working* dog — whether for competition or shooting — there are specific behaviours which we want to see from especially the questing breeds (HPRs and spaniels), when they are off-lead and in a rural environment.

To give an example:

I met up with a friend of mine for a walk with his dog. He has a hard-hunting HPR, which I hugely admire. He took the lead off the dog, and away we went. His dog instantly began quartering at pace and with intent, and my friend had to pay complete attention to his dog — in case the dog found game. No doubt about it, that was the dog's goal. This dog was not out for a walk in the park — it was a dog on a mission, and the mission was to put game in your game bag. The dog was under very good control and working *for* the handler — but a relaxing potter in the country, this was not. We could hardly talk because, at any moment, game could be put up. It was not really a social occasion, until the lead went back on and we could relax. It was an edge-of-the-seat exciting demonstration of some fantastic dog work! This is a good working dog. (He subsequently won an Open HPR field trial.)

On another occasion, I met up with an old friend and her HPR of the same breed. And we took a walk together in similar open terrain. This friend is a fellow dog trainer, but she doesn't work her HPR as a gundog. To meet her needs, as a pet dog, she has trained her dog to focus on her, to recall on cue, and to offer frequent check-ins. On our walk, her dog stayed close by, pootled around and sniffed things, and we were able to chat away easily — just keeping one eye on the dog. This dog will never win trials, and nor does my friend want that. Would the dog be much use on a shoot? Well, maybe, if covering a spaniel-sized beat. But the dog definitely isn't fulfilling the job description of a HPR.

For most pet gundog owners, this dog would be their ideal. But this book is not about achieving a well-trained *pet* gundog. And we need to be clear about that. This book is *not* written to teach people who have bought a gundog breed, how to walk a gundog breed whilst retaining control. Why? Because there are loads of books out there in the pet dog market, covering just these issues. And these are not even gundog-specific issues: Recall and check-ins and managing off-leash walks around distractions are issues relevant to any breed of dog.

This book is intended to teach you how to train your dog to be a successful working gundog, using force-free methods.

When it comes to creating a gundog you can compete with, there are some real difficulties with 'taking a walk':

- If a rabbit or hare gets up and runs and your dog decides to chase, it will be really difficult to prevent this — if you are 'having a walk'. Even a controlled walk, reinforcing focus on you. If your dog has any speed or interest in ground game, she will be away before you can say 'Bob's your uncle'. A traditional trainer may not think this is the end of the world, because they can always 'steady the dog up' again. However, such steadying the dog up involves the use of a huge dollop of positive punishment, which we don't use in force-free training. It is hard to emphasise how just *one* chase can be so reinforcing for a dog that it can require a ridiculous number of successful reps to steady her up, without aversives, after she has tasted the endorphin rush of a chase. If you really do want to train without aversives, and your dog is at all interested in ground game, I can't recommend taking a walk (of any sort) — unless you're holding the end of a long-line or in an area devoid of game.

- Dogs become conditioned to the degree of active attention they give to their handler when off-lead and in a rural environment. If you are *regularly* reinforcing the dog for looking at you during a 'focussed walk' or checking back in with you of her own accord, the dog is going to start offering this behaviour increasingly whenever outdoors. This is great if you have a pet dog, but can easily result in a working gundog almost popping out of hunting and being too handler-focussed. Nothing looks less stylish than you turning up for a test or trial, casting your dog off, and seeing your hunting dog giving up hunting and looking at you, or returning to you. (I've been there and got that T-shirt!)

- Dogs become conditioned to the distance they routinely range out to, from their handler. If you *routinely* keep a dog within a short distance from you, the dog will begin to habitually hang out in this range when outdoors. This may not be a huge problem for a close-hunting breed like a spaniel, but if you have a HPR and would like the dog to quarter fields independently and to cast off immediately in a trial situation for the nearest hedgerow, it is likely to cause problems if the dog typically spends day after day after day close to you and focussed on you — because that's what you want, on walks. (Similarly, with spaniels, if routinely ranging further away from you and finding game out there, you can be sure they will start heading for the hedgerows — which isn't in *their* job description!)

- Dogs become conditioned to the way they cover ground when you are out and about. This means their quartering patterns, thoroughly covering ground and not missing any, use of scent and wind direction, size of the 'bites' taken for each cast, and the way they treat game when they come across it. The UK J-Regs (field trial regulations) describe, in some detail, the ground treatment required for success in trials. It's a good idea to familiarise yourself with these regulations — or the equivalent regulations for the testing body your dog will be assessed under. A HPR or spaniel should learn that being outdoors in a rural environment, when not on a retrieve, means giving game-finding her *all* — as with my first friend's HPR. I do not believe it is a good idea to associate being outdoors in a rural environment with pootling along and focussing excessively on the handler. Or, alternatively, with bogging off to the horizon. It's important that the dog associates the working or competition environment with the behaviours you want to see from the dog, in that environment.

- If nothing else, walking the dog is a waste of time if you want to train a gundog up to a good standard. How will you walk her for an hour a day, *and also* train her to hold straight lines on retrieves, sit to whistle, heel under distractions, deliver to hand exiting water, mark at a distance and take casts? Having a well-trained dog involves so much that, just on the basis of time alone, for most people, it isn't feasible to add a one-hour daily walk onto all that and still meet training objectives. (Whilst also working and having a social life!)

Two provisos:

- Obviously a good gundog is not going to be destroyed by an occasional walk. But doing this with a young dog more often than doing anything else may cause problems.

- Of course, retrievers are not questing breeds and many don't have the same '*I must find game, now*' need coursing through their blood. But some do! It may well be more possible to walk retrievers than the questing breeds. But ask yourselves if you are still able to retain the retriever's focus in a working environment. If you cannot obtain and keep your retriever's focus in a rural environment, don't walk your dog. (And, of course, all the reasoning about there not being enough hours in the day to both train and walk your dog apply just as much to retrievers as other breeds.)

'Can't I just cue what I want?'

When you release your dog to run free, some people believe you can simply add in a verbal cue to tell her what you want: To focus on you more (for a walk), or to focus on the environment more (for hunting). And, that way, these folks believe that you can have the best of both worlds.

One problem with this, is that the cue is not (mainly) what is said. Humans are terrible at perceiving what their dog experiences as the cue for a behaviour. I often spot people in class, leaning over their dogs, with their hands on their chests, saying 'sit'. They believe their dog knows the cue for 'sit' and that it is the word 'sit'. I tell them to stand up straight, to put their hands by their side or behind their back, and to say the word again. Usually the dog can't respond. Because the cue wasn't the word — the cue was the leaning forwards, hand on chest and perhaps the word *as well.*

Humans are verbal creatures and put huge significance on words. Dogs are not verbal, and usually a cue, for a dog, is a whole package of stuff. This is also part of the reason why a dog may be able to respond in the kitchen, but not in the lounge or in the garden — the kitchen was part of the cue. Not to get too technical about it, but the environment itself becomes built into the cue.

So, being outdoors and off-lead in a rural environment quickly becomes a cue for the sort of behaviour expected from the dog in that location. If you mostly associate being outdoors with pootling around by your feet, or (the opposite) bogging off to the horizon, that's what *being outdoors* will come to cue, for your dog. If you mostly associate being outdoors with '*We are seriously trying to find game, here*' or '*We are focussed on only me, in this place*', that's what *being outdoors* will come to cue, for the dog.

Try as you might to create a verbal cue which differentiates for the dog between quartering and just having a walk, in all likelihood the significance of the environment itself is going to far outweigh, for your dog, the significance of a couple of words you say when you take the lead off.

Teaching the dog to associate the cue which the environment gives with pootling, focussed walking, is not going to lead to trail-blazing quartering when you want it, at other times, in the same sort of environment. Through repeatedly putting the dog into an outdoors environment and encouraging high focus on you, you are teaching the dog that this is the behaviour you want, in this environment. The environment is the cue.

Think about it... Good agility trainers teach agility dogs to relax at the side of agility rings. They teach the dog that this is the behaviour they want at the side of the ring — *in that environment*. Dogs which are service animals must learn to settle by their owners and relax in a pub or café. They are taught that this is the expected behaviour, *in that environment*. The environment is part of the cue for the desired behaviour.

On another note — as I've said above — what is reinforcing to a dog is learnt, by the dog. If a dog learns that, when off-lead, it is reinforcing to focus on you and hang around near *you*, they are going to grow into a dog which seeks their reinforcement in that way. If a dog learns it is reinforcing to hunt and to range, they are going to grow into a dog which finds *that* reinforcing — turning to the environment to provide reinforcement.

'But wait, isn't there a contradiction here?'

By now you might be thinking: 'You're saying on the one hand that I shouldn't walk the dog because I don't want the dog to get reinforced by the environment. On the other hand, you're saying that walking the dog and encouraging focus on me, isn't going to be good for the dog's hunting if I have a spaniel or HPR — because they should learn to look to the environment for reinforcement. So — do we want them to focus on the environment or not? Which is it?'

There is a difference between just walking the dog and training the dog to hunt or quarter. When we are teaching a dog to look to the environment for reinforcement (to hunt), we are 100 per cent focussed on the dog. We are looking to ensure good quartering patterns, good ground treatment and good use of the wind. We are not just having a walk, outdoors. We are not going to be walking on footpaths — we are going to be walking through cover and open countryside. This is not a walk — it is training in the environment where we want performance to happen later. (We cover this training in Section 3.10, Hunting or quartering.)

If we find that the dog lacks focus on us and is not looking to us enough for reinforcement — if we find that she is instead excessively interested in the reinforcement coming from the environment — then we might need to reduce, or even stop altogether for a while, the environmental reinforcers, and work just with reinforcers coming from us. We cover this in Section 3.5, Focus and engagement.

Equally, if we find that a questing breed is *too* focussed on us, and is becoming a 'boot-licker', taking a step back and allowing the environment to 'teach' the dog that it is reinforcing, is the solution. (That means more quartering work, especially on gamey ground, and less engagement with the handler.)

Whichever way you look at it, if you want to have a working gundog, you are not just walking the dog. Even if you are allowing the dog to find the environment more reinforcing, you are thinking about ground coverage, use of the wind and scenting ability, pace and style, and all the other concerns that come with training a dog to hunt.

'How much exercise does my dog need?'

From adolescence onwards, most fit and healthy young gundogs from field lines will happily take all the exercise you can give them — and they will still want more.

A problem arises when people try to respond to their dog's demand for more, by providing more. The dog gets used to the increased daily exercise, and comes to want that amount — plus a little more. (The dog will always want more.) And so, the owner now gives the dog even *more*. This can reach quite ridiculous proportions.

If you have created a dog who expects huge amounts of exercise each day, the bad news is that she will be stir crazy at first, when you reduce this. But, after a week or so, she will adjust to the new regime.

The ideal — what you're aiming for — is that your dog's *physical* exercise needs are being met mostly at the same time (within the same training exercises) as her *psychological* exercise needs. Two for the price of one!

For example: Maybe you are working on your sit whistle, with your dog trailing a long-line. The dog is running freely, and then stopped on the whistle. Or, maybe you are working on some element of retrieving and your dog is running retrieves. If you have a HPR or spaniel, maybe you are practising quartering. The point is that the physical exercise is not a separate element to the psychological exercise. Instead, we try to provide physical and psychological exercise at the same time, and within the same exercises.

The other thing to bear in mind, is that research shows that dogs (like people) learn best in short and focussed sessions, followed by a rest, to consolidate and process that learning.

My training sessions (which include physical exercise) last on average about 30-45 minutes.

TRADITIONAL GUNDOG 'HUSBANDRY' (AND WHAT WE CAN LEARN FROM IT)

One of the most important things we can learn from traditional gundog training is what's around the training itself: It's the daily routine of the dog. It's the structure of the day. It's the amount of exercise given. It's where the dog's reinforcers are. Because there's a lot, in all this, which differs for your average *pet* dog.

Most large-scale professional traditional trainers have a set-up something like this:

They have kennels outside, in a purpose-built facility. They have many dogs, sometimes a dozen or two dozen. The dogs may be kennelled together, in pairs or even threes. There is probably a larger confined area outside the kennel — the exercise yard — where the dogs are let out in larger groups, to mill around, to toilet and to stretch their legs a few times a day. They may actually go for a walk on the property, but this will be a walk through the same relatively boring and safely fenced paddocks and exercise areas which do not contain game.

With that many dogs in kennels, each dog is not going to get a 1.5 hour session on a daily basis. Logic dictates that there wouldn't be enough hours in the day to provide that and run a business, clean the kennels, feed the dogs, run training classes, answer and return phone calls, test and trial dogs, and so on.

Each dog, according to their stage of development, gets relatively short focussed quality time, working on a specific training need. Quality over quantity.

Let's compare what learning experiences there are for dogs kept either as traditional gundogs, kennelled outside - or for pet dogs:

1) OTHER DOGS AS MOTIVATING

The traditional gundog learns:

- Other dogs are boring. (*'I am kennelled with one or two. I socialise in the exercise yard with 15 others. Other dogs are everywhere, they are two-a-penny and I get my fill of them. They are not especially interesting to me.'*)

The pet dog learns:

- Other dogs are incredible. (*'I live on my own, without any other dogs. I'm kinda deprived of my own kind. Once a day, I go on a walk and I spy other dogs from a distance. Desperate for some contact with my own species, I bog off to play with them. I have to get as much play in as I can, because my owner is after me, to take me away from them. I associate other dogs with wild games and high excitement.'*)

Possible solutions:

- It's great if you have a multi-dog household. Your puppy is much less likely to grow up to be excessively fixated on other dogs. If you don't live with other dogs, find a couple of good adult doggie playmates that your dog relates well to and which may not be especially playful. Spend frequent regular time, letting the dogs hang out together until bored (as long as interactions are consensual, equal, and well-supervised. Do not let the pup harass the older dogs — use a puppy house line to restrain the pup, should her advances be unwelcome!). Do this preferably *not* on a walk (due to environmental reinforcer problems, and the risk of dogs going off hunting together!) and also so your dog doesn't associate being outdoors and away from the house with seeking out other dogs for play. Instead, try it at each other's houses if possible.

  I can't stress enough how important it is that you meet frequently and that each session continues to the point of boredom (and longer) and that the contact is not wild and over-excited. If the dogs end up ignoring each other, bored, or sleeping, you are doing great. Why? This is about satiety and habituation. You want it to be almost as if the dogs lived together. If you meet 1) infrequently or 2) if you stop the play at the peak of excitement, the dog will only form an even greater belief that other dogs are 1) not always available (and therefore more desirable, because scarce) and 2) highly exciting.

For many people, this option isn't possible. It is hard to find dogs that are available frequently enough, for long enough. If that's the case, move on to these other ideas:

- Teach your dog to focus on you, in the presence of other dogs. Investigate Leslie McDevitt's most excellent *Control Unleashed* exercises. And read this book, specifically Section 3.5, Focus and engagement.

- Do not allow your dog to go running off to other dogs, for play. Other dogs should become a cue to focus on *you* more.

- Join some group gundog training classes. Gundog work is all about learning to concentrate and work whilst surrounded by other dogs, in an outdoor environment. What more could you want? Find out if there is a Gundog Club instructor in your area, running courses. All Gundog Club instructors are force-free.

2) HANDLER AS MOTIVATING

The traditional gundog learns:

- My handler is amazing. (*'Since I spend most of my time without human company, when I get some it's amazing stuff. My handler strokes me and tickles me and is also associated with retrieving and game and hunting and fun — since this is the stuff we do together, when I come out my kennel. I love to come out of my kennel and work with my handler. The two things are associated. My handler also punishes me and sometimes I am scared of him — but I am so much into hunting and game, nothing can take away my enthusiasm for that and so it rubs off onto how I feel about my handler, despite the punishment.'*)

The pet dog learns:

- My handler is pretty boring. (*'They are always around. They stroke me all the time anyway, and, although I love it, it's nothing which makes me want to stick around them when we're out — because I get stroked all the time. Daily, my handler takes me on a walk, and my handler is the most boring thing on this walk — they just plod along behind me. Far more interesting are all the smells and the other dogs and the game to chase.'*)

Possible solutions:

- Stop walking the dog. Start training the dog.

- Despite the 'findings' above, I am still not a fan of kennelling dogs outside. Research suggests that dogs need human companionship and have evolved to form close ties to their humans. Shutting them away from their people therefore seems wrong, to me — even if it results in enthusiasm and focus. Achieving such enthusiasm and focus through making the rest of a dog's life impoverished seems ethically questionable. I appreciate that may be controversial for some people reading this.

- However, there's no denying that to keep a dog in the house, successfully, prevention needs to be implemented at every turn. That means — access to areas where dogs can't be trusted is restricted. And people need to be ready to turn everything into a training opportunity. (*'You stole my underwear? Ok, let's work on the 'Drop' cue. Where are my training treats and clicker?'*) Working with the handler to earn treats becomes the highlight of the day, for the dog. So, for a dog living indoors, the handler is always around and is always available. But it is the handler *plus training* which equals fun.

3) ENVIRONMENTAL REINFORCERS AS MOTIVATING

The traditional gundog learns:

- The environment is great, but access to it is contingent on my handler. (*'I love bunnies and scent and birds. But I must access them in the way determined by my handler and only when allowed to by my handler. If I sit, I get to run and sniff where rabbits just were. If I take a cast correctly, I end up with a bird in my mouth. Doing whatever I want to get these goodies and ignoring my handler, doesn't work. In fact, it frequently leads to painful experiences when my handler punishes me!'*)The pet dog learns:

- *'The environment is great, and it's there for the taking. It has nothing to do with my handler. When I want it, I go get it. Bunnies. Birds. Dead things. There for the taking. Simple. They can't stop me, anyway.'*

Possible solutions:

- Prevention. Prevention. Prevention. Long-lines. Supervision. Prevention. Did I mention prevention? Then use these opportunities to proof the behaviours you have taught the dog. Don't allow free, unrestricted access to environmental reinforcers. Don't walk the dog — train the dog. In short, everything in this book!

HOW TO IMPLEMENT 'TRAINING THE DOG'

I'm going to tell you some *good* news about training the dog instead of walking the dog.

The good news is: It doesn't take any longer. Really. It will not take any more time out of your daily routine, to train the dog instead of walk her.

When people see a well-trained dog, they say things like '*Wow, what a lot of time that must have taken.*' The truth is that it doesn't take any more time than they spend walking Fido round the block on a daily basis. Honestly. So, if you are thinking that you don't have time to achieve a well-trained dog, you can scratch that one from the excuse list.

It's not about time spent. (It's not about quantity.) It's about what you do with the time you have. (It's about quality.)

Remember that traditional gundog trainers sometimes have dozens of dogs in kennels, and they are often extremely successful in trials and tests with these dogs. They don't provide each of them with four hours of training a day. There are not enough hours in the day. They just use the time they have, with each dog, in a very focussed and productive way.

For busy people, this is a good thing to know.

Research shows that an effective training session is short. If training continues for too long, results start to deteriorate. New trainers often don't realise this. They get results, and then they become 'greedy' and want to see even better results... and are disappointed when things deteriorate and end up worse than they started. So, keep it short and sweet. Stop when things are going well.

Don't worry about your dog needing more physical exercise: Training, which involves their minds, is going to tire dogs out much more deeply than bombing about everywhere. Whilst resting afterwards, your dog will process what she has learnt; latent learning is powerful. If you want to train harder, have another session later in the day.

Remember that training is not just running a retrieve. Training is walking at heel from your house or car, to the start point. Training is quartering, under control. Training is focussing on you when another dog appears.

Training is taking place every moment your dog is out of the house with you. If you are not providing reinforcers, the environment is. *Do you want to leave it up to the environment to train your dog for you?*

Before you leave the house, know what your training plan is to be for that outing. Each session, there will probably be a few different issues or exercises you'll be working on. Whatever's on the menu, you need to have a rough plan in mind. You need this plan to know what equipment you need to take with you (dummies? how many? what type? what colour?), and where you are going. (Do you need a field of short grass? Terrain for quartering? Water? Walls?)

It is hard to get out of the car in an unfamiliar place and have a useful training session. It is easy to fall back into walking the dog, if you're making the agenda up as you go. (It's amazing how everything disappears out of your head when you're standing in the cold, with a dog desperate to get out of the car.)

So, formulate your training plan before you leave the house, and *then* think about where you need to go, to realise that plan.

2.3

EQUIPMENT

Here's a list of basic equipment you'll need to make a good start with gundog training:

ACME GUNDOG WHISTLE Whilst other whistles are available, I recommend you use only Acme since other brands are not consistently pitched. This means that you can't easily buy additional or replacement whistles of the same pitch. The pitch is part of what the dog recognises and responds to and, if it doesn't sound the same, you may not get the same response from your dog.

The different Acme pitches are numbered — for example 212, 210.5, and 211.5 — with 212 being the highest pitched and shrillest whistle. As a result, traditionally, the 212 is used for dogs which find themselves working further away from their handlers (retrievers, HPRs, pointers and setters), whilst the other two pitches are slightly lower and are more commonly used with spaniels, who work much closer to their handlers. In reality, it doesn't really matter which pitch you choose and any dog can be trained with any whistle.

Each person who exercises or trains the dog should have their own whistle and you might want to buy a spare. (I especially recommend keeping a spare whistle in your car.) Acme whistles can come with 'peas' in them, as an option, but I don't recommend this type of whistle as the peas can get stuck in damp or freezing weather — and there's no advantage to the pea anyway.

LANYARD This is just to attach your whistle to, so you can wear it around your neck.

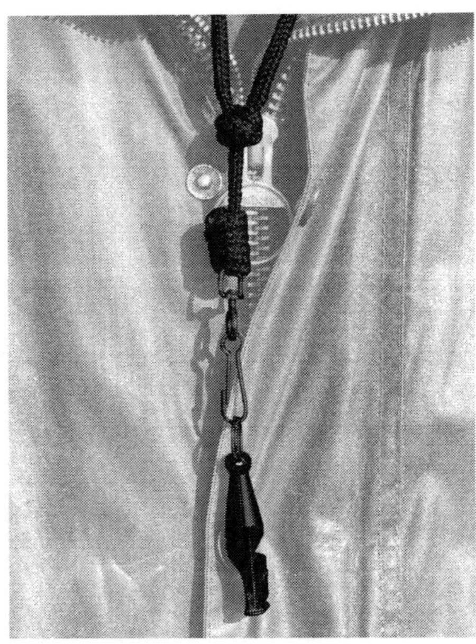

An Acme gundog whistle on a lanyard

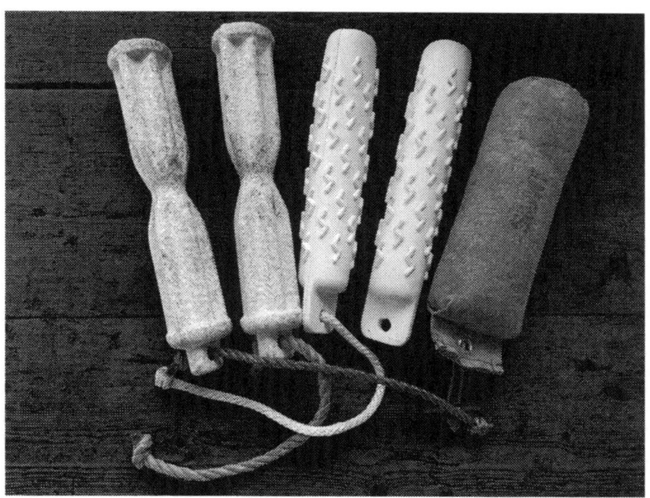

An assortment of dummies: Two Airflow Bumpers (left); two DT Systems Soft Mouth Trainers (centre) and a one-pound green canvas dummy.

WHITE DUMMIES (AT LEAST SIX) (in the US: 'bumpers') Dummies need to be white (or black and white) to assist in developing marking skills (using eyes, rather than nose, to find the dummy). White dummies will 'flash' in the air and will be clearly visible on the ground. They are also useful for sight-blinds and all types of lining and handling, as they are visible on the ground from a distance.

To do drills properly, you will need a good number of white dummies — ideally around six to nine.

Dummies are made from either canvas (UK style) or hard plastic (US-style). Carrying multiple one-pound canvas dummies around with you is pretty back-breaking. The white canvas dummies also tend to pick up dirt easily and they don't remain white for long, so my preference is the hard plastic US-style. These are lighter and they stay cleaner — and, therefore, whiter! However, if you compete in the UK — or you attend a mainstream gundog training class in the UK — you will be expected to bring two green one-pound canvas dummies, so it is a good idea to pick up a couple of these, too.

My preferred US-style dummies, for years, have been either the DT Systems Soft-Mouth Trainer dummies (in small) or Avery Hexabumpers. I have recently discovered the new AirFlow Bumpers, which are BPA-free. Whilst these dummies are manufactured in the US, they are available online from UK gundog supply stores.

A biothane long-line is highly recommended. Your long-line should be 10 metres long. The dog also has a training tab attached to the back of her harness.

TRAINING 'TAB' This is another fantastic US invention comprising a very short clip lead — about a foot long — without a handle. I have not seen them for sale in the UK, but you can make one by cutting down an old lead.

We use tabs for steadiness: The handler can keep a hand on the tab and then let go, when sending the dog. The tab stays attached to the dog whilst she is running the retrieve, ensuring control until the very last minute and preventing unsteadiness without the need for any '*No*!' or '*Ah ah*!' punishers, should the dog run in. It's important that the tab is kept slack so the dog is unaware anyone is holding onto her — unless she tries to go before being sent.

10 METRE LONG-LINE I highly recommend biothane long-lines as they do not absorb water to become heavy anchors behind the dog, and do not collect mud, twigs and leaves. They do not smell or need to be washed, and are comfortable to use.

Called 'check cords' in North America, long-lines are a favoured tool for almost all traditional gundog trainers so you should have no problems sourcing one. My favourite brand is a mom-and-pop US-brand called Permatack (www.permatack.com), which does ship to the UK, but we now have UK-based long-line manufacturers. I'd recommend checking out Zooplus.co.uk for the Heim biothane tracking line. This is a rolled biothane line, which pulls free from undergrowth easily and is slightly preferable to a 'flat' line.

WHITE ELECTRIC FENCE POSTS (THREE) These are incredibly useful for training blind retrieves, directions and handling (subjects for the next book, but included here to create a comprehensive equipment list).

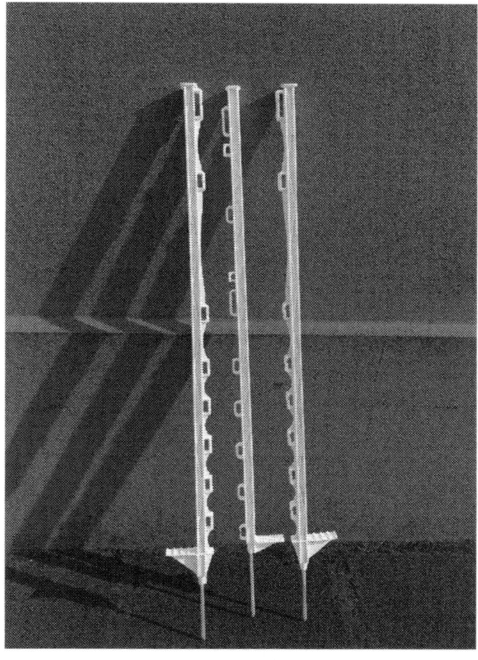

Three white electric fence posts are essential for training handling and blind retrieves.

BAG You don't have to buy a game bag specifically, but you do need something to store your dummies and your long-line, plus any other kit you use. You could always use an old ruck-sack to start with. My favourite brand of game bag is Firedog.

HARNESS To understand why a harness is recommended, we need to look at some other equipment choices, first.

Slip-leads are the conventional 'uniform' of a gundog in the UK. They tighten around a dog's throat when she pulls and, in traditional gundog training, are used to give corrections (positive punishment). Being force-free trainers, we wouldn't use a slip-lead in this way — however, most dogs pull at times, sometimes in a sudden way. Consequently, even if the handler is not actively giving corrections, the dog will be giving them to herself. By virtue of the handler holding onto what is effectively a noose, whilst not letting the dog lunge or pull towards something, this is inevitable. It is just physics and biology. Sometimes traditional trainers in the UK try to rationalise the use of slip-leads by saying that they are for safety purposes. They believe that the dog must wear nothing or the dog could get caught up on undergrowth and strangled. This is despite the fact that, in many other countries — including North America and mainland Europe — gundogs work and compete in collars, with no mishaps. And pet gundogs run around in all kinds of undergrowth wearing collars and harnesses, with no one judging this equipment unsafe — even though the world of pet dog owners is very concerned about safety issues. I've never been convinced by the safety argument against collars and harnesses.

Does this mean there's no place for slip-leads in force-free gundog work? No. We are part of the wider gundog community and it's important that we don't isolate ourselves. Whether we like it or not, slip-leads are part of the uniform for gundog work. Moreover, if we want to compete with our dogs in the UK, we will need to be using a slip-lead — because a dog cannot run in competition here, wearing a collar or harness.

But, just because we use a slip-lead when working our dogs or competing with them, doesn't mean we have to use one at all times. Think about your dog's total lifetime 'number of hours spent on leash'. Compare the hours spent working and competing with the hours spent *not* working or competing. Most dogs will have far more of the latter, and all of those hours, can be hours the dog wears something other than a slip-lead.

Even when you are working or competing with your dog, I would recommend a ***'limited' slip-lead***. This is a leash which doesn't tighten like a noose, but tightens to a certain point (which you set), and no further. A limited slip essentially converts a slip-lead into a flat-collar and leash. Yet it looks the same as the usual slip-lead and few people will notice it is not.

One final word about slip-leads. Sometimes I come across people who want to 'look the part'. They have just brought home their first puppy, which they want to work as a gundog, and the slip-lead is part of the 'image' — it is the uniform of a working gundog. So they turn up to puppy class with a slip-lead on their dog. Anyone can dress up in shooting gear and put a slip-lead on their untrained dog. It is always best to be the part, rather than just *look* it — so I'd recommend these people focus on training (substance) and less on appearance (image)!

So, what about a ***flat-collar and clip leash*** when we are not working or competing? Certainly this is preferable to a slip-lead, but the flat-collar still goes around the dog's throat. Anatomically, dogs' throats are not markedly different to those of humans. Both canine and human necks contain lymph nodes, thyroid glands, spinal cords, tracheas and larynxes. Research demonstrates that intra-ocular pressure (the pressure inside the eye) is much higher when dogs pull into collars, compared to dogs pulling into harnesses. No matter how good your training is, young or inexperienced dogs *will* lunge into a flat-collar when they see something which grabs their attention. Wearing a collar, they *will* at times rear up on back legs with full body weight on their necks — even to the point that their necks look bisected. Again, this is just physics and biology.

Only ***harnesses*** take the pressure off a dog's neck. The most common type of harness available is the ***back-fastening harness***, where the leash clips onto the dog's back. For owners of all small puppies — and even small breeds, like cockers — a back-fastening harness is usually the best option. These dogs don't have the power to tow an owner along — the owner will be able to stop walking when the leash is tight. Similarly, once a dog of any breed or age has been trained to walk at heel, a back-fastening harness works well because additional control just isn't needed. The leash (used in any way), by that point, is only an insurance policy.

The difficulty with back-fastening harnesses occurs when dogs that are large or strong wear them — and attempt to pull. Due to their size and strength, these dogs will successfully pull their handler forwards a few steps towards something they want to reach. These few steps will reinforce the pulling — the dog sees that she gets closer to her desired goal, through pulling you — and so the dog will continue trying to pull. And dogs can really throw their weight into a back-fastening harness. After all, these are what sled dogs wear, to pull sleds! Dogs can end up focussed 'outwards' (forwards), and the handler can find it difficult to 'access' the front of the dog to regain the dog's attention. In short, many handlers don't feel in adequate control of their large or strong dog when she is wearing a back-fastening harness.

The solution is a harness with a ***front-attachment point*** — on the dog's chest or sternum. This gives the handler control, takes a lot of power out of the dog's pull, enables the handler to prevent jumping up, and enables access to the front of the dog to gain her attention with a treat or lure. Most front-fastening harnesses also have a back-attachment point, offering more options: You can use a double-ended leash to clip to both front and back of the harness for control. If you are working on recalls or the remote sit, and have a long-line attached to the dog, you can clip this to the back-attachment point alone.

There are many different brands of harnesses on the market today and it is important to find one which fits your particular dog well. Ideally, and for most dogs, ensure you choose a harness which has a 'Y'-shaped front piece which sits high up above the dog's shoulders — almost where a collar might sit — so it does not restrict the freedom of movement of the dog's shoulders.

CLICKER

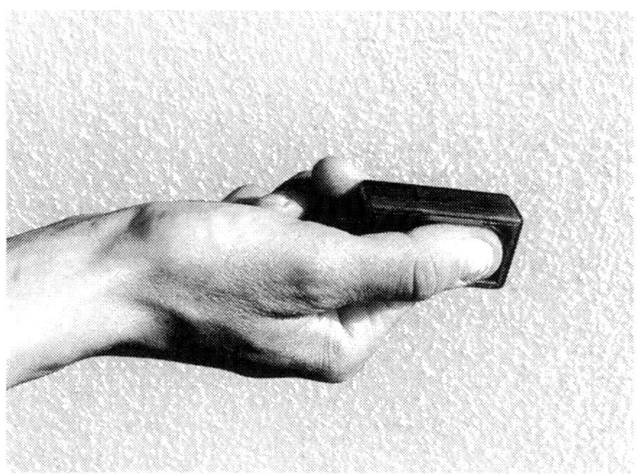

A clicker. The loudest clickers for training outdoors are Karlie box clickers.

TREATS I really can't over-emphasise the importance of getting your treat usage sorted if you want to be successful using reward-based methods. Too often, I see people whose idea of using treats in gundog training is having a few hard dry bits of biscuit inside a piece of cling-film, which they fumble about with, to give their dog very occasionally. This is not what we're about here!

When you are training in the house, use your dog's ordinary meals (if kibble or Ziwipeak) for training purposes. See Section 2.1, Food motivation, for more information. The only exception to this, is when it comes to your recall —

whether verbal, or whistle. For this, you will need your amazing recall treats, even when you're training in the house.

When you are training away from the house, you will need two separate categories of treats with you: 1) Your recall treats and 2) your normal/regular (but still very tasty) treats. Suggestions for recall treats include sardines, mackerel, paté and gourmet dog food. (You can use a spoon to feed some to your dog, or to splat on the floor. You may like to have a small pouch of wet-wipes with you!) Suggestions for normal or regular treats include mild cheddar, any unprocessed meat or organ meat and blueberries.

Training is very treat-intensive, and, when you run out of treats, that's it — you're going home. Similarly, if your treats are ginormous and your dog gets full, you can't train. So cut your normal/regular treats into small pieces to ensure they go a long way... but not *so* small they become fiddly, or you might drop them on the floor accidentally. This can lead to broken stays, or distracted sniffing.

TREAT CONTAINERS My favourite treat pouch is the Australian-made Trainer's Pouch, made from silicone. This is the largest treat pouch ever(!) — so you will not run out of treats! It can alternatively hold four tennis balls. Being silicone, it can go in the dishwasher daily and doesn't get dirty or smelly. And it is also the only treat pouch I've found that's practical and comfortable to wear over a Barbour jacket!

If I'm attending a traditional class or a shoot and I want an option which is more subtle and discreet than any treat pouch, I like to use two Addis screw-top beakers — one in each pocket of my coat. These fit well in any deep and straight coat pockets. I keep my normal/regular treats in my left pocket (on the same side as the dog, for heelwork) and my recall treats in my right pocket. Addis beakers are, of course, dishwasher-safe.

Addis beakers fit well into deep coat pockets and are a more subtle way to carry treats on your person.

The treat pouch here, is the Trainer's Pouch.

2.4

FORCE-FREE GENERAL TRAINING CLASSES

You can achieve a huge amount by attending well-run, excellent force-free general training classes — even better if they are clicker classes.

If you can't find a clicker training class, you will need to add the clicker into what you are doing in your non-clicker class. I like the book *Click for Joy* by Melissa C. Alexander as a good clicker primer. There are also some great online clicker training resources. (I recommend the Karen Pryor Dog Trainer Foundations online course, if you want something structured.)

But nothing really replaces finding an excellent clicker trainer in your area and going through their general training classes as far as you can and just generally getting 'into' training your dog with a clicker.

Check out the following lists to find a clicker trainer in the UK:

- Association of Pet Dog Trainers (UK): apdt.co.uk
- Pet Professional Guild (UK): ppgbi.com/PetGuildMembers
- Institute of Modern Dog Trainers: imdt.uk.com
- Karen Pryor Certified Training Partners: karenpryoracademy.com/find-a-trainer
- Academy for Dog Trainers (Jean Donaldson): academyfordogtrainers.com

In North America, try the latter two above.

WHAT'S WRONG WITH JUST GOING RIGHT INTO GUNDOG TRAINING CLASSES WITH A PUPPY?

It is hard to find force-free gundog training classes, as very few exist. It is (comparatively) easy to find many excellent, well-run force-free *general* training classes.

Gundog basics (sit; heel; stay; un-cued and cued attention; sit-at-my-side) are the basics of any force-free general dog training class. Learn them from an excellent force-free general trainer, not a traditional gundog trainer. Dog training is firstly about *your* learning, not your dog's, so give yourself the best teachers around.

If you attend traditional gundog training classes with a completely untrained puppy, you will probably find yourself told to push your puppy's bum down into a sit, check your puppy with the leash, say 'no' to your puppy for various behaviours, smack your puppy on the nose for whining, run intimidatingly at your puppy for various misdemeanours, and so on.

Take what you can from good general classes and then move onto gundog training when you really need that gundog specific material — which won't be until you are done with the basics.

Then you can turn up to your gundog training class with a dog which sits when asked, heels well on a basic level, pays attention to you in a class environment, and can stay.

When you are ready for gundog classes, I would highly recommend getting started with a Gundog Club instructor. The Gundog Club is now entirely force-free, so you can get a force-free start in gundog training if you are fortunate to have an instructor in your area. Check out www.thegundogclub.co.uk

• • • • •

This section provides training 'recipes' to work on with your dog. Each part covers a different behaviour or issue.

Use this section of the book as you need. It's not expected that you would train one behaviour entirely and complete the section on it, before beginning the next. Rather, you may be starting out several behaviours at once.

Please don't skip over material to find 'the place you're at' with your dog's training – thinking you can just start from there. We need to ensure there are no gaps in what you have taught, and we need your dog's understanding of a behaviour to be the same as a dog which has gone through these specific exercises. Without this, future training may break down.

Remember that you can do all this training *indoors* to begin with, with your dog's regular meals. Only once a particular exercise is working well indoors, should you take it outdoors to the field.

SECTION 3

TRAINING (BASICS)

3.1

SITS – (IN THE PLURAL!)

In gundog training, it's not 'all about that bass' — it's 'all about that sit, about that sit, about that sit'. Perhaps the sit *is* the bass of gundog training!

Sit *can* be a basic behaviour: Imagine a sit, lured with food, such as a baby puppy might do. But a sit can also be advanced, occurring in response to a rabbit flushing and with the handler a considerable distance away — and therefore a complex behaviour — requiring self-control and deferred reinforcement.

Whether it's sitting steadily at heel during a drive, sitting to the 'sit' whistle remotely, or sitting to flush — this behaviour is pivotal and occurs during some of the most important moments. In fact, we could say that the 'failure' of this behaviour is in itself responsible for many dogs getting eliminated from competitions: The dog that breaks and runs in for a retrieve, the dog that fails to sit-to-flush (or shot or whistle!) and chases, and the dog that moves forwards out of heel position when the handler stops walking.

There are multiple cues for 'sit', for a gundog. We have:

- sit to the word (verbal 'sit')
- sit to the hand signal ('stop' hand signal)
- sit to the whistle (single whistle peep)
- sit aligned with my side (a different verbal cue)
- sit at heal (when I stop walking)
- sit to shot
- sit to flush.

As you can see, there is not just one 'sit' that is needed for gundog work: There are sits in the plural!

SIMPLE SIT

We need to ensure that you can: Say the word 'sit' (once), click when your dog's bum touches the ground in a sit, and then throw a treat for the dog to collect. (The click functions as a release — the dog can move on hearing the click.)

There are three stages:

1. ***The lure:*** Begin by placing a treat on the dog's nose and — keeping your hand low so the dog can nibble at the treat — move your hand slowly back over the dog's head, towards the dog's tail. The dog will usually sit to better follow the food lure over the top of her head. At the precise moment that the dog's butt touches the floor, you click and release the treat. At this stage, the dog is getting both click and treat whilst in the sit position. If the dog doesn't get up from the sit for the next rep, just throw an additional 'freebie' treat without clicking to get her up again. Repeat x10 or until the dog is fluent.

   If you get any jumping up at the treat, whilst you are trying to lure the dog, it means you are holding the treat too high. Keep it low enough that the dog is nibbling it constantly without taking her butt off the ground.

   Do not stick at this stage for too long, or the visible treat will get 'built in' as part of the cue to sit. Move on quickly to the hand signal.

2. ***The hand signal:*** To move from a food lure to a hand signal, think first about the hand signal you want to use. Most handlers use a flat 'stop sign' hand — such as the sign a policeman uses to stop traffic.

   To achieve this: Trap a treat between your thumb and the palm of your hand, keeping the rest of your hand flat like the stop hand signal. Do a few more food lures, moving your hand with the trapped treat over the top of your dog's head, clicking when the bum touches the floor and releasing the treat.

   Now repeat this, *without the treat there* — just with the hand held flat, moving over the top of the dog's head. Keep your thumb against your hand for a few reps, so that it looks the same at first. Click when the bum touches the floor and throw a treat for the dog to collect. This is now becoming your hand signal.

Repeat this many times, working on gradually presenting the hand signal further away from the dog. (A hand signal that you have to move on top of the dog's nose over her head isn't very useful!) Try to ensure you can stand up and show the dog your stop-sign hand up at chest or shoulder height — and she will sit for you to click and throw a treat. You will probably want the dog to respond to *either* of your hands, held in this stop-sign way — so ensure she can recognise both left and right hands as the sit hand signal cue.

You can stay at this stage (the hand signal) for as long as you like. Unlike the food lure, there's no reason to rush to move on from the hand signal to the word — so take your time.

If your dog ignores your hand signal, don't keep showing it to her over and over — and don't hold it out for a while, waiting for the dog to respond. Instead, go back to the food lure for a few more reps, then try again.

3. ***The word (or verbal cue):*** It's pretty easy to attach the word now, as you've done most of the hard work. Say the word 'sit' and then give your stop-sign hand signal cue. Click and treat the sit. So it goes: 'Sit' > stop hand signal > click (the sit) > treat.

   It's important that you say 'sit' only once, and that you say it first — before doing the hand signal. Repeat this x10. Then try just saying the word and waiting — your dog will almost certainly sit because she anticipates the hand signal. Congratulations: Your dog now sits on verbal cue.

Tip: Not everyone uses the word 'sit' as their verbal cue. I use 'hup' and so do many other gundog handlers. I do this because I got tired of strangers approaching my dogs to 'say hello' and then repeating 'sit-sit-sit-sit', endlessly — and then not providing a reinforcer when my dog sat! You can use any word you like, as long as you're consistent.

Generalisation: You now need to practise this in different locations (different rooms of the house, the field, the garden) to generalise it. You may need to return to earlier steps in the process, when generalising to new locations.

COMMON 'SIT' MISTAKES

These principles actually apply to all cues, not just the 'sit' cue. Wherever you see 'sit' in the following mistakes, you can replace it with any cue whatsoever — the principles hold the same.

- ***Mistake #1: Saying 'sit' when you have no treats available.*** Don't do it. Your dog will soon learn that sitting when asked leads to precisely nothing for them — and therefore they will stop responding. They will also learn that *if* you have food on you and show it to them, and ask them to sit, then there *is* something in it for them. End result is a dog which sits if you show her food and not the rest of the time. Then you will start contacting dog trainers saying: '*My dog only does it when I show her food!*' This is because you've trained her to know that reinforcement is given, only if it is shown first! Only cue a behaviour if you have reinforcers available — but preferably not visible at the moment of cuing the behaviour. If you don't have reinforcers available, don't ask for the behaviour. This means that, every time you leave your house with your dog, you need to have some treats on you. It's best if you can also have a little pouch or pot on you, in the house — to reinforce behaviours you like, at home.

- ***Mistake #2: Saying 'sit-sit-sit-sit' many times over, before the dog sits.*** If you want your dog to respond to one 'sit' cue, then you need to say it only once in training. If your dog gets used to hearing 'sit-sit-sit-sit-sit' before they sit, you will always need to say 'sit-sit-sit-sit-sit'. Say it once. If the dog doesn't respond, give a hand signal or food lure — *do not repeat the word.*

- ***Mistake #3: Saying 'sit' at the same time as giving the hand signal.*** Dogs are not verbal creatures. In the presence of a mesmerising physical hand signal, they won't even notice the word. In addition, we need to teach the dog that the word 'sit' *predicts* the hand signal — so that they will begin to sit to the word alone, in *anticipation* of the hand signal. If you give word and hand signal at the same time, the word no longer predicts anything — both word and hand signal are simultaneous. The dog will then not sit to the word — because they can't anticipate the hand signal. Say 'sit' first, wait a second, then give the hand signal.

- ***Mistake #4: Generating excess frustration whilst training — and then accidentally training frustration-related behaviours into the sit.*** Frustration has been recently seen as an entirely negative emotional state for dogs — undesirable and to be avoided at all costs in training. But there is *some* degree of frustration involved in any learning. *Some* degree of frustration is the inevitable outcome of asking a dog to do something and providing a reinforcer, contingent on the dog's response: Time passes between the cue and the reinforcer, and in that time between cue and reinforcer, the dog experiences some degree of frustration. Frustration and motivation are therefore inextricably entwined and *optimal* frustration is not punitive — it is desirable and motivational.

What is optimal frustration for one dog, however, is excessive frustration for another. One dog may be able to tolerate you giving the 'sit' cue and then waiting for five seconds for her response. Another dog may experience that as too frustrating — giving rise to unwanted behaviours, like barking at you, vocalisation, jumping on you, sniffing the floor, paddling her front feet and so on.

If your dog barks at you, and then sits, or paddles front feet back and forth and then sits, or does any frustration-related behaviour and then sits — and you still click the sit when it occurs and throw a treat — then *you are training that preceding frustration-related behaviour into the response.* And if you do that repeatedly, you will strongly train in that unwanted frustration-related behaviour. You will end up with (for example) 'sit'> dog barks> dog sits> click> treat.

How to prevent this? Monitor frustration levels in your dog, whilst training. If you start to see any frustration-related behaviours, adjust your training to reduce frustration:

- If you are giving a cue and waiting for the response, help the dog with a hand signal or food lure earlier — before the frustration behaviour begins. Don't wait five seconds — get in there with a hand signal or food lure after one second, if necessary. Your particular dog may need your help for longer, before they can respond to the verbal cue without signs of frustration.

- Increase the frequency of reinforcement to reduce the frustration — perhaps by breaking the behaviour down into smaller steps so the dog is able to offer you something reinforceable more frequently.

- Frustration can build over a training session, so take a break and give the dog a chance to calm down with some slow petting or sniffing.

- Train the dog to do a behaviour which is calming or self-soothing, so this behaviour can be cued at times of frustration. For more information on this idea, see Section 3.5, Focus and engagement — specifically, the 'Close Your Mouth' behaviour.

DEFAULT SIT

You can think of the default sit as the 'sit-to-say-please'. A default behaviour is a behaviour which the dog offers you *without being asked to do it.* That means — without the verbal cue or a hand signal. They just 'guess' the behaviour when they perceive a reinforcer which they would like to have. In a way, they are saying '*Please can I have it?*' by sitting.

In gundog work, there are many tempting situations where a dog is going to want to run after something they want: The flushing rabbit, the birds exploding from a bush, or the shot pheasant lying on the ground, fluttering.

If a dog learns, from a young age, that the best way to get what they want is to sit and *ask* for it — and if this is a strongly conditioned unthinking response — then you are more likely to end up with a dog which sits in these situations. The dog will learn that sitting results in the best chance of being allowed to have (flush or retrieve) the desired thing. (You will still need to do further work on sit-to-flush, but this earlier training will speed things up.)

The default sit also helps with no-jumping-up and, in general, a dog which doesn't attempt to *take* something she wants from you (even attention) — instead, sitting herself politely to *ask* you for it.

BASIC DEFAULT SIT

To reduce the risk of frustration-related behaviours developing, be sure to have first trained the simple sit (above). Then, stand in front of your dog with some treats and your clicker. Wait and watch your dog. If she leaps up on you, just turn away so she jumps off you. If she needs additional help, mime eating the treats in your hand with maximal lip-smacking and '*Yummmm, these are nice*' proclamations. (This sounds completely ridiculous, but it works!) Resist the urge to give the sit cue (verbal or hand signal) — just wait. Providing you don't see frustration-related behaviours from the dog, *it doesn't matter how long it takes* — it will get quicker each time. As soon as your dog's bum hits the floor in a sit, click and throw a treat. Be sure to throw the treats, or your dog will get superglued in a sit and you won't be able to get her up for the next rep!

Keep practising until your dog is slamming her bum down into a sit as soon as she has eaten the previous treat. We want this to be a fluent default behaviour. This is a great warm-up for training sessions. Remember that we don't want to give any cue to the dog, to sit. But, if your dog finds this difficult or is showing signs of frustration, intervene with a minimal 'sit' hand signal for a few reps — just to get her started.

Keep in mind that cues are not only what we intend them to be: Sometimes people lean forwards or step into their dog, and believe they are not giving a cue because they are not actually saying 'sit'. Well — they *are* giving a cue. They are training the dog to learn that being stepped into or leant into, is a cue for 'sit'.

The purpose of the default sit exercise is partly for the dog to have a way to *ask* for what she wants — be that bird, bunny, affection or treat. Cues are not part of this — giving a cue defeats the purpose of the default sit. The default sit is known as 'manding' in the puppy-rearing system which is 'Puppy Culture': Puppy Culture's creator, Jane Killion, considers manding part of the 'Communication Trinity' — called such, because it gives the dog a voice, enabling her to communicate her needs to her handler. To function as communication from dog to handler, the default sit must be un-cued.

DEFAULT SIT IN OTHER SITUATIONS

Think about all the moments during the day when your dog wants something:

- She wants to go out to the toilet.
- She wants to be let into a room.
- She wants to get out the car to start exercise/training.
- She wants to be let off the leash.
- She wants some fuss or physical attention during the day and comes to find you for it.

In all of these situations, the reinforcers are not food reinforcers. Still, you should wait for a sit before giving her what she wants. Resist the urge to give the 'sit' verbal cue — instead just talk to her in a tempting way: '*Would you like to go out to pee, would you really? Don't you have to do something first? Do you remember?*' (said with hand on door handle, waiting).

You are unlikely to have your clicker on you at these times — and the clicker also tends to lead the dog to expect a food reinforcer by this point (rather than these alternative reinforcers), so you won't be using the clicker.

However, when we click, we tell the dog: '*You can stop doing it now*'. With the sit, the dog can get up from the sit if we click. If we're not using the clicker in these other situations, then we need to give an alternative release. Otherwise the dog has really broken a stay: The dog should not get up just because a door opens in front of her, for example. We will be talking more about sit-stays and the release word in the next section.

For now, you have two options:

- Use your release word to release the dog from the sit *before* she has released herself. You can praise ('*Gooooood*') whilst the dog sits, and then release ('*Okay*'!) and give the dog the reinforcer (let her outside, give her some fuss, or allow her out the car). If a release word seems an unclear concept to you at this point, read the next section (3.2, Sit-stays).

- Use a verbal marker ('*Ace!*' or '*Ex!*'), which replaces the clicker and functions as both a marker and a release, in one. Then let the dog have the reinforcer.

Whichever option you choose, at the moment when you release the dog, she should be sitting. If the dog has already started to get up, you cannot give your release word or marker word because you are *reinforcing what happens at the moment you release*. Be sure that your dog is sitting when you release.

What I often see in class is a dog which just starts to get up, and the handler somehow thinks they can get in there if they release the dog at that instant. You can't beat time itself! You are not a time-traveller! You will only be reinforcing the dog for breaking the stay, if you give the release word at this point.

DEFAULT SIT – TO A MOVING REINFORCER

At this point, we can move onto an exercise which replicates the idea of game flushing. The crucial variable we are going to work with, is a moving reinforcer. After all, when game flushes - or when game is shot and falls - we have ourselves a moving reinforcer!

Leslie McDevitt's ace book *Control Unleashed* has an exercise which has a few things in common with what I'm about to describe here — but our goal is slightly different. Leslie's exercise is called 'Leave It' — which puts the emphasis on leaving a falling treat.

The emphasis we want to put on this idea, for gundog work, is that the stimulus of something-falling-from-the-sky is a cue to sit. We are not so interested in the dog just standing or resisting the temptation (although you can split the behaviour by reinforcing this, initially, if the dog offers it) — and we're not so interested in aiming for more complex 'leave its', such as heeling the dog around multiple treats on the floor, or being able to throw handfuls.

Instead, for us, it's all about 'movement-means-sit'. We begin with falling movements using dropped treats, but then move onto rising movements — after all, birds flush upwards! We also want the dog to begin each rep standing or moving around naturally — since this most closely imitates how things will be when game flushes, later in training.

Let's take a look at how to train the default sit to a moving reinforcer:

1. ***Warm up:*** Do some basic default sits to get the dog thinking about sitting. (If the dog is not able to perform default sits yet, don't attempt this exercise.)

2. ***Treat under shoe:*** Take a treat and place it under your shoe, holding your foot above it so you don't squish it. Your dog may scrabble and scrape at your shoe or lie down and attempt to get the treat. Wait a few seconds to see if she will sit. If she is really focussed on the shoe (rather than you), mime eating the treats in your hand with maximal lip-smacking and '*Yummmm, these are nice*' proclamations — which you can fade out after a few reps.

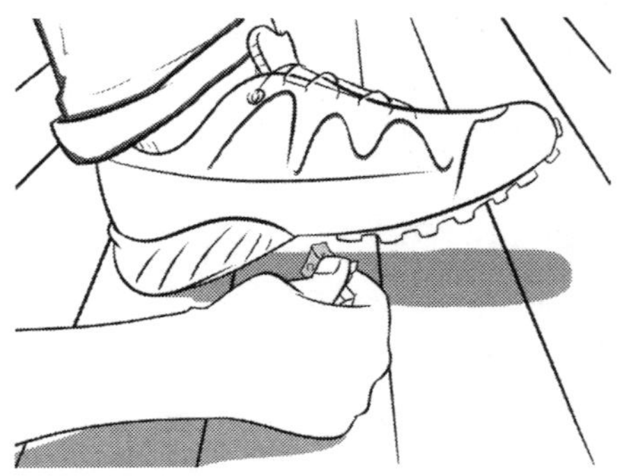

PLACE A TREAT UNDER YOUR SHOE, AIMING FOR THE ARCH OF YOUR FOOT

When she sits, click and give her a treat from your hands (*not the one on the floor*). Deliver this directly to her mouth — don't throw it on the floor. She is probably still staring at you, now she knows you also have treats. So swivel your foot off the treat on the floor so she can see it again. If she still doesn't notice it, using your foot, tap the floor by the treat. Be ready to cover the treat quickly with your

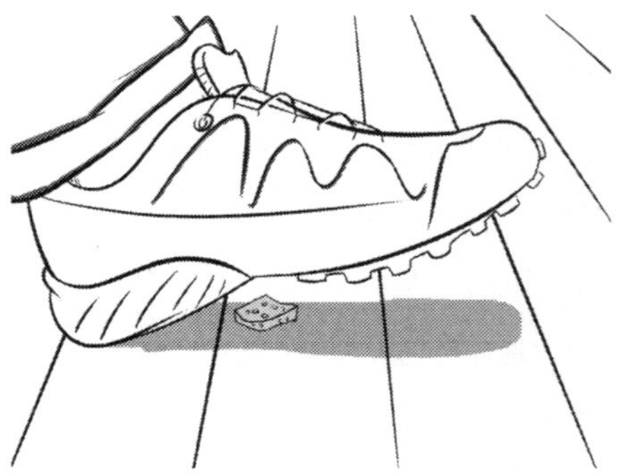

SUSPEND YOUR FOOT OVER THE TREAT, ENSURING YOUR DOG CAN'T REACH IT BY KEEPING THE FOOT AS LOW AS POSSIBLE WITHOUT SQUASHING THE TREAT. USE YOUR HEEL TO PIVOT ON AND TO BALANCE.

shoe because she will likely go for it, especially when you tap. Again, wait for a sit, then click and treat from your hands.

Remain at this stage until she isn't really paying much attention to the treat on the floor, even when you tap the floor. (The behaviour of trying to get it, has extinguished.)

3. ***Falling treat:*** Next, pick up the treat on the floor and hold it in the hand furthest away from the dog. You are going to drop the treat from just 10cm above the floor. You are going to be ready to cover it with your foot, should the dog go for it. Don't drop it from higher up than 10cm yet because, the higher you drop the treat from, the more erratic and unpredictable its movement — and so the dog may be able to get it.

   So, drop the treat and cover it with your foot when the dog moves to get it. Wait for the sit, and click and treat — again, always using a treat in your hand to reinforce and never giving the treat on the floor. Pick up the treat on the floor and repeat until the dog has stopped making any effort to attempt to get the treat — *the dropping of the treat has become a cue to sit, in order to earn a reinforcer from you.* (Later in training, the flushing of a bird will be a cue to sit for a reinforcer from you - for example, a thrown tennis ball.)

4. ***Advanced falling treat:*** You can start to drop the treat from slightly higher up, still with the hand furthest from the dog and still ensuring you can cover it before she gets it — should she try. Wait for the sit, then click and treat.

   Some dogs start to put themselves into the sit *before* you've dropped the treat. The sit occurring from free-movement (dog standing freely) is what you really want to achieve, because it more closely replicates the freely moving dog which flushes game and has to sit: The dog is not already sitting, when the game flushes! So, if your dog sits herself before you've dropped the treat, just encourage her to stand up again using your body language and voice — or give her the release word and throw her a freebie.

5. ***Rising treat:*** Here, we pop the treat *up* from the floor — rather than dropping it *down* onto the floor. Game rises *upwards* when flushed, after all. This means that you will again begin with a freely moving dog and then do a tiny throw upwards beginning at floor-height to about a foot in the air. Be ready to cover the treat with your hand, should the dog go for it — it should not land that far away from you and you must be quicker than the dog, so begin with very little 'pop-ups' at first. Click and treat when the dog sits.

WHISTLE 'SIT' (UP CLOSE)

In gundog work, the cue to sit is one peep on the whistle. Eventually we want this to work wherever the dog is, at any distance. For now, we start up close with the 'sit' whistle.

I like to train this after the default sit (above), because I can pretty much guarantee that the dog is going to sit after I've peeped — because she is in default sit mode.

It goes like this:

1. Practise some default sits, as above.

2. Do one peep on the whistle, just before your dog sits. If your dog is fast and manages to sit before you've peeped, just throw a freebie treat without clicking to get her up again — and peep earlier next time.

3. Click the sit and throw the treat on the floor in such a way that the dog has to get up to eat it.

4. To cement together the whistle cue and the sit behaviour, you need many reps of whistle > dog sits > click > treat - across multiple training sessions. Don't forget to generalise to new locations as well.

SIT-AT-MY-SIDE

The goal of this behaviour is to teach a dog to sit at your *left* side, with her spine aligned perfectly with the direction you are facing. It is very important that the dog does not sit partially rotated towards you — the dog's spine should be facing forwards and her shoulders should be level with your leg (level with the seam in your trousers).

Why is this important? Firstly, it looks bad if your dog sits wonkily. You won't create a good impression in the minds of anyone watching and it communicates a sense of your training and precision being sloppy, generally.

Secondly, for marked retrieves, you need your dog looking forwards at the same field of vision that you are — to be sure that they see the mark.

Thirdly, for blind retrieves, you want your dog to run in a straight line from your side and to maintain that straight line. Your chances of achieving a good line are far better if you start out with the dog straight than if she starts out at 90 degrees to where you are sending her. You should be able to indicate, through pivoting with the dog at heel, which retrieve a dog should get.

I sometimes have students who don't appreciate just how important the sit-at-my-side behaviour is, and they skimp on the training. They end up pulling and shoving their dogs around by the harness to *make* them line up straight at their side, for retrieves. That isn't force-free training. And you can't touch your dog in competition or assessments.

Do not click efforts from your dog which are not straight. There is no such thing as 'good enough' with this one, even starting out — it's going to be perfect (in terms of straightness) from the start. Often, the dog's head can make it look like she is straight from a cursory glance — whilst her rear is sticking out behind you. To prevent this, check back over your left shoulder as the dog sits, to ensure her rear is also straight before you click.

DO NOT CLICK IF THE DOG SITS WITH HER REAR OUT AT AN ANGLE.

The sit-at-my-side involves the exact same initial moves as the repositioning move from Section 3.4, Heelwork. The only difference is that the repositioning move does not involve a sit at the end — it's a way to get your dog back to your side after she has pulled or moved in front during heelwork. The repositioning move is the exercise to start with, as it is slightly simpler. When that is fluent, you can add the sit-at-my-side.

Take a look at the following illustrations. Images 1-5 recap the repositioning move, to remind you of this manoeuvre. (Do take a look at Section 3.4, Heelwork, for more details on how to train this.) Images 6 - 7 show how to add the sit-at-my-side onto the end of the repositioning move.

BEGIN WITH

THE REPOSITIONING MOVE

(SEE SECTION 3.4 HEELWORK PAGE 225)

1 BEGIN WITH THE DOG IN FRONT OF YOU. TO ACHIEVE THIS, JUST TURN YOURSELF TO FACE YOUR DOG. TAKE A BIG HANDFUL OF TREATS IN YOUR LEFT HAND FROM YOUR TREAT POUCH OR POCKET (ON YOUR LEFT SIDE).

2 LURE THE DOG STRAIGHT BACK BEHIND YOU ON YOUR LEFT SIDE, WHILST TAKING A STEP BACK WITH YOUR LEFT FOOT. ENSURE YOUR HAND IS PALM-UP AT THIS POINT.

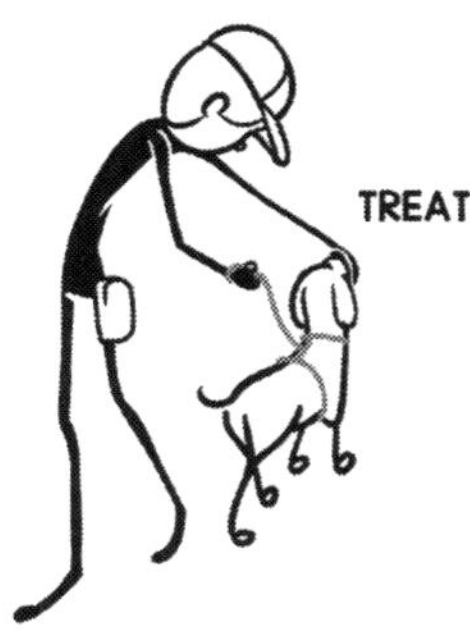

3 WHEN YOU REACH THE FURTHEST POINT BEHIND YOU, RELEASE A TREAT. THIS WILL ENSURE YOUR DOG CONTINUES TO FOLLOW YOUR HAND RIGHT BACK TO THIS SPOT.

4 TURN YOUR DOG TOWARDS YOUR LEG, SWITCHING YOUR HAND OVER ON THE DOG'S NOSE AS YOU DO THIS. YOU ARE NOW LOOKING AT THE BACK OF YOUR HAND – IT IS PALM-DOWN.

5 LURE YOUR DOG FORWARDS AGAIN AS YOU STEP YOUR LEFT FOOT FORWARDS TO MEET YOUR RIGHT. ENSURE YOU ARE LOOKING AT THE BACK OF YOUR HAND AS YOU DO THIS AND USE THE LURE TO KEEP THE DOG'S BODY ALIGNED STRAIGHT AT YOUR SIDE.

(CONT...)

CONTINUE WITH
SIT AT MY SIDE

6 WHEN THE DOG IS LEVEL WITH YOUR LEFT SIDE AND IN LINE WITH YOUR LEFT LEG, KEEP YOUR TREAT ON THE DOG'S NOSE – AND THE DOG NIBBLING ON IT – TO LURE THE DOG BACK INTO A SIT. FOCUS ON ACHIEVING A STRAIGHT SIT AT YOUR SIDE.

7 WHEN THE DOG'S REAR TOUCHES THE GROUND IN A STRAIGHT SIT, CLICK AND RELEASE THE TREAT FROM YOUR HAND.

As with most behaviours, there are three stages we move through:

1. ***The lure:*** *For the first many moves of sit-at-my-side, go to Section 3.4, Heelwork — and ensure your dog can do the repositioning move, before progressing to this material.*

    Once you have done the repositioning move, you just need to get a sit on the end of it, to achieve sit-at-my-side. But, no matter how tempted you are to speed things up here — you must *not* use your dog's 'sit' verbal cue! Why? Because your dog knows 'sit' to mean 'sit, anywhere, facing any direction, in the vicinity of me' — not 'sit at my side, facing forwards'. If you say 'sit', your dog may just move out of position and plonk her bum down in a lovely sit — and then not understand why you don't reinforce that, when it was a great sit!

    So, instead of saying 'sit', you're going to keep a treat on your dog's nose at the end of the repositioning move and, *with your dog nibbling away at the treat*, you're going to lure her back into a sit. Be sure not to take your hand away from the dog's nose at any point — do not allow her to sit herself yet: Many dogs will move their butts out of position to the side if you let them sit by themselves. Keep your hand and treat on her nose for maximal control and steerage to ensure straightness. Click the sit and release the treat.

THIS HANDLER HAS TAKEN THE LURE AWAY FROM THE DOG'S NOSE BEFORE THE SIT – LEAVING THE DOG TO DECIDE WHERE TO SIT. THE DOG WILL TYPICALLY SIT AT AN ANGLE.

2. ***The hand signal:*** Once your dog is fluent at following a treat to get into the correct position on your left, with her spine nice and straight — and you are happy with the positioning (which will take many sessions) — you will use your hand, *without* a treat in it, to get her to do the exact same behaviour. Click the sit at the end, and then deliver a treat. (It doesn't matter if the dog moves out of position to collect the treat — it only matters what she is doing when you click.)

   You can stick at this stage as long as you like and, the more you practise it, the less you'll need to do with your hand to communicate that you want her to sit at your side — until eventually you are just doing a tiny hand movement to achieve this behaviour, perhaps tapping the top of your thigh once.

   A functioning sit-at-my-side hand signal is very useful and can be given in a very subtle way to a dog — much less obviously than any verbal cue. Since extra verbal cues will see you lose points in tests, it's worth ensuring you've got this hand signal working well.

3. ***The word (or verbal cue):*** You're not going to use your sit verbal cue for sit-at-my-side, for the same reason mentioned above. We need a cue that tells the dog to sit in this very specific place on our left side, facing forwards, spine aligned with our body. Suggestions include: 'Close' or 'left'.

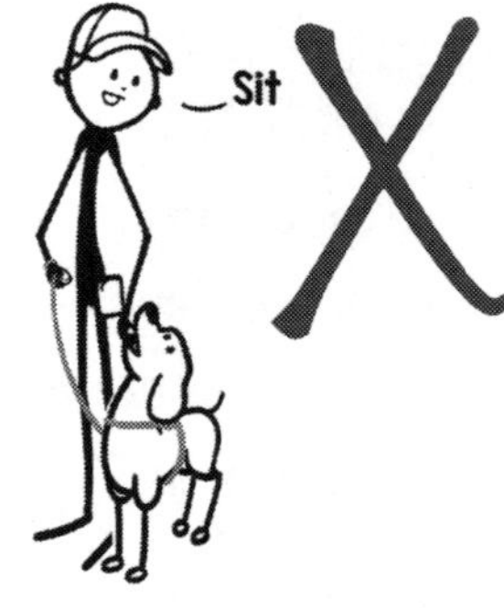

THIS HANDLER IS USING THE DOG'S ALREADY-LEARNT VERBAL 'SIT' CUE TO ACHIEVE THE SIT AT THE END OF THE BEHAVIOUR. DON'T DO THIS, EVEN IF IT TAKES LONGER TO FIDDLE AROUND WITH THE LURE TO ACHIEVE A SIT. WE WILL USE A DIFFERENT VERBAL CUE FOR THIS BEHAVIOUR.

To teach your verbal cue, just as with teaching the sit itself, we are not going to say the word at the same time as giving the hand signal — or the the word will not come to *predict* the hand signal.

So, say your word once and be absolutely sure you are not doing anything else at this time, other than saying the word! *Then* give your hand signal for sit-at-my-side and click and treat.

After many reps of this, pause a bit longer after saying the cue — to see if the dog will start to position herself to the word alone. If not, just keep repeating word > pause > hand signal > click > treat.

This one is quite a complex behaviour for dogs to learn, so expect the dog to need some hand signal help for a while. Uphold straightness at your side, at all times, and do not click efforts which result in a non-straight sit — use a hand signal or even food lure to achieve a straight and clickable sit.

3.2

SIT-STAYS

A dog on a peg, waiting during a drive, is doing a sit-stay under very high distractions. A spaniel or HPR (versatile dog or bird dog) that has sat to flush, is doing a sit-stay during the shot and fall of game. We will talk later about proofing your stays against such distractions as these — but the basic concept of a stay, is not gundog-specific.

The most successful methods for teaching stays involve an *immediate consequence* for the dog moving. This doesn't mean using positive punishment when the dog moves; it means using *negative* punishment. In other words: Removing the reinforcer. And making it clear to the dog that her action of moving has *caused* that reinforcer to be available no longer. This cause-and-effect is what we need the dog to understand.

The trick, here, is in making that connection (between moving and losing the reinforcer) clear to the dog. Holding treats in your hand and feeding the dog for remaining in a sit, makes it hard to communicate that anything has been 'lost' when the dog moves.

The best version of the 'consequence of moving' approach which I've come across, is that encapsulated by Anne Bussey in her great e-booklet called *Teach your Dog to Want to Stay: The Pot Method of Stay Training*.

In Anne's method, a pot of treats is placed on the floor in front of the staying dog. If the dog moves, the pot of treats disappears. This makes it really easy to communicate with the dog: Keep your butt on the floor, and the pot stays on the floor and treats occasionally come from it. If your butt leaves the floor, the treats disappear and all reinforcement stops. The devil is in the details and there is more to it than that, but I don't want to repeat Anne's method here — we have so much gundog-specific material to cover. Please do buy her book!

COMMON 'STAY' MISTAKES

Mistake #1: 'Greedy trainers', waiting too long before reinforcing the dog — raising criteria too fast. The dog gets up or breaks before you've made it back to reinforce — and not only do you have an unwanted pattern developing (dog breaking stays), you've lost an opportunity to reinforce. Always be conservative in terms of the time you wait before returning or the distance you are walking: It is *your* job to get there and reinforce your dog before she has moved. Don't be greedy and push it. Consolidate a good foundation by really reinforcing those baby stays so that you can build on them later.

Mistake #2: Increasing distance, duration and distractions at the same time. Adjust only one criteria if you are making things harder. I recommend you *first work on duration, achieving a reliable one-minute stay with you right by the dog* — before introducing any distance. When you do start to introduce distance, do it gradually. There has to be some duration to your distance (since you are not a magician and can't click your fingers to be instantly 20 yards away!) so don't add even more duration by waiting too long before you return. Remember that it is your duty to get back to your dog before she has moved.

Mistake #3: Immediately re-setting and reinforcing your dog after a break. The dog breaks — the handler goes to the dog, gets her attention with a treat, asks for a sit, reinforces the sit, and begins another stay. What has the dog learnt? '*If I keep staying, I might have to wait ages for another treat. If I get up, my handler comes back to me and immediately gives me one!*' Pretty soon the dog is breaking almost to 'call' the handler back with treats!

Instead: If your dog breaks and you are past the 'baby' stages of stay training (that is, your dog can stay for 10 seconds with you next to her), then take hold of the leash (if you are outdoors). Hold the leash short enough that your dog can't sniff the ground and self-reinforce. Turn your back to your dog and wait at least 10 seconds, with your dog losing your attention during this time. Check your mobile phone for messages or admire the sky! If you are indoors, you don't need to hold a leash — just lean on your kitchen counter and text someone. Read the paper on the kitchen table. The message you want to give to your dog is that you are not currently involved in training her. This avoids the pattern of 'dog breaking and owner immediately re-setting for another rep'. After 10 seconds of 'hanging out', you can set up for another attempt without reinforcing the break — but this time, don't push it — get back to reinforce much earlier than last time. You don't want to get multiple breaks in a row.

Mistake #4: Not reducing criteria when something goes wrong. If a dog breaks a stay, you should absolutely not be immediately re-attempting the same distance/duration/distraction criteria. You need to make the exercise easier by reducing the distance/duration/distractions. If you attempt to repeat exactly the same exercise, the majority of dogs will break again. Then you have not just one break to deal with, but two — consecutively. Dog training is a slippery slope and once your dog has broken two stays in a row, you have put yourself at crisis point for developing the wrong habits on your stays. At class, I see time and again dogs breaking and handlers immediately trying the same criteria again. It's as if the handler thinks '*Oh, we were so close, I'm sure we can do it next time — let's try again*'. Instead, once your dog has broken a stay, she is at a hugely increased risk of breaking the next one. So you need to be ultra conservative in what you ask for, to enable you to get back to her and reinforce her, *before* she has moved. You need to rebuild your foundation to get back to where you were, in a secure way.

Mistake #5: Reinforcing after the release. There is a difference between a 'wait' (for something to happen) and a stay. I will talk more about the wait behaviour below. What I say here relates to the stay.

Sometimes handlers release the dog — and then reinforce the dog. Some reinforce with food, others with a ball. Reinforcing after movement can result in a dog doing a stay 'on the starting blocks', desperate to move because the reinforcement comes after moving. You will get a very different quality of stay: It won't look like a secure, relaxed and calm stay — more a 'seat-of-your-pants', '*When is the reinforcer appearing?*' kind of a stay! Remember that we are always training associated emotions into behaviours, not just training the behaviour by itself.

Similarly, sometimes people want to use balls, thrown for the dog, to reinforce a stay. It is impossible to reinforce the dog with a ball (and for the dog to derive reinforcement from it) whilst the dog is actually staying — so, again, we are reinforcing after the dog has moved. The anticipation of such an exciting 'event' can often lead to the dog breaking. If they do stay, it is again a 'nail-biting' and highly-aroused stay. We really don't want to associate that emotional state with our stays.

When we do steadiness training (whether steadiness to retrieves, or to the flush with spaniels or HPRs), we *do* end up with an exciting reinforcer (retrieve) happening afterwards — but the control occurring here, is the 'wait' behaviour and not a stay.

We don't want to train our basic stays in the first place with high arousal reinforcers occurring after the release. It's not going to lead to a calm, relaxed stay lasting many minutes. For now, focus on achieving a calm, relaxed and bomb-proof sit-stay at this point — by ensuring the reinforcer is food and that it arrives in the mouth of a sitting dog.

Mistake #6: Accepting lying down on stays. Dogs should remain in the position in which they are left. If you ask the dog to sit and leave her in a sit-stay, the dog should maintain that position. This is just 'good practice' for training purposes and it is the standard across all other dog sports.

But it also makes practical sense with a gundog: A dog in a sit-stay during a drive can better mark falling retrieves. If you have walked some way off, and a dog is lying down in cover, you can no longer see your dog to handle her — should you decide to. If you need to have a pee behind a bush(!), you will be better able to see your dog in cover if you leave her in a sit-stay.

If your dog lies down during a sit-stay, you need to treat that as if the dog has stood up and broken the stay. You can't accept it and continue reinforcing the dog — or you will be reinforcing the lying down. If you are having problems with your dog lying down during stays, again it is best to *remain up close to her and focus on duration* first and foremost — until you can get to one minute without her lying down. Only if you are right next to the dog, can you remove the reinforcer and thereby communicate immediately that lying down is what led to the loss of that reinforcer.

Mistake #7: Sometimes problems with stays are actually problems with the release word. This is the word (or words) you give your dog to release her from a stay. Handlers are notoriously slack at using this cue consistently. Some handlers will walk up to the dog, praise with '*Good dog*' and the dog will get up — they don't even have a release word. Or perhaps the dog believes 'good dog' is the release. Others may ruffle the dog around the scruff to pet her at the end of a stay — and the dog gets up — believing physical contact is the release. Other handlers will garble their release word quickly *after* the dog has already moved — as if they can somehow fudge time itself(!). This doesn't work.

No matter if you release a fraction of a second after the dog has got up, your cue is not releasing her — therefore it is not functioning as a release word. Your dog has, in fact, released herself. If your dog gets up before the release word, she has broken a stay — no matter if it is half a second before the release word!

Mistake #8: Not realising that, every time the dog is asked to sit, she is doing a sit-stay. Once you've asked the dog to assume a position, the dog should remain there until released. The dog should not get up of her own accord. Whether you are doing a formal sit-stay or asking the dog to sit whilst you unpack your gear at class. The handler needs to uphold sit-stay standards, any time the dog is asked to sit. *The only ways out of any cued sit are: 1) the sit is clicked (the click has a built-in release), 2) the release word is used, or 3) the dog is asked to perform another behaviour.* If none of these three has occurred, the dog has broken a stay.

RELEASE WORD

'What is it?'

Think about a stay as a pair of brackets: ('*Sit*'... ... ... duration... ... ... '*ok*').

The 'sit' cue is the start of the stay — the opening bracket. Then there is duration on the stay, which is what's contained within the brackets. And then there is the release word at the end of the stay — the closing bracket.

Just like brackets come in pairs — opening and closing — so the stay *must* have a clear beginning and end to it. People generally provide clear beginnings — everyone remembers to say 'sit' and perhaps 'stay' — but it's the clear *endings* which get messed up.

A stay is defined by its beginning *and its end*. If you don't provide dogs with a clear endpoint, they will never quite understand when they can move. And if the dog does not understand when she can move, she does not understand the concept of a stay. This lack of understanding leads to stays being broken.

'Which word or words should I use as my release word?'

With other cues, my answer to this question is always: '*Whatever word or words you choose.*' But the release word requires more thought. For the majority of handlers, I really believe that the simplest and easiest approach (for the human in the relationship!) is to use 'ok'. Because this word makes sense (to the human in the relationship), across all the scenarios where you might need to use a release word.

That's the simple answer. So, if that satisfies you, use 'ok' and skip onto the next section! If you want the nitty-gritty, read on!

Think about all the situations in which you need to release the dog: To tell her she can jump out of the car, to tell her she can move after a stay, to tell her she can bite the tuggy now, or to tell her she can get a treat she's been showing self-control around. The release word is a verbal cue which applies in all these situations and it means 'you can stop the self-control now'. Dogs really do generalise the release word to different situations easily: The dog, herself, seems to understand self-control around what she desires to be the same skill in these different contexts. Furthermore, using one release word across different scenarios greatly simplifies things for people who are starting out in training. They need only remember one word ('ok').

You *can* have different verbal release cues for these different scenarios — but these releases also typically function as *markers*. They are used at the exact moment we want to mark something, in the same way as the clicker. For example: I use 'tag' to tell the dog to bite a tuggy. I use 'cookies' to tell the dog to get the treat in the bowl I've put on the floor. I use 'find it' to tell the dog there is a treat on the floor near me, which she needs to sniff out. So, I could say 'sit' and, instead of clicking when the dog sits, say 'cookies' and the dog races to her bowl. Or 'tag' and the dog races for the tug. These marker words tell the dog 1) which type of reinforcer to expect (toy or food) and also 2) where to access it (on my person or elsewhere).

We don't want to reinforce the dog after we've released her from a stay. So our release word just releases her. Unlike a marker cue, it does not predict any reinforcement — other than the inherent reinforcement there is, in ending the self-control. The release word also isn't precisely marking a behaviour, in the same way that a marker is. It is just telling the dog that the self-control can stop, now.

When I've told people to choose any word they like, I've had people use words like 'free' to end stays, for example. But if you're playing tug with a dog and tell them to leave the tug, you're unlikely to say 'free' to tell the dog they can get it again. Of course you *could*, if you wanted to — but it doesn't come naturally to the human in the relationship! If you are considering not using 'ok' as your release, ask yourself what other word you would use instead — and would it make sense in all these various scenarios? Is it going to occur to you to use it? Or are you prepared to have multiple different release words (perhaps alongside multiple marker words)? Having given this some thought myself, I came to the conclusion that 'ok' is the one word I can think of which makes sense (to the human) in all these scenarios.

Sometimes people are worried about 'ok' being a word which they often say in conversation and which might accidentally release a dog. I suggest that you say it in a sing-songy happy tone when releasing from stays — so that your dog learns to listen out for this tone of voice. It is very rare that your dog is performing a behaviour which requires a release and you happen to use the word 'ok' in conversation to someone else, at the same time.

HOW TO TRAIN THE RELEASE WORD

In this exercise we want the dog to:

- move immediately on hearing 'ok'
- not move when hearing any other words.

1. Ask your dog to sit. Don't click (because the click has a release built into it and we don't want the dog to move), just give a treat. The dog should remain in a sit. (If she gets up when you give a treat, then forget about saying words to her and focus on her maintaining a sit for five treats before your release word.)

2. Say a nonsense word to your dog (like 'banana'). Quickly give her treat before she moves.

3. Say another nonsense word ('strawberries'). Give her a treat. (NB — Nonsense words do not have to be fruit!) This is quite rapid fire and not about duration between treats.

4. After about three nonsense words and a treat after each, say 'Ok'. Try to say 'ok' in a sing-songy and easily-recognisable way. If your dog releases on 'ok', click the moment her rear leaves the floor and throw a treat. If your dog doesn't move when you say 'ok', move your hands encouragingly, bend forwards and physically tempt her to get up — watching her rear closely. As soon as the dog's rear leaves the floor, click and throw a treat. The 'clickable moment' is when there is any air between your dog's rear and the floor.

5. Repeat, many times.

Make sure that you say the nonsense distraction word first and then feed the treat a millisecond later. Don't do both at the same time. The distraction word is a temptation. Does the dog resist it? Then reinforce that. Give the dog half a second to show that she is resisting that temptation before you reinforce.

If you have a dog which is really into offering you behaviours, you may find that, when you say the distraction word and pause, she offers you another behaviour. She may 'guess' a down, for example. If this happens, then reinforce much sooner after saying the word — (before she has a chance to guess something else) — to communicate that remaining in position is what you want.

'Hey! Why are we now reinforcing after the release word? Didn't you say not to do this?'

Well spotted! As explained above, we usually want all the reinforcers to occur *during* the stay — and then none afterwards.

But, at this early stage, we are teaching the dog what the release word means. So, we need to communicate to the dog that moving after it is the correct behaviour — that's the whole purpose of this exercise. Therefore, in this particular exercise *only*, we click when the dog's rear leaves the floor — and throw the treat. A little chase on the treat when you throw it provides additional reinforcement.

When you can say your release word and your dog immediately moves without any encouragement from you (and doesn't move when you say other words!), you can stop reinforcing after the release word. Just release and praise the dog.

THE DIFFERENCE BETWEEN 'STAY' AND 'WAIT'

Many handlers find it useful to differentiate between 'stay' and 'wait'. Not everyone does. Some don't use *either* cue, instead only cuing the dog to assume a position (like sit) and then training the dog to remain in that position until she hears the release word or is given another cue.

Whichever you choose, consistency is key. For me:

STAY

- 'Stay' is used to tell the dog that she need not focus on the handler — no cue for another behaviour is going to be given whilst she is staying.

- The handler is going to return to the dog at the end, and release her.

- Any reinforcement will come during the stay — not afterwards.

- We can think of a stay as a more passive, settled and often longer-duration behaviour. I put my dog in a stay when I lay a track, as an example.

Or if I am setting up a retrieving drill by putting dummies out in different locations before returning to the dog.

- All the preceding material in this section relates to the training of the stay. (In my opinion and experience, it is the harder behaviour to train.)

- The emotional state relating to the stay is one of calm relaxation.

WAIT

- 'Wait' is used to tell the dog that she should pay attention to the handler as the handler leaves her, because she will be given a cue for another behaviour. This may be a cast in a retrieving drill, for example. A wait is also occurring at the moment when a dog sits to a flush, waiting to be told to hunt on or to retrieve.

- 'Wait' tells the dog that the handler — from a distance — is going to give her a cue to do something — and *often this is going to be a release to some form of reinforcement.* That is: Unlike the stay, the reinforcement in a wait is usually going to come *after the release.*

- Wait is typically of shorter-duration and is a more active behaviour, with very alert attention being required from the dog.

- Whereas handlers should not reinforce after the release word when training stays, reinforcing after the release word is perfectly fine — in fact, recommended — when training a wait. After all, it's what a wait is all about: Wait to get the cast to retrieve (reinforcer), wait to get the cue to hunt on (reinforcer), or wait to get the cue to flush. Great preparation for this is to wait to get the tennis ball. Or wait to be released to the treat on the floor!

- The emotional state relating to the wait is one of anticipatory excitement.

'TEMPT THE DOG' SIT-STAY

This exercise is the beginning of proofing your stays — and the sit itself — against distractions.

With this exercise, we are going to present the dog with a deliberate temptation during a sit-stay. We are in complete control of this temptation (unlike those in the natural world!). If the dog resists the temptation, she gets the treat. If she breaks the stay and tries to get the treat, the treat disappears. We need to make it easy enough that the dog is successful at least 85 per cent of the time — since it is very punishing to lose treats.

1. Ask the dog to sit and reinforce this with a treat. Your dog has probably sat facing you.

2. Make space by turning yourself 90 degrees — you need some space in front of the dog.

3. Hold out a treat in that space — for just *one second*. To ensure the dog is successful, begin by holding the treat higher than the dog — at the height of your chest to begin with. In terms of the distance along the ground, you should always hold the treat two feet away from the dog's mouth and no closer. (With each successful rep, lower the treat until it is level with the dog's mouth — still two feet away.)

4. If the dog remains sitting when the treat is held out for just one second, quickly reinforce her — in the sit. When you reinforce, I recommend you get into the habit of lifting the treat up in the air to your chest and then coming down quickly from above, to deliver it to the mouth. Because, when the treat comes directly towards the dog's mouth from the temptation position

— especially when at the same height as the dog — it tends to result in her standing up to meet the treat because it's low and looks so reachable. *It is important that the dog's rear is on the floor in a sit when she eats the treat*, so if she stands up to meet the treat — we can't deliver it.

To try to prevent the dog from getting up to meet the treat, do not dilly-dally with the treat on the way to the dog's mouth. This is not 'temptation-time' — the dog has successfully resisted the treat at the temptation position and now we need to get it to the dog's mouth, fast. So, zoom the treat to her mouth so she has no reason to get up. And deliver down from above, to the mouth.

5. If the dog does not remain sitting when the treat is held out, snatch the treat away to your chest and wait for the sit again. For the next few reps, hold the treat higher and ensure it is less tempting — before you reduce the height again.

6. You are not finished with this exercise, until you can hold the treat *level with the dog's head in terms of height* — still two feet away in terms of distance — with the dog resisting the temptation of the treat. Just for a second. You want to reinforce that refusal as soon as you see it.

7. When you want to finish your 'Tempt the Dog' sit-stay, remember to release the dog using your release word ('ok'). You should release your dog after every four or five treats so she gets a mini-break — rather than expecting her to keep staying, endlessly — only for her to get up and break the stay.

Tip: This exercise is not about duration, so we are not holding the treat out for prolonged amounts of time — it is about a momentary resisting of temptation. It is very rapid-fire — since every successfully resisted temptation earns a reinforcer.

3.3

THE RECALL

A gundog needs a bomb-proof recall away from high distractions — both a functioning whistle cue and a verbal cue.

Since there are two cues you need to train, you will need to cover the exercises described here with both the whistle cue and the verbal cue — so that both cues become well-trained.

I have a very specific programme I like to follow for training the recall, which I will outline after discussing the cues themselves.

THE WHISTLE CUE

Most gundog handlers in the UK use an Acme whistle. The whistle cue for a gundog recall is conventionally four or five quick peeps on the whistle (as in, choose whether you want yours to be four or five and be consistent).

I'd recommend you take your whistle to somewhere your dog can't hear you (maybe shutting yourself in your car) and experiment till you find a cue you're happy with — so you can be consistent from the beginning. Think about the speed of your peeps, since this is also something the dog is going to learn to recognise — and again try to be consistent.

Lastly, if you can blow your whistle using your tongue to start each peep — 'toooo' — instead of 'oooo' — it will be much easier for you, and clearer for the dog. (If you have ever played a wind or brass instrument — even the recorder — you will know how to do this!)

THE VERBAL CUE

You will also need a functioning verbal recall. You may not always have your whistle with you, or it may break or get lost. It may be inside your shirt at a crucial moment, leaving you with only your voice.

The verbal recall should be more than your dog's name: It should be 'Fido, come' or 'Fido, here' or 'Fido, this way'. Not just 'Fido'. Because you don't always mean '*Come here as if your life depends on it*', every time you say your dog's name.

In addition, think about the sing-songy pitch and volume of your voice as you call — and try to keep this the same, each time you give the recall. The pitch of the call is part of what the dog is learning — not just the words themselves.

When you are training the verbal recall, call it exactly as you will outdoors — loudly, in a sing-songy way.

Dogs tend to generalise whistle cues better than verbal cues: People's voices differ greatly in pitch and intonation, so that even using the same verbal phrase can sound very different when it is called by different people. A whistle, on the other hand, will sound similar to the dog — even when different people are blowing it. As a result, the whistle cue is more transferable between handlers. This is especially useful if multiple people are training or handling a dog.

REINFORCERS FOR THE RECALL

You need super-duper extra-tasty treats for recalls. Your treats are competing with other dogs, decomposing animals, flushing pheasants, and people: All those environmental reinforcers we've discussed.

I've found that the treats that get the best results are always messy things. My hypothesis is that squishy moist things get around the inside of the dog's mouth — and so she actually tastes them. Solid treats are often just 'down the hatch', without any chewing and without the dog even processing what they are.

As mentioned previously, my list of top recall treats would be something like:

- sardines (e.g. tinned)
- smoked mackerel
- paté
- gourmet wet dog food (different varieties).

You are shooting yourself in the foot if you go out into the world without the most amazing treats: You are going into battle against dead rabbits and other dogs and horse poo — you need the best 'weapons' on your side to combat those environmental reinforcers which rival your treats.

Sometimes people say that their dog recalls incredibly well at home — or even at class — for *just* a hotdog slice or cheese. So, why should they use anything better?

Even when you are training at home, you need to use the amazing stuff for recalls. Why? Because you are creating an association for the future — a reinforcement history. You want your dog to remember that the recall is *wow*! We want these recall cues causing a Pavlovian response for the dog's salivary glands. Remember that we are always training an emotion, alongside a behaviour. And we want the dog to feel very excited when hearing that recall.

A 10M LONG-LINE

Check out Section 2.3, Equipment, for more information on this item and my biothane recommendation.

Why 10 metres? Any longer and it becomes unwieldy and has too much drag behind the dog. Any shorter and your dog doesn't get to move very far away from you.

At this point, it is important to have read and understood Section 1.2, Prevention.

COMMON 'RECALL' MISTAKES

Mistake #1: Calling a dog more than once. If you call 'Fido come, Fido come, Fido come' before your dog comes, you will always need to call 'Fido come' three times before she will come. Your dog will learn that the recall cue is this phrase, repeated three times. The same goes for repeated whistle cues.

Repeating recall cues also teaches a dog to ignore them: Giving the recall cue and allowing the dog to ignore it, is associating the recall cue with *not* coming — the opposite of what you want. It is pairing together 'Fido come' with the *absence* of coming. It will soon become just another thing you sometimes say to your dog, which your dog sometimes responds to (and often doesn't).

If you want a reliable recall, give the recall cue (whether verbal or whistle) *once only*. If you see the dog is not responding, get your dog's focus using your treat and lure her towards you. Outdoors, if your dog does not respond, she should always be trailing a 10 metre long-line. You can use this to gently 'detach' or disengage her from whatever she is distracted by — enabling her to turn and respond to your recall.

Mistake #2: Raising the criteria too fast, too soon. If you don't do enough training indoors first but just take your dog out and start attempting to recall her away from other dogs — you will fail. It is essential that you do initial recall training inside your house and then in your garden or yard, before ever attempting it out when exercising your dog.

Even once you start practising out and about, at first only use the recall when the dog looks back at you anyway (of her own accord). If that is successful (many times), then recall the dog when she is sniffing a plant or the ground. And so on. So there is a gradual progression of the level of distraction under which you expect your dog to respond.

If you unexpectedly meet a higher level of distraction (say another dog) when you haven't trained up to that yet, don't even attempt the recall — just reel your dog quickly but gently in on the long-line and march away in the opposite direction.

Mistake #3: Using the recall phrase casually (to get attention from the dog) and then not providing a recall treat when the dog responds. Whilst training heelwork, a dog gets a bit distracted by, say, another dog and loses focus on her handler. To get the dog to focus on the heelwork again, the handler says 'Fido, come' — using the recall phrase to regain the dog's attention. If the dog responds, sometimes no treat is given — and if a treat *is* given, it's not an amazing *recall* treat, it's whatever bog-standard treat the handler had in her hand, for heelwork. The dog evidently wasn't *wowed* by it.

Don't use your recall phrase casually like this. If you just want your dog's attention, use her name and reinforce that response with a regular treat. The recall phrase does not mean '*Give me your attention*' or '*Look at me*'. It means '*Come here — from a distance — as fast as you can*'. Use the recall phrase *only* if you believe you have a good chance of getting a response, and *only* if you are going to reinforce a good response with a super-amazing recall treat.

Mistake #4: Not using a long-line (prevention) to stop a dog accessing environmental reinforcers. Long-lines can be cumbersome pieces of equipment. Many a handler has been tugged off their feet by one, or has tripped over one. It's not surprising that some handlers decide they would rather not deal with this piece of equipment or want to stop using it prematurely — or perhaps to leave it off sometimes and put it on at other times.

A long-line is not perfect — it can be awkward to use. However, it's what we have. Used consistently, it is extremely effective. In the US, the majority of pointing dogs are trained whilst trailing a long-line ('check cord') until they are steady to shot and fall — it is a standard piece of mainstream gundog training equipment. If you don't use a long-line, you will have no way of preventing your dog from accessing environmental reinforcers (such as other dogs, dead rabbits and people). If your dog chooses not to respond and bogs off to the horizon, you will have no options — other than admiring her disappearing rear end. She will seek the reinforcement she wants (chase the rabbit) and then be even more likely to seek that reinforcement again in future.

A 10m long-line is an essential piece of equipment and your dog should be trailing that from the moment she is old enough to begin off-leash exercise. Very occasionally, there's the odd dog which doesn't need a long-line. Typically, this is a Labrador with loads of food motivation, and a bomb-proof recall as a result — because food trumps all else. But the majority of dogs will need a long-line to achieve a reliable recall.

It is far better to put the long-line on *always* and then, if you have a very reliable dog, to stop using it, than it is to *not* use a long-line, see the dog get accustomed to ignoring you and bogging off after game, and *then* decide to use one. Under the latter circumstances, the dog then has a strong reinforcement history for chasing game and ignoring you. And you are then not just starting from some 'neutral' position, but have a lot of damage to undo. Remember that prevention is far better than cure.

Mistake #5: Using the long-line sometimes and not at other times. Once you start using the long-line, you want your dog to forget about it and experience it almost as an extra leg. You don't want your dog to learn that, when the long-line is off, she is free to pursue environmental reinforcers — and that you can't do anything to prevent it. If she learns this, you will never be able to remove the long-line — because, whenever you take it off, she will stop responding to you. She may be perfectly responsive with the long-line on — and not at all, with it off! She will have become 'long-line wise'. And you will be stuck using it forever.

Dogs only become long-line wise if you give them an opportunity to compare 'long-line on' with 'long-line off', through putting it on sometimes and not at other times during the training process. To avoid your dog becoming long-line wise, always put the long-line on when you exercise her.

If you should forget your long-line, don't use your recall cues (verbal or whistle): If you recall her and she doesn't come, you then risk her learning that when the long-line is off, she can access environmental reinforcers rather than your own — and you can't do anything about it to prevent her.

Mistake #6: Recalling before unpleasant things. Using your recall cues before a bath, before nail trimming, or at the end of exercise to put your dog on the lead and go home, will cause your dog to associate the recall with something unpleasant being done or — at the end of exercise — with the end of fun and freedom.

Go and get your dog when you need to do something slightly unenjoyable. At the end of exercise, reel your dog in on her long-line to go home.

Of course, once your dog has a bomb-proof response, as long as you keep practising your recall at other moments, you can also use it at the end of exercise without a problem. Just avoid letting it get associated with this, early in your training.

Mistake #7: Avoiding difficult distractions permanently. Sometimes there is a particular environmental reinforcer which handlers feel challenged by — typically other dogs or perhaps game. They 'resolve' this by completely avoiding all other dogs and all game, as far as possible.

This approach is positively reinforcing to the *handler* — because they get to feel successful during their training sessions: Everything is going so well, now! However, obviously, it is not going to teach the dog to respond around those distractions. And it is impossible to avoid these distractions permanently — so, when they are encountered, things definitely do not go well!

Whilst avoiding your dog's nemesis during earlier stages of training is essential (see Mistake #2), *permanently* avoiding her nemesis is not a good idea. How will things get any better? Instead, when your dog is ready and has done the preliminary training with lesser distractions, you need to *seek out* the nemesis deliberately and to be prepared to encounter it at those times. Being prepared to encounter it means you have put prevention in place, you have the highest level of reinforcers on your person, you have reduced criteria to a recall from two paces away, if necessary, and you understand that repetition is going to be required before you see good results. Then you train persistently around your nemesis, until you achieve reliability.

RECALL – A TRAINING PROGRAMME

There are three phases I use when training a reliable recall. The first two phases usually only take about a week each. These two phases are trained indoors (only). During this time, the handler must avoid using the recall cues when out and about with their dog. We must ensure there is a strong trained response before using the recall cues outside — because we don't want to teach the dog to ignore them. The third phase is outdoors and can be quite long-term, sometimes months — or even until adolescence is over. This phase is where the bulk of the generalisation and proofing against distractions is being done — since the environment is almost infinite in its variability. (See Section 1.4, Generalisation and distraction management, for more details.)

These exercises are best started as soon as you get a new puppy home, but they can be used with dogs of any age.

PHASE 1: ELASTIC RECALL

- *Practise 20-30 times a day, for a week*
- *Practise indoors only*
- *Practise with both whistle and verbal recall cues*

The repetition of this exercise is really important for 'drilling' a knee-jerk, reflexive, recall response into your dog's brain. (See Section 1.3, Repetition, for more information on why repetition is so important in training.)

Practise this exercise at least 20 reps a day, every day, for a week — training in the house only. If you can have two sessions a day, you will make even better progress. This might sound like a lot, but the elastic recall exercise is very quick. Even if your dog is doing this exercise perfectly, please keep going until you've done 20 a day, every day: We need to hit our 20-30 reps. It's about the repetition, here — not just achieving the result and stopping.

For this exercise, you'll need *throwable* treats. Messy treats just go 'splat' and don't throw far, even though they taste super-amazing. Having just recommended you use messy, squishy treats for recalls, you will need to downgrade slightly for this exercise, to things like cheese and frankfurter. This should be a temporary down-grading and for all other recall exercises, you'll be using the amazing stuff.

To prepare you for this exercise, we're going to visualise it first. Stand in the middle of a room. Look to your right. You are going to throw a treat there. Now look to your left. You are next going to throw a treat there. The distance you throw the treats can be determined by your available indoor space. I prompt you to do this looking about *before* you start training and flailing around with treats and dog — because it can all get a bit chaotic, especially if you have a very fast dog.

It's important that the treats and you yourself form a reasonably straight line: Left treat delivery spot — you in the middle — right treat delivery spot. Sometimes people get a bit uncoordinated on this exercise and start to do things in the wrong order — even trying to do everything at once!

Think about it: We are training the dog to *come to us* when we call. So it's important to call your dog when she is at a distance from you. Don't throw a treat out and call at the exact same time — or your recall cue will be associated with your dog's retreating backside — and that's never what we want to see after a recall!

'My dog didn't see a treat I threw. What should I do?'

You can give your dog a little time to find the treat if she is looking for it. Or you can go and point out the treat to your dog. Then quickly move away as she eats it, so you are back in the middle and ready to call again.

You can help by *rolling* the treats rather than throwing them, so the dog can more easily follow them. And also by choosing treats which contrast with the colour of your floor - so your dog can see them better. (Cheddar for dark floors!)

If you have a baby puppy, do this exercise 'in miniature' — up close to you. *Place* the treat at arm's length on one side of you and tap the floor by it until the pup sees it. Call the pup back to you, and *place* the next treat on the other side of you, again within arm's length — and again, tap the floor by the treat to draw attention to it.

PHASE 1 — Elastic recall

1 STAND IN THE MIDDLE OF THE INDOOR AREA YOU WILL BE USING. HAVE A HANDFUL OF TASTY-YET-THROWABLE TREATS.

2 THROW A TREAT OUT TO ONE SIDE OF YOU. DO NOT CALL OR GIVE ANY CUE AT THIS TIME. THE TREAT IS A FREEBIE TO GET YOUR DOG TO MOVE AWAY FROM YOU. THE DOG WILL RUN TO THE TREAT.

3 *AS* THE DOG EATS THE TREAT, GIVE EITHER YOUR VERBAL RECALL CUE OR YOUR WHISTLE RECALL CUE. IF SHE DOESN'T COME, JUST WAIT. DON'T REPEAT THE CUE.

4 THE DOG WILL TURN AND BEGIN TO RUN TO YOU. QUICKLY THROW THE TREAT (FOR THAT RECALL) OUT TO THE *OTHER* SIDE OF YOU.

5 AGAIN, WHILST THE DOG IS EATING THAT TREAT, GIVE EITHER YOUR VERBAL OR YOUR WHISTLE RECALL CUE.

6 AGAIN, THE DOG WILL TURN AND BEGIN TO RUN TO YOU. QUICKLY THROW THE TREAT (FOR THAT RECALL) OUT TO THE OTHER SIDE OF YOU. REPEAT FOR 20-30 REPS.

'What should I do when I exercise my dog, this week?'

Before you use any recall cue away from the house, we have to condition it and make it really strong in the familiar (and boring) environment of the house and garden. Next, still at home, we need to begin proofing it against some distractions. (That's coming in Phase 2.)

If you use your recall cues outside now, your dog may learn that it's possible to ignore the recall — and you will undermine all your training.

If you have a puppy, it will be very easy not to let your pup off-leash yet: Pups don't need much physical exercise, they need socialisation trips — and long-lines or house-lines are ideal for these.

Those of you with older dogs will need to let your dog off-leash for training and exercise though, and you might be worried about how to get her back without using your recall phrase.

There are a few different options, with this one. You can use some other verbal phrase to get your dog's attention — but not your recall cue! You can throw your hands in the air and wave them about whilst making silly squeaky noises and running away from your dog — inspiring your dog to chase after you. In short, do whatever you like to encourage your dog to return, when you need her to — but don't use your recall cues yet.

If your dog has control issues (which might be why you are reading this book in the first place!), I'd really recommend beginning to use your 10m long-line now. You can either allow it to trail on the ground near you whilst your dog is off-leash so you can grab it should you need to control her, or — for the far-ranging and independent dog — you can keep hold of it and change direction frequently. Just reel your dog in when you want to put her on the normal lead. (No recall.)

PHASE 2: RECALL FROM A DISTRACTION

- *Practise 20-30 times a day, for a week*
- *Practise indoors and (once it's working indoors) also in your yard*
- *Practise with both whistle and verbal recall cues*

Recalls malfunction largely because dogs pursue environmental reinforcers (dead animals, other dogs, other people, scent) over *your* reinforcers. As discussed in Section 1.4, Generalisation and distraction management, a 'distraction' is simply an environmental reinforcer, to your dog: It's all good stuff, to your dog. There is no innate reason why dogs should prefer your own reinforcers over those in the environment. We need to teach them this.

The recall-from-a-distraction exercise sets up the scenario where the dog is distracted by something — and is then called away from it. A dog which can recall away from something she wants, usually develops a much stronger recall away from *all* other distractions — it is a concept which the dog acquires. The beauty of this exercise is that we stay in control of the distraction and so we can prevent the dog from accessing it.

This exercise needs two people — one is the 'distractor' and the other is the 're-caller'. (If you don't have someone to help you train this exercise, you will need to skip it. This shouldn't make too much of a difference to the overall outcome of the programme — but it will help greatly if you can 'borrow' a helper to act as the distractor just a couple of days of the week.)

1. The distractor holds a treat in her fist. It's important that the dog can smell the treat, but not lick it or make contact with it. The distractor allows the dog to sniff at her fist with the hidden treat.

2. The recaller then calls the dog (whistle or verbal).

3. If the dog doesn't come immediately, the distractor removes the distraction from the dog's nose, making it easier for the dog to leave the distractor and go to the recaller.

4. If the dog *still* doesn't leave the distractor, the recaller comes forward with the recall treat and lures the dog away — then feeds the treat. (The recaller should not repeat the recall — they only call once in each rep.)

It's important that the recaller's food is the same or higher value than the distractor's food. (You can't call a dog away from smoked mackerel and give her a dry dog biscuit — it's not going to work!) This is when you will start to see some amazing recall responses if you are using paté, gourmet wet dog food, sardines or similarly amazing stuff.

As the dog gets better at leaving the distraction, the distractor can try to be even more distracting. They can do this by opening their hand to reveal the food, wafting the food under the dog's nose (never letting the dog actually eat it), moving it about and teasing the dog, speaking to the dog about how amazing the treat is, jumping about and being a loon, or by using equally tasty food as the recaller. In short, the distractor can use any means they like to try to tempt the dog to stay with them. The distractor cannot give any trained cues to the dog — they cannot give a recall cue, say the dog's name, or give any other cue.

If the dog is unsuccessful, the distractor should dial down the distraction. If the dog is finding it easy, the distractor should dial it up.

You are trying to reach the point where there is *nothing the distractor can do to keep the dog with her.*

PHASE 2 — Recall from a distraction

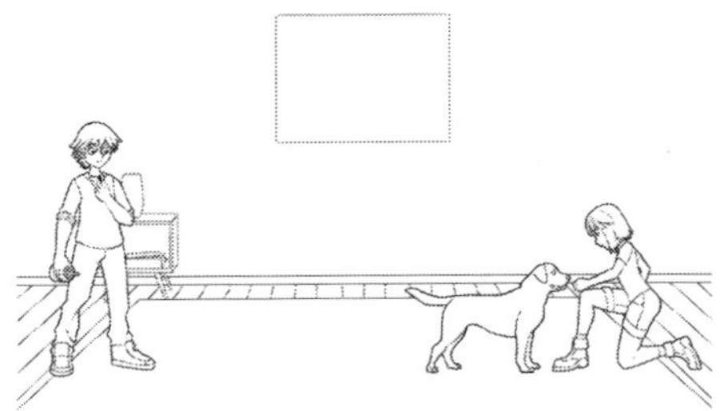

1 THE DISTRACTOR DISTRACTS THE DOG WITH FOOD, WHICH SHE ALLOWS THE DOG TO SMELL BUT NOT TO EAT.

2 THE RECALLER RECALLS THE DOG, WITH EITHER VERBAL OR WHISTLE CUE.

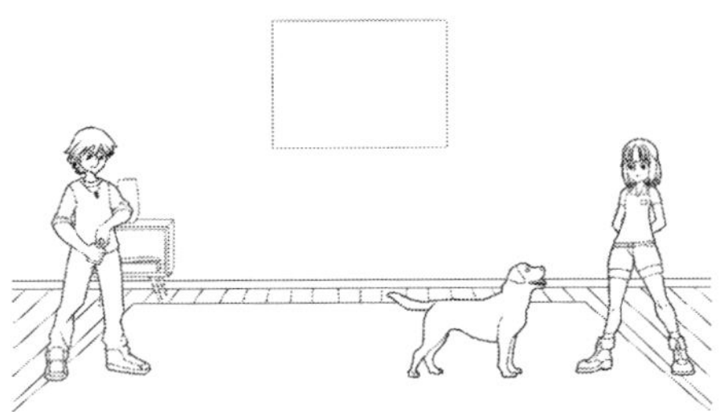

3 IF THE DOG IGNORES THE RECALL, THE DISTRACTOR PUTS THE FOOD BEHIND HER BACK TO REMOVE THE DISTRACTION AND BECOMES STILL AND QUIET.

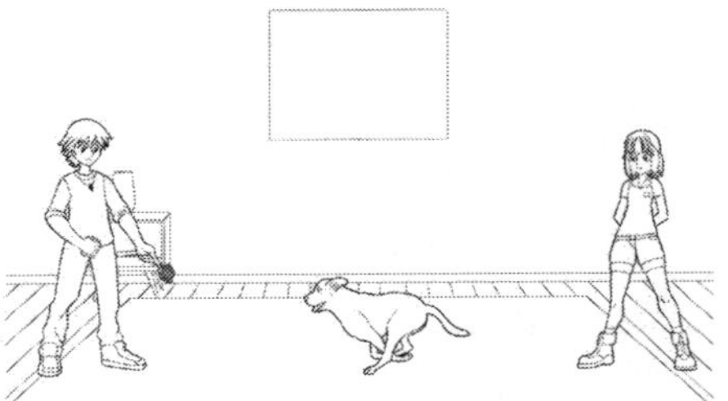

4 AT THIS, MOST DOGS WILL RUN TO THE RECALLER. IF THE DOG DOES NOT DO THIS, THE RECALLER SHOULD USE THE RECALL TREAT (WITHOUT CALLING AGAIN) TO GET HER ATTENTION.

5 THE RECALLER FEEDS THE DOG AN AMAZINGLY TASTY RECALL TREAT. THIS WILL USUALLY BE SOMETHING SQUISHY AND SLOPPY, DELIVERED FROM A PLASTIC TODDLER SPOON.

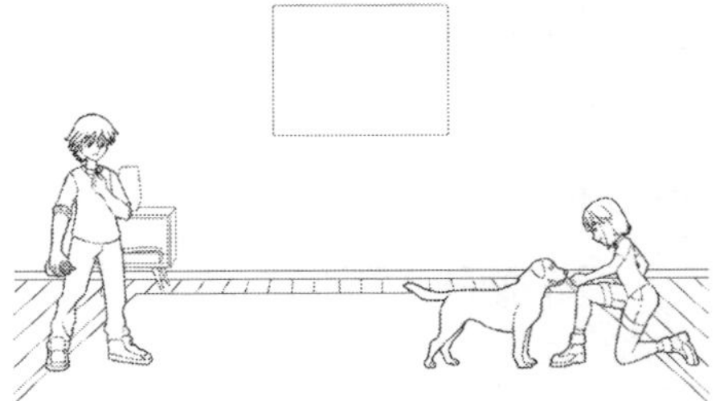

6 THE DISTRACTOR THEN GETS THE DOG'S ATTENTION FOR THE NEXT REP.

7 IF THE DOG IS SUCCESSFUL, DIAL UP THE LEVEL OF DISTRACTION PROVIDED BY THE DISTRACTOR. THIS MEANS THE DISTRACTOR USING HER VOICE AND HER BODY MOVEMENTS AND TREAT-HAND MOVEMENTS, TO INCREASE THE LEVEL OF DISTRACTION.

8 AS THE DOG IMPROVES, SHE WILL BE ABLE TO COME AWAY FROM THE DISTRACTOR IMMEDIATELY – BEFORE THE DISTRACTOR HAS REMOVED THE DISTRACTION: THE DISTRACTOR WILL STILL BE ATTEMPTING TO KEEP THE DOG'S FOCUS AS THE DOG RUNS TO THE RECALLER.

9 ALWAYS REINFORCE RECALLS WITH EXTREMELY HIGH VALUE REINFORCERS!

Be sure to drill the recall-from-a-distraction exercise for a full week before moving onto Phase 3. Remember that this is not about just doing the exercises once or twice to check your dog can do them — it's about repetition and deeply embedding things in the dog's brain. Even if it all looks brilliant, keep doing it for a full week.

PHASE 3: OUT AND ABOUT

- *Practise at least 10 times a day*

- *Practise whilst outdoors exercising, indefinitely, until you have a reliable recall*

- *Practise with both whistle and verbal cues*
- *Use a long-line every time your dog would usually be off-lead*

This is the phase of training that will take the most amount of time. For the majority of dogs, it will take a period of some months.

To use the long-line, let it trail on the floor while you walk. Don't hold the end of it all the time, but try to stay near it, so the end is near your feet. Try to forget about it most of the time — until you need it. Think of the long-line as an insurance policy — you hope never to have to use it, but it's there just in case. You do need to make sure you are near some part of it: There's no point having a long-line on your dog, if she is several fields away with it attached! Remember the principles discussed in Section 1.2, Prevention.

Some older dogs are used to bogging off to the horizon and maintaining a good distance between their handler and themselves. These may be hard-hunting dogs, which have learnt to be independent. If you have a dog like this, you *will* need to hold onto the end of the long-line at first. Every time your dog looks like she is going to hit the end of it, recall your dog and give her an amazing recall reinforcer — and then change the direction you're walking in.

Keep this up for a week and I can almost guarantee that you will end up with a dog that is paying much more attention to you, and that becomes reconditioned to hanging out nearer to you. At which point you can start to drop the line on the ground and allow the dog to trail it.

Don't worry that this will adversely affect your hunting if you have a HPR, pointer or setter: If your dog has already shown an inclination to range that far, it's not going to take much to bring that back out — but it needs to happen with the brakes and control installed first!

There are two exercises for Phase 3...

GIANT ELASTIC RECALL

This exercise needs two people and a fairly open outdoor area — so the two people can walk parallel but some distance apart. (If you don't have another person in the household to help, you can skip it as an exercise.)

The 'giant elastic' recall is a really good exercise to do at the start of any training session — especially when you are first transferring the recall from indoors or the yard to the field. It is an excellent way to introduce larger distances and to 'work' the distance variable. It is also great for conditioning the dog to respond to two different people's recall cues.

In this exercise, the dog is simply called back and forth between the two people for an amazing recall reinforcer each time. Work on both verbal and whistle recalls and also work on extending the distance to approximately 80 yards. Do at least four to six reps a session.

Once you've got the basic exercise working, you might find that the dog starts to go onto auto-pilot — snatching a treat from whoever called, and then immediately running to the other person even if they haven't called the dog yet. *Don't reinforce the dog for coming if you haven't called her!*

Instead, whoever the dog is furthest from should call again. This may mean that sometimes the same person calls for two reps in a row.

This particular exercise you can do daily for about one to two weeks, or until it is working well — and then discontinue.

This next exercise is the one you stick at indefinitely:

PHASE 3 — Giant elastic recall

1 TWO PEOPLE, EACH WITH WHISTLES AND POTS OF TASTY WET TREATS, WALK PARALLEL TO EACH OTHER ACROSS A WIDE AREA. THE DOG HAS A 10M LONG-LINE ATTACHED TO THE BACK OF HER HARNESS. LET THE DOG CHOOSE WHICH PERSON TO HANG OUT WITH TO START.

2 WHOEVER THE DOG IS FURTHEST FROM GIVES THE WHISTLE RECALL CUE.

3 THE DOG RUNS TO THAT PERSON.

4 THE DOG EATS A DELICIOUS WET TREAT – HERE, DELIVERED ON A PLASTIC TODDLER SPOON FROM A POT. WHILST THE DOG EATS THE TREAT, THE OTHER PERSON GIVES THE WHISTLE RECALL CUE.

5 THE DOG RUNS BACK TO THAT PERSON TO GET A TREAT FROM THEM IN TURN. AND SO ON, BACK AND FORTH.

RECALLS – FOREVER!

You're going to remain at this point until you can call your dog back confidently from any distraction which could realistically be expected to present itself — every day, for a week.

As I am almost umbilically connected to my whistle — every time my dog is off-leash, my whistle is in my mouth — I do tend to focus on whistle recalls from this point onwards when I am training my own dogs, just testing the verbal cue now and again.

It goes like this:

1. You call your dog. She ignores you.

2. Without recalling again, you quickly pick up the long-line from near your feet and reel her in gently. The purpose of this is not to 'force' her to do a recall — but to detach her from the environmental reinforcer. You want to act quickly here, because, every second your dog is interacting with the environmental reinforcer after you have recalled her, she is being reinforced for ignoring you.

3. If your dog begins to come towards you of her own accord (rather than being reeled all the way in), treat when she reaches you — the reinforcer most strongly reinforces the dog's last behaviour. So, even if she is reeled slightly reluctantly for a few steps to create the disengagement, if she then turns and comes willingly, reinforce this.

4. If your dog has to be reeled all the way in, don't treat. Hold her harness for the slow count of 10 and maybe talk to her in a calm 'normal' voice or give some gentle calming strokes or neck scritches — you don't want her to experience you as 'angry'. We are holding her because, if we release her *imme-*

diately back to the amazingness of the world, we may reinforce her for not coming. (Permission to 'hunt on' is actually a powerful reinforcer for many hunting breeds.) We are calming her and talking to her because high arousal levels can make responsiveness difficult — in all this, we are ensuring our next rep is going to work better. Then release her ('ok') and recall her *immediately* and whilst she is still near you — hopefully with a better response, which you can then reinforce. If she doesn't come to the recall often, you need to go back to drilling recalls around your house and garden before trying this exercise again.

5. If your dog comes to you when you call, then you don't need to touch the long-line. Just reinforce your dog and release with 'Go play'.

You want to be calling your dog back at least 10 times every session. You're not waiting until you actually need to call her — you are practising and drilling a recall response.

Be creative and interesting with your recall treats to keep your dog guessing about what she's going to get when she comes back. If you buy a tub of paté, when you finish it don't get more paté — that's an opportunity to switch to a different (but equally tasty) reinforcer. Keep changing it up: Rotate, and learn what your dog likes most.

Now you are in the big outdoors, keep working those distraction levels. For example:

- Level 1: *Call when your dog has looked at you, anyway.* At other moments with high distractions around, just grab the long-line and reel it in if you need to get your dog.

- Level 2: *Call when your dog is distracted by scent, in some way.* This might be a spot of grass or a doggie pee place she is smelling, or some feathers or fur on the ground, or sniffing where you know that game likes to hang out.

- Level 3: *Call when your dog has seen something she would quite like to run to, but it's far enough away that you know you can get a response.* Examples might be another dog which is far away and so doesn't have too much suction for your dog yet — but your dog has noticed the dog. These things are typically moving/animate distractions, which are harder because they trigger predatory responses or more interest from your dog. Don't pick something ridiculously close and tempting, like game flushing, just yet.

- Level 4: *Call when your dog has seen something tempting which is closer.* This may be another dog or a person (if your dog is distracted by people). Or it might be horses, bicycles or livestock. (Take care around these hazards with your long-line and hold it shorter than usual.)

At each stage in the above, you can also call away from the lower level distractions in the list, of course.

By this point, you are just about ready to use a recall any time you need one, successfully. You may not have reached a recall away from departing game or off a chase, yet — that's going to come later. (But — hint, hint — why not try a person (distractor) trailing a 'flirt-pole' with a rabbit skin tied on the end, which the dog starts to chase — whilst you stand a short distance away and recall?)

COMMON QUESTIONS ABOUT TRAINING THE RECALL

'Other off-leash dogs keep derailing things. How do I deal with this?'

Make sure your recall is functioning really well around other distractions before you go seeking out other dogs in any way. Whilst you are still perfecting recalls in other situations, it is a good idea to do all you can to avoid other dogs.

When you start work around other dogs, try to pick on-lead dogs as your decoys. You can even arrange for a friend to stand and hold their dog on a leash, so you can practise. Because it sucks if you recall your dog and she comes — and the other dog is off-lead and follows your recalling dog, to you, sabotaging your recall!

You can call away from an off-leash dog, but make sure first that the dog is not interested in your dog. Dogs which don't look that interested are unlikely to follow your dog back to you and are good 'decoys' to use.

If you come across a dog-obsessed dog, at first don't attempt to recall your dog if dogs are also a distraction for her. Just grab the long line, turn around and march off with your dog in the opposite direction, leaving it up to the other owner to get their dog back. (Usually, as the distance increases, the other dog will decide to go back to her owner.) Use a fistful of treats, which you continuously deliver into your dog's mouth, to keep her with you in this scenario — and to prevent her from engaging with the pursuing dog.

'Why don't you use a clicker when training recalls?'

Purely for practical reasons: When you start training recalls out and about, you will have your dog on a long-line, whistle, and treats to administer.

If you *were* to use a clicker during recalls, the moment to click would be when the dog — at a distance — has made the decision to come back to you. However, there are times when a dog starts out coming to you (and you may click), and then veers off or gets distracted on her way back. What to do then? You've clicked, but the dog has chosen her reinforcer — and it's not yours.

'Do I really, really need to use a long-line? My dog comes most of the time.'

There is always one person in each of my classes, who asks this question.

My answer is: If there are any occasions when your dog doesn't come back after you've called, then you need to use the long-line as described. If your dog comes back 80 per cent of the time, that's 20 per cent when your dog isn't coming. That 20 per cent of time, the dog is being reinforced for not coming — by an environmental reinforcer. And reinforced behaviour occurs more frequently. (Remember that when we reinforce something, we make it stronger.) So that 20 per cent will become 25 per cent, then 30 per cent. Before you know it, you don't really have a decent recall at all.

So - be honest with yourself. If your dog doesn't come back almost 100 per cent of the time, immediately, then you need to use the long-line. If there is any one category of distractions (other dogs, people, animals, dead things, etc.) which your dog cannot recall away from, you need to use the long-line — and target those distractions with long-line on, for many reps, until you start to see success.

Pretty much all dogs need to use a long-line to achieve a reliable recall. It is not the exception — it is the norm.

'How long do I need to use the long-line for?'

Until you can recall your dog, immediately and first time, away from anything you happen to encounter when out and about — every day for a week.

For most dogs, this will take a few months. But some may take a few weeks and some may take a year.

'Can I give treats only occasionally? Meaning not every time my dog recalls correctly? Can I move to a variable reinforcement schedule?'

The short answer is: No. Continue to give a high value reinforcer, for every single 'correct' response.

The long answer can be found in Section 1.4, Generalisation and distraction management.

'I'm doing everything I'm supposed to do, but things aren't working.'

Try returning to basics in the house and garden and really drill your recall phrase and whistle 20-30 times a day — both with the Phase 1 (Elastic recall) and Phase 2 (Recall away from distractions) exercises. If things work well in the house and garden, but every time you go out into the wider world, you are not very successful...

...then you need to think *hard* about food motivation. Read Section 2.1, Food motivation, and address this, first and foremost.

Secondly, ensure you are not 'walking' the dog. Read Section 2.2, How to stop 'walking the dog!' — and implement. Ensure you are not providing any 'hunting' practice yet, if you have a spaniel. This is especially important for young spaniels who, given their head too early, turn into hunting machines and often lose interest in their handler and in food reinforcers entirely.

Remember that you can shape a dog to favour certain reinforcers: What a dog finds reinforcing is not set in stone, genetically. If you allow a dog with strong hunting drive access to gamey fields and free-running, you can be sure she will teach herself that this is the most amazing thing in the world. Don't give her an opportunity to learn this before she's learnt to value *your* reinforcers. Install yourself as the source of favoured reinforcers before you give her access to all that the world has to offer.

Pick a defined area to exercise your dog, like the corner of a field — one defined location — rather than wandering over a vast landscape, as happens when people 'walk the dog'. That way, there is not a never-ending infinity of interesting things: There is a limited number of interesting things in that spot which your dog will habituate to, given time. Stand in that spot (or sit somewhere) with your dog on the leash for a good five minutes before you start training. This gives the dog time to habituate to the environment so it is not so novel and interesting.

Keep your recalls very easy — short distances with long-line on.

If you have a driven hunting breed, you need to focus entirely on obedience — retrieves, stays, recalls, heelwork. Read Section 3.5, Focus and engagement, and ensure your dog is able to relate to you in an outdoors environment — *before* you start any hunting training.

• • • • •

3.4

HEELWORK

IT IS NOT BASIC!

Heelwork is a deceptively difficult behaviour. Because it is included in almost every beginners' dog-training class — and because just about everyone who owns a dog wants her to walk well on the lead — it is easy to assume that heelwork is a 'basic' behaviour. While it might be universally *desirable* for all dogs and is probably a dog training *essential*, this does not mean it's *easy* — as demonstrated by the vast proliferation of devices and gadgets designed to enable owners to walk dogs on the lead.

If you struggle with heelwork — and you believe it is basic — you are likely to feel demoralised about your progress with your dog. (If you are struggling with something so basic, what does that say about your ability to train your dog, and your dog's trainability?) If you expect your dog to master heelwork in six weeks, you will likely consider yourself and your dog to be failures if you don't achieve this.

Heelwork is one of the hardest behaviours there is and you and your dog have every right to find it difficult. That's not a licence to give up, though!

Before we can talk about heelwork, we first need to define what it is...

HEELWORK VERSUS LOOSE-LEAD WALKING

Heelwork and loose-lead walking are not the same thing.

Heelwork, amongst the general public, is associated most closely with competition obedience. We are talking about dogs superglued to their owners' thighs, gazing up at them unfalteringly.

How close the dog is to the handler actually varies from one dog sport to another — and even from one country to another. In UK competition obedience, the dog is often very close whereas US competition obedience permits a looser style of heelwork. So the proximity of dog to handler is not an innate characteristic of all heelwork, everywhere.

But what *is* a consistent characteristic of heelwork in these other dog sports is that the dog is looking at the handler: It is considered desirable for the dog to maintain eye-contact with the handler *or* with some part of the handler's body. A dog looking around everywhere is going to lose marks in these other dog sports.

What makes the dog look at the handler? In training, the handler has been holding the reinforcer (typically food or a toy). And the dog looks at wherever the anticipated reinforcer is expected to appear. This is quite an important point, for gundog heelwork. We'll return to this in a moment.

Here's how heelwork can be practically useful for just about anyone, even someone training their dog using 'gundog skills' but having no intention of working her. You are out with your dog off-lead and you need to pass a child who is afraid of dogs. Or a horse. Or an elderly person. You call your dog to you and say 'heel'. You walk with the dog at heel until you pass the distraction. Then you say 'ok' and release the dog from heel to be free.

This example illustrates how heelwork is really an *in-motion stay*: The dog must maintain a position relative to the handler. Just like a stay, heelwork is a behaviour with duration and a defined beginning and end. Therefore, just like a stay, you will need to have a cue to ask the dog to begin heelwork (like 'heel') and a release word, at the end ('ok') — typically the same release word you have at the end of your stays:

'heel'… … … duration… … … 'ok'

The dog and the handler should move like a motorbike and sidecar: The handler is the motorbike, dictating the dog's movements via a *connection* with the dog (sidecar). This connection is not a physical one, though. It is a connection achieved through training.

You can do heelwork with the lead on, or off. The role of the leash, in heelwork, is preventative. The lead is important when you are starting out in a location with environmental reinforcers, because the lead prevents the dog from deciding to drift off to access those reinforcers. We've all seen dogs whose noses hit the floor, gradually taking them off on a scent trail — until they are well out of heel position. Even if you get them back with a food lure, they have been allowed to self-reinforce — so they will try it again. Using a lead until you reach a decent standard of heelwork will prevent your dog from being able to learn to do this. *Just stop walking the instant the nose drops* — and the dog can no longer follow a trail of ground scent: We have removed that reinforcer.

The lead, in force-free training, is not a piece of equipment used to punish a dog for moving out of position. This can be a difficult concept for people crossing over from traditional training, where heelwork is taught using a lot of lead jerks (positive punishment). For force-free training, the lead is just an insurance policy — to *prevent* your dog from choosing reinforcers other than your own. (For more information on this, see Section 1.2, Prevention.)

Many a gundog trainer decides their heelwork is good enough to take the lead off — only to regret this a few minutes later when they put up a rabbit and watch their dog take off after it! There is no need to rush to implement off-leash heelwork. Focus on achieving the end result in the long-term — not just on 'looking the part'!

Loose-lead walking requires the lead to be slack/loose at all times. However, the dog can look around at the environment, move around within the length of the lead — including in front of you — pee up lamp-posts you walk past, sniff things in passing, and so on.

The cue to walk on a loose-lead should simply be the lead itself, going on. This is just the way the dog walks, when the lead is on — you don't need to give your dog a verbal cue. When the lead comes off, the dog can stop doing it. Because you can't have loose-lead walking without a lead on! This differs from heelwork — which can happen on or off-lead.

In loose-lead walking, the dog does not look at the handler. Why not?

Remember that *dogs look to where the anticipated reinforcer is going to come from*. In loose-lead walking, the reinforcers don't come from the handler — the reinforcers are environmental.

The dog wants to reach a lamp-post? Then she has to maintain a loose-lead to get there. The dog wants the walk to continue with forward progress? Then she has to maintain a loose-lead to achieve that. The reinforcers, here, are not on your person — they are in the *environment*. So the dog looks at the environment. This results in a dog which is focussed on the environment — but (crucially) also understands that *her access to that environment is contingent on her behaviour*.

Loose-lead walking doesn't use (many) treats. If we do, we end up with the dog looking at us, and it morphs into heelwork, really.

The difference between heelwork and loose-lead walking is clearly demonstrated by many successful competition obedience dogs who tow their owners around on the lead outside the ring or away from competition, and then — at the sound of 'heel', in competition conditions — are transformed into impressive obedience dogs, superglued to their owner's side, before coming out of the ring and towing their owners around again!

In other words, it is possible for the same dog to have achieved *advanced* levels of heelwork, and yet not to have mastered loose-lead walking *basics*. That is the extent to which these are very different behaviours.

Often new handlers don't appreciate this, and see these two very different behaviours as the same thing — because, superficially, they look very similar. I hope I've explained why, under the surface, they are very different.

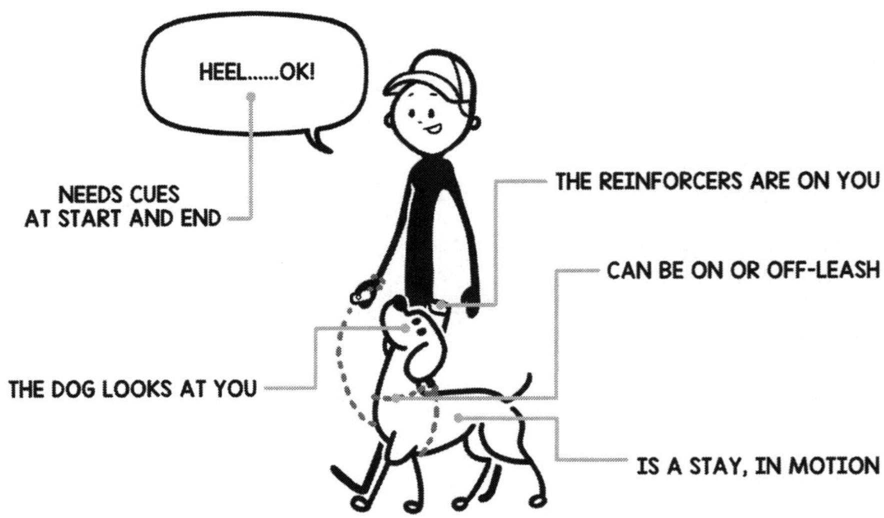

HEELWORK

WITH HEELWORK:

- the reinforcers are on you
- the dog looks at you
- the dog can be on or off-lead
- the behaviour is a stay, in-motion
- a cue (heel) to start and the release word ('ok') at the end, are required.

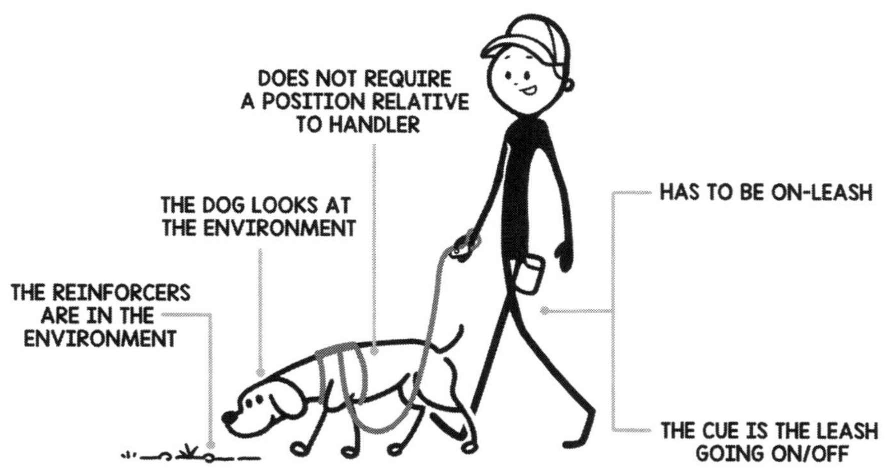

LOOSE-LEAD WALKING

WITH LOOSE-LEAD WALKING:

- the reinforcers are in the environment
- the dog doesn't look at you, she looks around at reinforcers
- the dog is on-lead
- the dog is not required to maintain a precise position, just a loose lead
- the cue is the lead going on and coming off.

We don't cover loose-lead walking in this book because it's not a gundog-specific behaviour. Whether on or off-lead, the majority of gundog handlers would want their dogs at heel when under assessment or when working — not just on a loose-lead.

Now we've explored heelwork and loose-lead walking generally, let's turn back to gundog work, specifically.

RETRIEVER HEELWORK: TO LOOK, OR NOT TO LOOK? THAT IS THE QUESTION.

At this point, things are looking beautifully clear-cut and relatively simple. For all dogs besides gundogs, they really are. But — now I'm going to have to muddy the waters.

What's the problem? In a nutshell, the problem centres on retrievers — specifically on training retrievers to walk at heel using positive reinforcement. So, if you have a spaniel or HPR, you can breathe a sigh of relief — things do remain relatively simple for you!

To bring the subject of retriever heelwork to life a bit, I'll describe how I first 'discovered' the quandary! What I describe here relates to British/European retriever training, trialling and testing. North American requirements are very different and do not involve walking at heel for long periods of time whilst simultaneously marking.

Many years ago, I thought I'd take one of my HPRs along to a retriever training class. She was a very keen retriever and I'd taught her to handle well. We'd won out of Novice and Graduate HPR working tests, she had her KC Working Gundog Certificate and I was just starting to run her in HPR field trials. So, I thought I could 'do' heelwork. And I like to learn from lots of different sources, and was curious about what went on at retriever training classes. So I took her along.

This is where I first discovered this retriever thing called a 'walk-up'. Off we set, in a row, across a field — handlers with dogs off-lead at heel. As we walked forwards in our row, our trainer in front periodically fired starting pistols, threw dummies and set off bolting rabbits. Each time a retrieve was thrown, the line stopped walking and the trainer nominated a dog for the retrieve.

At first I thought to myself: '*Wow, this is so much easier than HPR work. Because, at the moment the tempting thing falls from the sky, my dog is at my side. My influence is much greater than if she were off-lead, a hundred metres away from me — as a HPR would be. These retrievers have it good.*' Then I had my first retrieve.

I quickly discovered that my HPR was unable to walk at heel *and* look forwards. This is because her default heel behaviour was to look at me. This meant she was as steady as a piece of furniture by my side — because she wasn't even looking at the 'temptations' (environmental reinforcers). So what was the problem? The problem was that she didn't see marked retrieves and ended up running them as blinds, needing handling and making it all much harder than it needed to be. (A dog which runs a retrieve as a blind when it should have been a simple seen, is not going to score very highly.)

I figured that the reason she was looking at me was because I had the reinforcers (treats). So I decided to stop reinforcing her heel with treats — to allow her attention to wander forwards as we walked, so she stood a better chance of marking. But this resulted in unsteadiness: If we were walking when the retrieve was thrown, and she was looking forwards to mark, she would run in a few steps. Then I would say her name and ask her to heel again, and she would return to my side. If the line was already stopped when the retrieve was thrown and she was sitting at my side, in heel position, she was perfectly steady and marked accurately. (As her HPR training had taught her: She was able to *sit* and mark. Just not to walk at heel whilst marking!)

On the day, my choice seemed to be having either a 'looking-at-me' heel, where she failed to mark anything — or unsteadiness!

None of this mattered at all, because she was a HPR and walk-ups are not required for HPRs — I was only there for fun and to learn more. Heelwork is a very small part of HPR assessments, and the part it plays is well-served with a looking-at-me heel. (More on that, below.)

But I stored all this away for mulling over, because — in an epiphany — I realised that 'heel', for a UK retriever, has to mean '*Walk at my side whilst looking forwards/marking.*' In other words, this is a behaviour where the dog must maintain a pretty exacting heel position — and will be eliminated if she moves forwards by as much as one step out of heel. Yet, she cannot stare up unfalteringly at her handler or she will miss marked retrieves and have to run them as blinds.

You can see how these requirements borrow a bit from what I've defined as loose-lead walking, above (the reinforcement is in the environment — the retrieves), but also a bit from what I've defined as heelwork (the position is exact and by the handler's side, sniffing and peeing is not allowed, the leash is off, and there is a cued beginning and end to the behaviour). It is, then, a hybrid. As such, it needs some careful attention because it's not a behaviour which is covered by the standard fare — the distinctions I laid out above, between loose-lead walking and heelwork, which are commonly accepted in non-gundog, mainstream, force-free training.

How does traditional gundog training deal with this situation? Can it help us? To a great extent, this quandary only occurs when we bring together force-free training with retriever heelwork. In traditional training, heelwork is trained largely through leash corrections when the dog moves out of heel position — in other words, through positive punishment. There is less reason for the dog to look up at the handler — because the handler is not giving the dog reinforcers. (In fact, research shows that positive punishment leads to avoidance behaviours and a reluctance to engage, from the dog.) When retrieves are introduced as reinforcers, the dog learns that she must maintain an acceptable heel position to be sent for the reinforcer (retrieve) out in front. At this point, potentially, things start to become more reinforcement-based, since handlers base their decisions about which dog to send for a retrieve on steadiness and heel position — denying retrieves to those dogs which are unsteady whilst reinforcing those which are steady, by sending them. But those reinforcers (retrieves) are out in front of the dog — not carried on the handler. Dogs look to where they anticipate reinforcers will appear, so the problem of the dog staring up at the handler and missing marks simply doesn't occur in traditional gundog training.

This is a tricky corner which neither general force-free training, nor traditional gundog training, can completely help us with. We need to think outside the box...

'What are the implications of this for training retriever heelwork using force-free methods?'

Whilst the initial beginner heelwork exercises for retrievers will be the same as for other subgroups, once dogs are past the first stages of training heelwork, clearly we need to be working more intensively with exercises where the reinforcers are off the handler's body — and where the dog maintains heel position to gain access to them. This goes some way towards simulating the environmental reinforcer (retrieve or game) being located 'out in front' and so towards the acquisition of the skills we need in that situation.

There are many creative ways we can use food bowls placed on the ground at a short distance from us, containing a treat, and permit access to them after the click — contingent on heelwork behaviours. This would allow rapid reps of heelwork-specific behaviours — more than is possible using a retrieve, each time. This would also enable training on a smaller scale and indoors, even, with young dogs — yet still permit the practice of key skills. I have included an exercise towards the end of this section called the Food Bowl game, which is along these lines and works well.

The other issue up for consideration with retrievers is the issue of loose-lead walking — and what to do with that behaviour. With our *heelwork* training, we are teaching retrievers that access to *environmental reinforcers* is contingent on maintaining an exacting heel position — whether the leash is on or off. (The presence of the leash is irrelevant when it comes to the behaviour of heelwork.) So, are we making things harder for the retriever to grasp heelwork if, at other times, we are also using environmental reinforcers in *loose-lead walking* (when the dog is allowed to mill all around us, sniff, urinate, stop — as long as the lead is loose)? Since we are using environmental reinforcers for *both* heelwork and loose-lead walking for retrievers (and since the leash can be on for either behaviour) there is much less that differentiates the two behaviours, for retrievers, than there is for the other subgroups. Does it muddy the waters for retrievers to have a loose-lead walking behaviour and a heelwork behaviour?

I can see two options here. Option one is simply not to do loose-lead walking with retrievers — at all. Every time the retriever is at your side (in any way or context, on or off lead), uphold excellent standards of *heelwork*. The dog is not wandering around on the lead, ahead and behind and sniffing things at will. It's not 'just' about the lead being loose. For retrievers (in this version of things), it's black or white: The dog is at heel, offering the sort of heelwork you'd like to see in the field. Or the dog is not at heel at all — is off lead and 'free'. If this sounds a bit hardcore, remind yourself that, on a shoot or during a trial, a retriever may end up maintaining heel position almost all day. It needs to be an unconscious and automatic behaviour, requiring little effort from dog and handler. We want the dog to achieve complete unconscious auto-pilot about maintaining heel *position* always. This is not to say that the dog should be robotic and denied the pleasures of sniffing things completely — but sniffing is reinforcing and, as such, we want to use it to reinforce good heelwork. We will explore this concept later in this section, with the Go Sniff game.

Option two for retrievers, is — like spaniels and HPRs — to maintain a separate loose-lead walking behaviour, separate to heelwork. I can foresee many people wanting to walk their dogs to places sometimes, without having to uphold excellent heelwork all the time. Rather than letting your heelwork deteriorate, it would be better to have a separate loose-lead walking behaviour. But, if you opt for this, you must be very clear with your cues and their associated behaviours — so that the dog understands the difference between heelwork and loose-lead walking. The leash is clearly a big potential clue (and cue!) here: Since loose-leash walking isn't possible if there is no leash! So you could have: Leash on and loose-lead walking is required. Leash off and heelwork is expected. Whatever you decide, be consistent. And be aware that in baby puppy classes and early Gundog Club grades, heelwork on leash is going to be needed. Just when you thought you had it figured out!

For best results in terms of dog training and the dog's comprehension, I think the first option for retrievers — 'heelwork is always required' — is ideal. But I recognise that this simply isn't going to be realistic for some handlers.

'What about spaniel and HPR heelwork?'

Spaniels and HPRs are not required to walk at heel (at all) for field trials. There's no doubt that heelwork is very useful for spaniels and HPRs on shoots: In between drives, they should be kept at heel. And, when it comes to other forms of assessment, there is often a heelwork component: For working tests, often there is off-lead heelwork in the Puppy or Novice classes. And there is off-lead heelwork involved in the KC Working Gundog Certificate, too — as well as The Gundog Club's graded assessment scheme for spaniels and HPRs, from Grade 2 upwards.

But, if a HPR or spaniel owner *only* wanted to run in trials, there would be absolutely no need to train their dog to walk at heel. That is, it is possible to be extremely successful at arguably the highest level of achievement (field trials) with HPRs and spaniels, when the dog can't walk at heel — at all.

When heelwork *is* required in other assessments, for spaniels and HPRs, the situation is not a walk-up — as it is for retrievers: The dogs are not walking at heel when the retrieve is in the air. In other words: Spaniels and HPRs are not expected to mark retrieves whilst walking at heel. If they are at heel, they will be *sitting* at heel to mark the retrieve.

Most people would agree that it is far easier to teach a dog to look at you and walk at heel than it is to teach a dog to look ahead at all the great stuff out there — and yet maintain heel. That is: *Teaching heel, as it's taught in most good force-free pet dog training classes, is perfectly fine for spaniel or HPR heelwork.*

If you have a spaniel or HPR, my advice would be to simplify this complex subject and just train the dog to pay attention to you and look at you, when at heel. She might look around sometimes or look away, and that's fine too — this isn't competition obedience, it's practical heelwork in the field. We also don't want the dog superglued to your leg, salivating on you, competition obedience-style. But the dog can frequently visually check in with you — and, more importantly, *you should have no worries about clicking and reinforcing the dog for looking at you whilst walking at heel, and for making that behaviour ever-stronger.* You can't really end up with a dog which is looking at you too much, and not seeing marks. Unlike those unfortunate retriever folk!

Since spaniel and HPR handlers are using reinforcers on their person for heelwork and seeking eye-contact from their dogs, they can easily have a loose-lead walking behaviour, which is separate to their heelwork — without confusing the dog or muddying the behaviours, as I described above.

HPR and spaniel folk have enough to worry about with getting their dogs steady to flush and fall, and achieving stylish hunting — they don't need to get too bogged down in heelwork technicalities.

IN SUMMARY

For retrievers:

- Heelwork is hugely important in all forms of assessment — including field trials — and a high standard of heelwork is considered an essential.

- They need to develop the ability to maintain heel position, whilst also looking forwards to mark retrieves. To achieve this, reinforcers in the environment have to be used in training — since the dog will look to where the perceived reinforcer is.

- Because heelwork involves using environmental reinforcers — yet maintaining an exact heel position — the distinction between loose-lead walking and heelwork is potentially blurred.

- Handlers have to decide:

    - whether to uphold heelwork standards any time the dog is at the handler's side (on or off-leash) — so there is a very black or white approach to what is expected

    - whether to train a loose-leash walking behaviour which can be used at times when the dog is permitted to mooch around on the lead. If choosing this option, handlers will need to be crystal clear with their cues and when they are cuing heelwork versus loose-lead walking.

For spaniels and HPRs:

- Heelwork is not assessed in field trials and a high standard of heelwork is not considered an 'essential' by many successful field triallers. Heelwork *is* assessed in other types of assessment and is useful on a shoot.

- They do not need to develop the ability to maintain heel position whilst also looking forwards and marking retrieves in a walk-up situation. There is therefore no need to use environmental reinforcers in training their heelwork: It is fine to use reinforcers on the handler, and for the dog to look at the handler (and away briefly) during the short periods of heelwork needed by spaniels and HPRs. (And this is much easier to train, too.)

- It is fine to have separate loose-lead walking vs heelwork behaviours.

WHEN TO TRAIN HEELWORK

In an ideal world, just as with any other behaviour, you would first practise heelwork in the house until it was working well (including various different rooms), then in the garden/yard, then in the street, and then in the field. And you would never practise it somewhere highly distracting until it was really working somewhere less distracting. This is the case for every other behaviour, and it's the same for heelwork too.

But the reality is that many owners need to 'transport' their dog, from one place to another. And often this involves a period of time on-leash. It may be that you park your car on the street and then need to walk your dog to your house. Or perhaps you drive somewhere to exercise and train your dog off-leash — but you have to walk on leash for a while first.

The problem is that your priority will be reaching your goal and destination. It won't be dog training, en route. Distractions are likely to be high and your dog may be eager — resulting in intense pulling. You are likely to get frustrated with your dog, which is counterproductive to achieving training results. Or you may just give in and allow your dog to pull. And that is a bad idea — because the pulling is reinforced by the dog's forward progress.

From the dog's perspective, *learning is happening all the time.* There is no neat division of 'we are training' and 'we are not training'. Your dog is always learning and *something* is reinforcing her behaviour — whether it's you, or something in the environment.

So, think about ways you can reduce the amount of time spent on-lead if your attention isn't going to be completely on training your dog — or if your particular dog is going to struggle with the duration or distractions involved.

Tip: Replace walking on-leash with driving (wherever possible). If you have to park some distance from your house, walk (without the dog) to get the car — and then quickly drive by the house to collect the dog. And the same in reverse, when coming home: Drop the dog off and then go and park the car.

Tip: If you still must walk some short distance, consider this part of your training for the day. Training doesn't just start when you get 'there' (wherever that is!), it starts on the way there — every moment your dog is out of your house. Uphold excellent standards of heelwork and turn this into a training session.

Tip: The final option is to use loose-lead walking for these times when you must walk on-leash. If the walk is going to be extended, and you can't avoid it, then this may be the best option. Be very clear with your cues for heelwork, in this case — so that your dog clearly understands when heelwork is expected, and when loose-lead walking is required. And be advised that loose-leash walking isn't 'easier' than heelwork, it's just a different behaviour.

Whatever your solution, you also need to ensure you are spending *5-10 minutes every day* training heelwork. The priority here should be quality over quantity: This should be dedicated heelwork time, when you are not trying to 'go' anywhere: When you begin training outdoors, you must be quite happy to walk back and forth over the same few yards for the entire session, if necessary. If you have a goal or destination in mind, you will only be frustrated and the behaviour will deteriorate.

Instead of having a destination as a goal, be time-focussed: 'I will train for 10 minutes and then stop' or '*I will train until my dog has finished her dinner, and then stop*'.

Once your training is working well in the street outside your house, you can start to integrate some heelwork into your main daily training session away from the house — where distractions are higher. At this point, you can drop the separate 'at home' heelwork session.

The 'Class 2' (regular) treats are held either in the handler's left pocket or in a treat pouch, on the handler's left hip. The handler's right pocket contains 'Class 1' (recall) treats. The leash and clicker are held in the handler's right hand.

As your gundog training grows more advanced, small 'bits' of heelwork will be needed within it: For example, throwing dummies out into particular locations will require you to heel the dog around whilst you set things up, and doing memory retrieves will require you to heel the dog away from the thrown dummy. Short bursts of heelwork within drills and exercises is an ideal way to practise heelwork, at this point.

Finally (if you have a retriever), you will start to use heelwork around high distractions, like bolting rabbits, rabbit pens, and in walk-up situations.

HOW TO HOLD EVERYTHING

For some reason, people often think that how the equipment is held is optional or down to individual preference. Perhaps because holding equipment is not exactly training itself. But it's not optional! All the following exercises assume you are holding equipment as explained here:

In the UK, gundogs conventionally heel on the left side of the handler. We position the treats on the same side as the dog — the left. So your left hand takes the treat and delivers it to your dog's mouth. That's the only role for your left hand.

If you are using a treat pouch or pot, it should also be on your left hip or in your left pocket. It can be slightly behind your left hip, if you prefer it not to be on the side of you. But make sure it doesn't slip around in front into a more central position. (Your dog will want to get to where the food is. If your treats are in your *right* hand, or if your treat pouch is centred on your belly, your dog will start to move in front of you, to get closer to the food. This is definitely not heel position!)

Your lead is held in your right hand. The handle should go around your wrist for maximum security — and then the lead should run between your thumb and forefinger — wedged up into what Grisha Stewart calls your 'thumb armpit' (thanks, Grisha!). With your leash in your right hand and

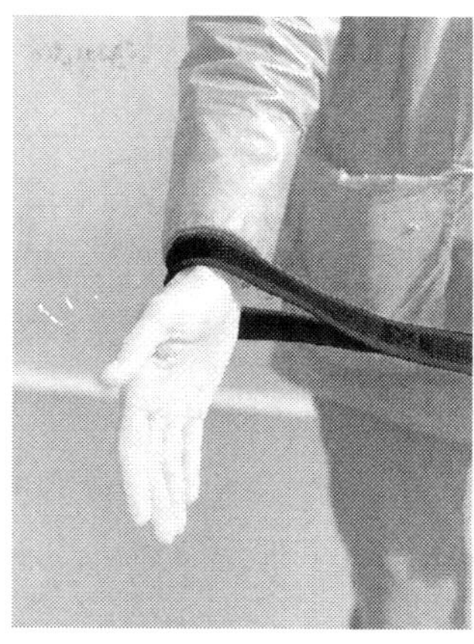

The leash goes first around the wrist.

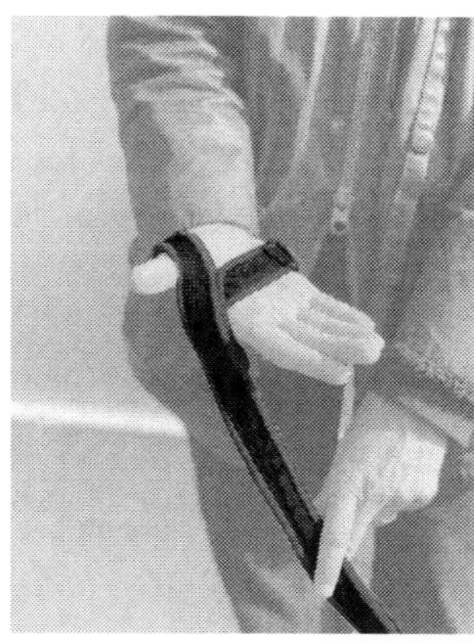

The leash is then wedged firmly into the 'thumb-armpit'!

The clicker is then held between thumb and fingers, so that the leash does not interfere with the action of the clicker.

your dog on your left, your leash will cross in front of your body. This is normal and correct.

Your clicker is also held in your right hand. It should be held in such a way that you don't press it by accident when the lead tightens! That would be counter-productive. (To prevent this, ensure your leash is wedged up into that thumb armpit — so your clicker is separate to the leash and not held against it.)

People can be resistant when it comes to holding things in this way. Sometimes they have previously been holding equipment very differently and it can feel strange and maybe clumsy to change things. It will all become easier and more familiar the more you practise. But there are reasons behind this set-up, which will become clear when we start the training.

HAND GOES UP AND DOWN – GETTING STARTED WITH HEELWORK

For everybody — retrievers, spaniels and HPRs

The 'Hand Goes Up and Down' is how I begin teaching heelwork — whether it's with a tiny puppy or with an adult dog learning for the first time.

You'll need to be holding the equipment as described above.

PHASE 1: HAND DOWN ALWAYS

1 TAKE A BIG HANDFUL OF TREATS IN YOUR LEFT HAND, FROM THE TREAT POUCH ON YOUR LEFT SIDE. THE CLICKER AND THE LEASH ARE HELD IN YOUR RIGHT HAND.

2 PUT THE HANDFUL OF TREATS ON THE DOG'S NOSE AND CONTINUOUSLY FEED TREATS WITH EVERY STEP YOU TAKE. BE GENEROUS!

Keep your hand with treats, level with your trouser seam. Ensure you are looking at the back of your hand whilst you are doing this. your hand should not be palm-up — since this will cause the dog's rear to pop out to the side to get better access to your hand. We need to keep the dog's body straight.

3 WHEN THE HAND RUNS OUT OF TREATS, STOP WALKING AND REFILL THE HAND TO REPEAT.

Your dog is constantly eating treats. (Do not keep the dog following the treats without actually feeding them to her — the point here is to be extremely liberal and generous and pump those treats into your dog's mouth as rapidly as your dog can eat them!

Why are we doing this? Because we are teaching the dog that your hand is the most reinforcing thing in existence — *that's* where the reinforcement is. Your hand is more reinforcing than the floor. Your hand is more reinforcing than anything immediately around the dog. Nothing can compare to a bazillion treats a second from your hand. When we take our hand away, we want the dog to be mesmerised by it — and continue looking at it. This is why we must keep the reinforcement ratio high, at this stage.

Your hand should be in full contact, always, with your dog's mouth. Make sure that the pressure of your dog's nose on your hand doesn't push your hand forwards so you end up reinforcing the dog for being in front of you. Aim to keep your hand by your trouser seam.

PHASE 2: HAND UP AND DOWN CONSTANTLY

After at least two fistfuls of treats have been fed in this way:

1 PICK YOUR LEFT HAND UP TO YOUR CHEST. THE DOG WILL CONTINUE LOOKING UP AT YOU FOR A SPLIT SECOND. CLICK IMMEDIATELY TO CAPTURE THIS.

It's fine if the dog is looking at the treats, or your person generally — as long as she is not drifting off to check out the floor or the environment.

2 THEN QUICKLY MOVE YOUR HAND DOWN TO DELIVER A TREAT TO THE DOG IN HEEL POSITION.

Ensure you are looking at the back of your hand. After this, immediately pick your hand up again, as in the previous image. Cycle back and forth between hand-up (click for focus) and hand down (deliver treat) — over and over.

When you raise your hand to your chest, imagine that you are asking the dog '*Are you able to look at me, without the treats right on your nose?*' We are 'testing' or checking this.

POSSIBLE PROBLEMS

If the dog begins to sniff the floor when you take your hand away:

- Put your treat hand back on her nose again.
- Deliver a higher ratio of reinforcement from your hand, for longer, before removing your hand again.

If the dog jumps up and down at your side when you take your hand away:

- Make sure your hand is held really high up against your chest between clicks and treats. If you hold your hand above your dog's head, but in the air, or just out of reach, she will try to jump up to get it — because it looks so tempting.
- Ignore any jumping and keep walking. Eventually your dog will stop jumping, even if only for a few seconds — and then you can click and treat. Make sure you don't click *immediately* after a jump though, or your dog will think you are clicking the jumping. If she jumps, wait at least a step or two without jumping before you click and reinforce again.

If the dog jumps up *after* the click — to get the treat, on the way down:

- This is quite an easy one to fix. If the dog jumps up to meet your hand coming down with the treat, just don't release the treat from your hand into the dog's mouth whilst the front paws are off the floor. Continue moving your hand down to the floor, and release that treat when all four paws are on the floor. If you repeat this, the dog will stop jumping up — because it doesn't achieve anything. It's quicker to wait on the floor for the treat to come down.

PHASE 3: TAKING A FEW STEPS WITH THE HAND UP, BEFORE GOING DOWN

Now take two or three paces after picking your hand up to your chest, before you click and treat.

By this point, your dog will be giving you lovely eye-contact sometimes — but perhaps not always. The dog may look at something nearby and then turn to look up at you. Stop walking if your dog looks away from you at this stage in your training. Watch your dog and click the second your dog looks back at you.

Remember that you can be very precise with the clicker — you can click that exact moment your dog does something you like. Your dog is making decisions all the time. When you start training outdoors, your dog is making decisions to see another dog or a leaf blowing in the wind — and to decide to stay with you. Your task is to observe those decisions she makes and to mark them (with the clicker) — then reinforce.

POSSIBLE PROBLEMS

If the dog's body starts to crab out sideways, at 90 degrees to you:

- It is probably because of the way you are holding the treat hand when you deliver the treat. If you deliver the treat into the dog's mouth *palm up*, the dog will tend to crab out to get better access to the treat. If you hold your hand *palm down*, so you are looking at the back of your hand, you can ensure the dog's body stays straight next to you as you deliver the treat. Observe the way you hold the treat hand, and how it affects the positioning of the dog's body when you reinforce.

- You may be delivering the treat too close to your leg. The treat should be delivered level with your trouser seam — but not directly against your leg. It should be about a foot to the side of your left leg. If you deliver too close to your leg, the dog's rear will move outwards in relation to the head. Deliver the treat with your left hand in such a way that the dog's body is straight and facing forwards at the moment she eats the treat.

If the dog gets interested in scent on the floor (which is more likely to happen away from the house):

- Bend down and put your handful of tasty treats on your dog's nose and lure that nose up off the floor, giving many tasty treats rapidly whilst keeping your constantly-feeding hand on the dog's nose for a step or two.

- Prevention is essential: *Stop walking* as soon as your dog's nose hits the floor. Any time your dog's nose goes down, she is self-reinforcing — and sniffing the floor is not heelwork! The leash will prevent her from having continuing access to new scent on the ground.

- If necessary, walk backwards slowly but firmly, until you have detached her nose from the floor. This is not about 'correcting' the dog — or positive punishment, it is about removing the dog from the reinforcer on the ground. Whilst we are not going to do this in a jerky or scary way, it's important to respond *quickly* — since every second that passes, is a second of reinforcement for sniffing around and ignoring you during heelwork.

  This is one reason that *we need to keep the lead on, in distracting environments.* Without the lead, we couldn't do anything here should the dog decide to access environmental reinforcers.

  Sometimes, when the leash is attached to the back of the dog's harness, it is still difficult to disengage the dog from the floor: A dog in a back-fastening harness, throwing weight fully forwards, presents a difficult challenge when it comes to gently disengaging the *front* of that dog from the ground. If you are experiencing this, use a leash with a harness that has a front-fastening attachment point. This will allow you to gently disengage the front of the dog's body from the ground.

PHASE 4: THE MAINTENANCE STAGE FOR THE HAND GOES UP AND DOWN

Phase 4 is not really a 'step' but more of a maintenance stage for the behaviour. It is really just to continue doing Phase 3, indefinitely!

It's important that you stick to clicking after two to five paces for now — whenever you happen to see something great from the dog, within that time frame. Do not become a greedy trainer! A greedy trainer is someone who wants more 'bang for their buck' — someone who always wants more 'behaviour' for their click and treat.

For example, a greedy trainer thinks: '*Ah, my dog can do three paces for a click and treat, so let's try six paces for a click and treat*'. Many is the time I've seen handlers attempt this in class, only for the dog's attention to wander off at pace five! It's as if the handler thinks: '*Wow, Fido, you're doing great — let's keep going and see how much more of it you can do*'. When the behaviour falls apart, you've lost the opportunity to click and reinforce *any* of it: If you wait too long to reinforce, you lose the behaviour you want to reinforce. Click it whilst you've got it! Catch it when you can! Don't be greedy.

'When should I add in a verbal cue?'

Whenever you add a cue to a behaviour, you want to be pretty sure you are going to be offered the behaviour by the dog, after you give the cue. That means: Make sure that you are getting heelwork happening (consistently) before you say 'heel'. Why? Because what happens after the cue, is getting attached to the cue. If you say 'heel', and your dog ignores you and sniffs the floor, you are attaching the cue 'heel' to the behaviour of ignoring you and sniffing the floor!

You might have a consistent heel in the house, but not yet in the yard. In which case, you would be saying 'heel' when you train in the house — but not yet when you train in the yard.

When you are ready to add in a verbal cue, just say it a second before you set off, with your dog at your side.

Do not use the word 'heel' to nag the dog ('*heel...heel...HEEL!*') when she is *not* heeling. Doing this 1) makes you into an unpleasant (punishing) thing which the dog would rather ignore and avoid — not someone they want to engage with and respond to — and 2) it associates the word 'heel' with not-heeling!

'How can I make things easier when we move heelwork outside?'

Don't give the cue at all. Reduce the criteria for a click down to what the dog can be successful with. This may just be standing at your side doing 'un-cued attention', with no walking involved. Try not to focus on *words* so much as on observing and reinforcing *behaviours* — no matter how small they are.

'Is there a non-verbal cue for 'heel'?'

Silent handling is valued in gundog work. Some handlers like to teach their dog to heel only if they move off using their left leg (the leg nearest the dog). If they move off using the right leg, it's a 'sit-stay' and the dog should remain.

Personally, I find I am concentrating on too many other things to choose which leg to move off on! Instead, I would just show a flat 'stop' hand signal to my dog if the dog is expected not to heel — and would expect the dog to heel if not shown that. But it may give the dog an extra advantage to have one more sneaky cue in there — so, if you want to try the leg cues, go for it!

'Doesn't this exercise teach the dog to look at the handler? Is that ok for retrievers?'

Yes, the early heelwork exercises are the same for all subgroups. Towards the end of this section, I introduce some exercises which will develop the 'focus forwards' type of heelwork required from retrievers.

THE REPOSITIONING MOVE - GETTING THE DOG BACK INTO HEEL

Back in Section 3.1, Sits (in the plural!), we covered the sit-at-my-side behaviour. The sit-at-my-side is actually the repositioning move — with a sit on the end. As such, the repositioning move is actually the easier behaviour of the two, since it is slightly simpler.

I would recommend training the repositioning move (here) first, before the sit-at-my-side.

'When do we use the repositioning move?'

During heelwork, your dog will inevitably get in front of you occasionally. (If you have a spaniel, this might happen more than occasionally!)

When this happens, the two most useful ways to deal with it are:

- Stop walking. About-turn to your *right* (180 degrees, clockwise). And walk back the way you were coming — keeping a close eye on your dog. When your dog catches up with you and is briefly in heel position, quickly *capture* that with a click and treat — before she shoots past you! This is a really nice way to set the dog up for success — you arrange antecedents so that the behaviour you desire (dog at your side) occurs, giving you an opportunity to click and reinforce. You can just keep walking back and forth, using this magic change of direction to reposition the dog and give you a 'clickable moment'.

- Use the repositioning move. This enables you to go from a dog out of heel in front of you — to a dog back in heel position. You will not be changing direction when using the repositioning move.

Begin with both feet together.

Take one step back with the left foot. The right foot does not move.

Step the left foot back to its original position so that both feet are together again.

HOW TO DO THE REPOSITIONING MOVE

THE HANDLER'S MOVES

Before we talk about the dog, let's talk about the handler's moves during this exercise. I highly recommend you do this a couple of times, without your dog!

- To begin with, stand still and look down at your feet. Your right foot is not going to move throughout this whole exercise. Imagine that it is superglued to the floor!

- Your left foot is going to take one step back and pause.

- Then step forward again — back into line with your right foot, so that your feet end up together.

PUTTING HANDLER AND DOG TOGETHER

1. Start with your dog in front of you and take a few treats in your left hand. To get the dog in front of you, don't pull her there by the leash or harness — simply turn your own body to face your dog. (When you are practising your heelwork, you won't need to do anything to get the dog in front of you like this — this is where the dog will naturally stray to, occasionally, and you will then use the repositioning move to get her back in the correct place.)

2. Lure your dog straight back behind you on your left side, whilst simultaneously taking a step back with your left foot — just as we practised above — to enable the dog to have space to turn.

3. You may find your dog is reluctant to follow your hand *all the way* behind you. If so, be sure to give a treat at the furthest point behind you — to reinforce her in that spot.

4. Turn the dog *towards you* whilst she is behind you. (Make sure you are not turning the dog *away* from you — a common mistake!)

   Until this point, the palm of your hand has been facing upwards — whilst luring the dog back behind you. When your dog is at that furthest-behind-you spot and you are starting to turn her towards you, switch your hand on her nose so that *you are now looking at the back of your hand.* Why? Because otherwise the dog is not likely to come forwards straight — the dog's rear will move out at 90 degrees to you, to get better access to the palm of your hand. You will only control the alignment of the

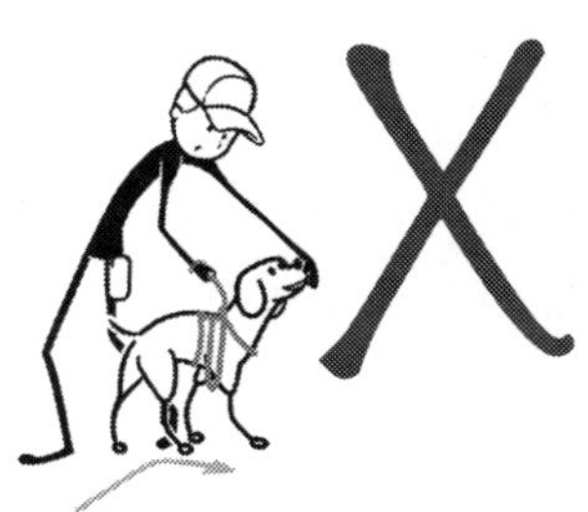

WHEN TURNING YOUR DOG BEHIND YOU (SEE 4) TAKE CARE TO TURN HER TOWARDS YOU – AND NOT AWAY FROM YOU. TURNING HER AWAY FROM YOU WILL PUT A HUGE DISTANCE BETWEEN YOU.

dog's body if you are looking at the *back of your hand* from this point onwards.

5. Lure the dog forwards as you step your left foot forwards to meet the right again. So now you and your dog are lined up, facing forwards. The shape in which the dog is travelling is a 'U' at your left side: Straight back behind you, curving towards you, and then straight forwards again.

THIS HANDLER IS TRYING TO LURE HER DOG FORWARDS AT THE END OF THE MOVE (SEE 5, ABOVE). THE DOG'S REAR IS SWINGING OUT TO THE SIDE. CAN YOU SPOT WHY? TAKE A LOOK AT THE HAND POSITION. THE HAND IS STILL PALM-UP, WHICH IS HOW WE LURE THE DOG BACK BEHIND US. TO BRING THE DOG FORWARDS, WE NEED TO SWITCH THE HAND OVER ON THE DOG'S NOSE WHEN SHE IS BEHIND US – SO THAT WE ARE LOOKING AT THE BACK OF THE HAND AS WE LURE THE DOG FORWARDS.

6. Click the moment that the dog and your feet line up, facing forwards — and release the treat or lure.

Isolate this behaviour and practise it away from your heelwork until it is fluent. Then you can start to use it during 'the hand goes up and down' exercise, when your dog gets out of position.

REPOSITIONING MOVE

1 BEGIN WITH THE DOG IN FRONT OF YOU. TO ACHIEVE THIS, JUST TURN YOURSELF TO FACE YOUR DOG. TAKE A BIG HANDFUL OF TREATS IN YOUR LEFT HAND FROM YOUR TREAT POUCH OR POCKET (ON YOUR LEFT SIDE).

2 LURE THE DOG STRAIGHT BACK BEHIND YOU ON YOUR LEFT SIDE, WHILST TAKING A STEP BACK WITH YOUR LEFT FOOT. ENSURE YOUR HAND IS PALM-UP AT THIS POINT.

3 WHEN YOU REACH THE FURTHEST POINT BEHIND YOU, RELEASE A TREAT. THIS WILL ENSURE YOUR DOG ALWAYS FOLLOWS YOUR HAND BACK TO THIS SPOT.

4 TURN YOUR DOG TOWARDS YOUR LEG, SWITCHING YOUR HAND OVER ON THE DOG'S NOSE. AS YOU DO THIS, YOU ARE NOW LOOKING AT THE BACK OF YOUR HAND – IT IS PALM-DOWN.

5 LURE YOUR DOG FORWARDS AGAIN AS YOU STEP YOUR LEFT FOOT FORWARDS TO MEET YOUR RIGHT. ENSURE YOU ARE LOOKING AT THE BACK OF YOUR HAND AS YOU DO THIS AND USE THE LURE TO KEEP THE DOG'S BODY ALIGNED STRAIGHT AT YOUR SIDE.

6 CLICK WHEN THE DOG IS LEVEL WITH YOUR SIDE AND ALIGNED WITH YOUR BODY, BOTH OF YOU FACING FORWARDS. RELEASE A TREAT TO THE DOG'S MOUTH. THEN – TURN YOURSELF TO FACE YOUR DOG AGAIN, AND REPEAT THE SEQUENCE.

PIVOTING

'Why do we need to teach dogs to pivot?'

Pivoting is important because it's how we 'steer' the dog. We are not allowed to touch the dog in competition, and she is off-leash. How, then, do we communicate that we want the dog to turn to face the left retrieve and to leave the right retrieve? How do we communicate that a bird is about to come down behind us and the dog might mark it if we can only turn swiftly and catch it in time?

A large part of the answer is the 'motorbike and sidecar' principle: The dog is attached to our side by our relationship with her and through training. And if our body moves, so does our dog — as the sidecar moves with the motorbike. Think of pivoting as *steerage* for a dog handler!

Retrievers need to be particularly adept at pivoting, since they have such demands placed on them during heelwork — they will be at heel (typically) when retrieves come down, and the ability to steer a dog at your side enables you to turn (difficult) blinds into (easier) marks. But spaniels and HPRs also need functional pivoting, for working tests particularly — when they may encounter split retrieves of various types. Or, in a trial, when they may be sent from the handler's side for a blind.

'How do we teach dogs to pivot?'

After dogs have a reliable sit-at-my-side, they don't find it difficult to implement pivoting — almost seamlessly. After all, they have been taught to sit straight, aligned with the handler's side. If the handler rotates herself, the dog should automatically realign herself to the handler's side in the new location.

Firstly, ensure your dog is fluent with the sit-at-my-side behaviour — covered in Section 3.1, Sits (in the plural!).

You can then practise pivoting by rotating 90 degrees at a time, and giving your 'sit-at-my-side' cue — clicking and treating as the dog aligns with you.

Be sure to practise rotating both clockwise on the spot and counter-clockwise, with your dog able to realign themselves at your side as you do this.

If your dog is not straight when you pivot — don't click. Use the treat to lure the dog into a better position and then click and treat this. Keep repeating that particular direction until the dog improves. Reduce the angle of your pivot to make things easier for your dog if necessary.

GO SNIFF – A HEELWORK GAME FOR DOGS DISTRACTED BY SCENT

AN INTRODUCTION TO HOW THE GO SNIFF GAME WORKS

The main reason heelwork 'fails' is because an environmental reinforcer tempts the dog out of heel position: In that moment, the dog is motivated more by that environmental reinforcer than by the prospect of our own reinforcers. The environmental reinforcer is frequently not even something we can see — since, often, it is scent which tempts a dog to break heel and investigate.

It can easily seem that it is *us* versus *the world* of environmental reinforcers (birds, rabbits, faeces, scent, etc.). That is, often handlers experience themselves as almost at war with all those distractions out there — pitting themselves against them when they go out with their dogs.

How much easier would it be, if we also had environmental reinforcers on our side and under our control? Think about clicking, and somehow being able to give the dog a scent they would like to smell... But that's a fantasy, right? Wrong. It's totally possible.

And this is the basis for the Go Sniff game. It's a game that uses scent in the environment as the reinforcer: When the dog gives us great focus, we release her with '*go sniff*' and she reinforces herself by sniffing great smells. Once we have great focus from the dog, we can ask for more — a step or two of heelwork, for example — before we release with 'go sniff' and allow the dog to reinforce.

The beauty of the Go Sniff game is that the more intense (and desirable) the scent — the more the dog wants that smell — the better the focus she shows you, once she understands the game. She is desperate to be released to investigate it and *you* are the route to that.

So, instead of a situation where it is us versus environmental reinforcers, we have enlisted those environmental reinforcers to our side. There's no war anymore, and we're all on the same team. The more distracting the world, the more focussed the dog!

The Go Sniff game could easily be located in Section 3.5, Focus and engagement, but, since I use this game almost exclusively for training heelwork, I'm including it in this section instead. But you should know that it very much straddles both these sections.

The Go Sniff game is a gundog-friendly take on Leslie McDevitt's 'Give Me a Break' game from her seminal book *Control Unleashed.* This game (as devised by Leslie) typically requires a confined area, defined by ring-gates, for example — so the dog doesn't have an infinity of environmental reinforcers available when she is released. The game involves a chair for the handler to sit on, whilst the dog has the 'break'.

Obviously, we don't typically have access to 'rings', in gundog training — they are not a part of our sport. So we're going to use a leash (later a long-line; even later — nothing at all!) as a portable way of restricting the area the dog has access to. If there is somewhere suitable to sit (like a wall), then we can sit down during the break — but often there isn't, so we stand there in a neutral and disengaged way at these times.

PHASE 1: ATTENTION AS THE CRITERIA

Attention is a lower criteria than heelwork because the dog needs only to offer you a fleeting glance — which is much easier than sustaining focus on you, and maintaining heel position, whilst moving forwards. Therefore, I suggest you begin with *attention* as the behaviour you are reinforcing, until your dog becomes fluent at offering attention in that session. (At that point, you can switch to Phase 2 below — heelwork as the criteria.)

1. Stand near something interesting for the dog to sniff, with the dog on-leash. It helps if the leash is at least six feet long — to enable the dog to reach what she wants to sniff when released. Sniffing is going to be the reinforcement - and it's not going to be that reinforcing if your dog doesn't want to explore the smells. You might be near a hedgerow, a gamey-smelling area — or locations where you know from experience the dog finds interesting scent. If you have a dog interested in smelling where other dogs have urinated, you can stand near likely pee-places.

   Hold the leash short enough that the dog does not have access to the ground and cannot self-reinforce to start with. Do not let the dog pull you closer to the smelly place. If your dog is really interested in whatever it is, move further away — so it loses some suction for your dog.

2. Click the dog when she looks at you - even the briefest of passing glances. You may need to wait a while for the dog to offer a glance towards you. If

you are really stuck, you can prompt this with a smoochy noise for the first couple of reps — but quickly try to stop the prompt, so that she is offering attention un-cued. The dog does not need to be in heel position — we are clicking *attention only* for Phase 1.

3. Jackpot the dog (after the click). This means delivering multiple treats, one after another, whilst being verbally very excited and happy and animated. Deliver the treats directly to the dog's mouth and don't place them on the ground (which you are still not letting the dog reach). You need to keep the treats coming so frequently that the dog doesn't disengage between them, so you may need to rapid-fire them from both hands, one after another. (You don't need to maintain the jackpot once the dog starts to understand the game — but in these early stages, the jackpot helps to establish you as extremely reinforcing, and therefore makes it more likely that the dog is going to look back at you fairly quickly.)

4. Stop delivering treats — and whilst the dog is still looking at you, release her to sniff with 'go sniff'.

   IMPORTANT: *At the moment you say 'go sniff', the dog must be offering you focus.* You must release the dog, *before* the dog releases herself back to the environment. Watch closely as your jackpot ends and ensure there is a nanosecond of attention from the dog — at which time, you release. If *you* cue the 'go sniff', it becomes a reinforcer which you are giving the dog for that focus — the sniffing is working *for* you, 'on your side'. If you don't cue it and the dog just does it anyway, the dog is learning to disengage and to stop focussing on you when she feels like it — the sniffing is then working *against* you — reinforcing the dog for something you don't like. So much of dog training is in the details and the timing!

5. Immediately after saying 'go sniff', encourage your dog to sniff by running your hand through the grass or cover. At first you will really need to bend over and actually touch the grass, to encourage your dog.

6. Stand up when you see your dog's nose hit the area to investigate. Step back and be quiet and still whilst she sniffs. The dog may sniff for as long as she likes and you should not interrupt her. Allow the lead to be loose whilst she sniffs within the length of it — but, if your dog tries to drag you off following a scent, don't allow this. Imagine that your feet are superglued to the floor: Be an anchor and don't give new ground to the dog. The rule is: '*You can check out everything you can reach within leash length*'.

   Whilst the dog is sniffing, you are watching her closely — whilst also feigning disinterest and not crowding her. Since you have limited the area that the dog can sniff — through the leash length — at some point the dog will get her 'fill' of sniffing this spot. She will then disengage from sniffing and look back at you. You may have to wait quite some time at first, and that's fine — be patient and observe. Don't give up and pull her away. Wait for her to have her fill. She will get quicker as she understands the game...

7. Click when your dog looks back at you, even briefly.

8. Jackpot again after your click — whilst also being very chatty in a happy and praising way. There should be a big contrast between how you are when the dog is sniffing (silent, disengaged, still, boring) and how you are when the dog turns to look at you and whilst you are jackpotting (happy, talkative, giving rapid treats, interesting). The dog's attention should appear to transform you — like a coin put into an arcade game makes something happen.

   Then you just keep cycling around this loop: Quickly, and before your dog looks away by herself — release her with 'go sniff' again.

As the dog improves, you will be able to click and treat multiple reps of a glance at you before you release to sniff. You do want to *aim* at multiple reps of focus before releasing each time — but you need to make sure you don't get greedy and expect more than the dog can manage, leading to the dog disengaging before your release.

If your dog is finding it easy to offer you focus, you can move to giving a single treat rather than a jackpot. If, at any time, you notice that it gets harder for the dog to offer you attention, return to a jackpot when she offers you this.

At some point, you will say 'go sniff' and your dog will say 'nah, I don't want to'. Your dog will say this by either refusing to sniff anything, or by making a weeny token gesture to sniff where you are indicating — and then turning back to you instantly for your click and treat. You should definitely click and treat this 'refusal' to go and sniff, a lot. Your dog is 'saying' they now find you more reinforcing than the environment. This is the whole purpose behind what we are doing. At this point, your dog is ready to do more than just look at you — and you are ready to move onto Phase 2: Heelwork as the criteria.

Alternatively, you can walk on a few paces to find new smelly stuff which your dog is a bit distracted by, and which you can use in the same way. This would be keeping the criteria the same (un-cued attention) and working on generalisation to a novel location. Another idea is to put the long-line on, and to work un-cued attention within the length of the long-line — rather than a six foot leash. You can eventually move this across to work entirely off-leash.

This game is a great way to warm up in a new training location. A few minutes of playing Go Sniff will result in a dog which is focussed on you and ready to work.

GO SNIFF - PHASE 1 — Attention as the criteria

1 WITH YOUR DOG ON A REGULAR-LENGTH LEASH, STAND NEAR SOMEWHERE WITH INTERESTING SMELLS. KEEP THE LEASH SHORT ENOUGH THAT YOUR DOG CAN'T YET ACCESS THE SMELLS. WAIT PATIENTLY AND BE READY WITH THE CLICKER.

2 WHEN YOUR DOG LOOKS AT YOU, EVEN FLEETINGLY, CLICK THAT PRECISE MOMENT.

3 JACKPOT THE DOG WITH MULTIPLE RAPID TREATS, ONE AFTER ANOTHER. BE GENEROUS AND DON'T ALLOW ENOUGH TIME BETWEEN TREATS FOR THE DOG TO THINK ABOUT DISENGAGING BY HERSELF.

4 WITHDRAW YOUR TREATS. HOPEFULLY THAT JACKPOT MADE A BIG IMPACT ON YOUR DOG AND SO YOU WILL BE OFFERED AT LEAST ONE SECOND OF ATTENTION. SAY 'GO SNIFF' RIGHT AWAY, WHILST SHE IS STILL LOOKING AT YOU. IF SHE LOOKS AWAY BEFORE YOU SAY 'GO SNIFF', RETURN TO STEP 1 – AND BE QUICKER NEXT TIME!

5 AFTER SAYING 'GO SNIFF', RUN YOUR HANDS THROUGH THE GRASS OR WHEREVER THE SMELLS ARE – TO ENCOURAGE SNIFFING.

6 STAND UP AND ALLOW THE DOG TO SNIFF FOR AS LONG AS SHE LIKES. THE DOG CAN SNIFF ANYTHING WITHIN THE REACH OF THE LEASH BUT DO NOT GIVE FRESH GROUND BEYOND THAT. BE QUIET AND OBSERVANT OF YOUR DOG – AND PATIENT!

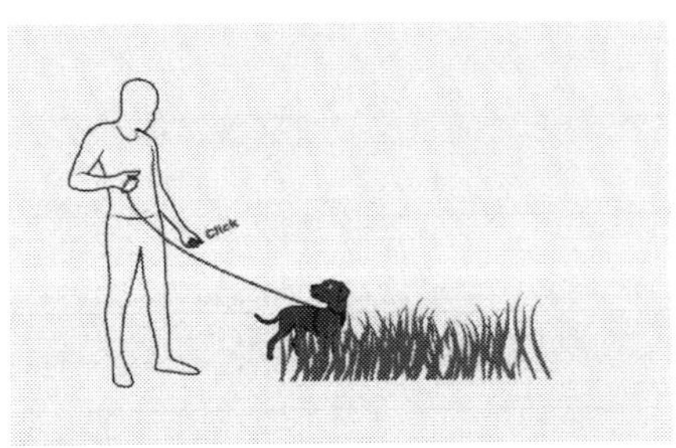

7 WHEN YOUR DOG STOPS SNIFFING AND GLANCES IN YOUR DIRECTION, EVEN MOMENTARILY – CLICK THAT MOMENT TO CAPTURE IT.

8 JACKPOT THE DOG AGAIN, AS IN STEP 3. AND CONTINUE, CYCLING AROUND STEPS 4-8.

PHASE 2: HEELWORK AS THE CRITERIA

Now, instead of just clicking a split second of focus when your dog looks at you, you will instead cue 'heel' — the moment your dog looks at you. Do one or two steps of heelwork. Click and treat. And then — whilst the dog is still looking at you — give your 'go sniff' cue. Over time, you will be able to build up the number of steps you take before you release the dog with 'go sniff'.

In this way, you are integrating environmental reinforcers into your heelwork. Your dog is allowed to sniff things and 'be a dog' — but, all the while, your heelwork is getting stronger and stronger. Everyone's a winner here!

If you practise this enough, the more distracting an environment, the more your dog will focus on you — in order to be released to investigate that environment. And your heelwork will gather all the enjoyment of sniffing: The 'feeling-state' the dog experiences when heeling and when sniffing will be connected. (Your dog will enjoy heelwork.)

Tip: Remember the role of prevention. If your dog is sniffing the ground before your 'go sniff' release, take hold of the leash where it attaches to the front of the front-attaching harness and gently hold it so it is too short for her to reach the ground with her nose. Having now removed that reinforcer, wait and see what her next choice will be. Will she engage with you? If so, skip the treats this time — because the most reinforcing thing in that moment will clearly be a release back to what she was just helping herself to: Just say happily 'go sniff' and let her return to what she was doing — but, this time, as a reinforcement for focus!

Tip: If your dog is sniffing something in the air, with nose raised up high, before the release — interrupt the scent. Do this by standing in front of her nose and blocking that scent being carried on the air. Remove the reinforcer! If she looks at you when you do this, click and say 'go sniff' — move out of the way of the scent and release her to sniff.

This concept of the dog complying with you to be released back to the environment will become very important later on for HPRs and spaniels: Frequently, the most reinforcing thing after a stop whistle is a release to hunt on. In order for the dog to experience the stop whistle as an opportunity to earn a reinforcer — rather than an interruption of their previous reinforcement whilst hunting — it really helps if they have a history of playing the Go Sniff game with another behaviour, like heelwork.

When your dog can do the Go Sniff game on a regular lead, try using your 10m long-line instead. Now, when you release her to the environment, she has a 10-metre radius to explore before choosing to check-in with you.

GO SNIFF - PHASE 2 — Heelwork as the criteria

1 AS BEFORE, STAND NEAR SOMEWHERE WITH INTERESTING SMELLS. KEEP THE LEASH SHORT ENOUGH THAT YOUR DOG CAN'T YET ACCESS THE SMELLS. WAIT PATIENTLY AND BE READY WITH THE CLICKER.

2 WHEN THE DOG LOOKS AT YOU THIS TIME, CUE 'HEEL' INSTEAD OF CLICKING THE ATTENTION ITSELF.

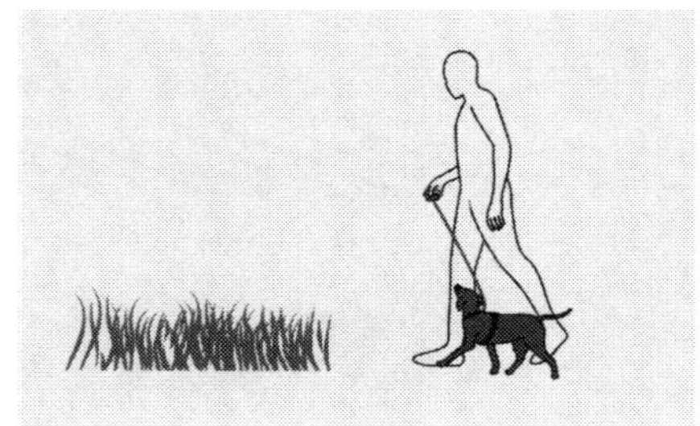

3 DO SOME HEELWORK USING THE HAND GOES UP AND DOWN. AT FIRST, KEEP IT TO JUST 1-2 STEPS OF HEELWORK AT A TIME.

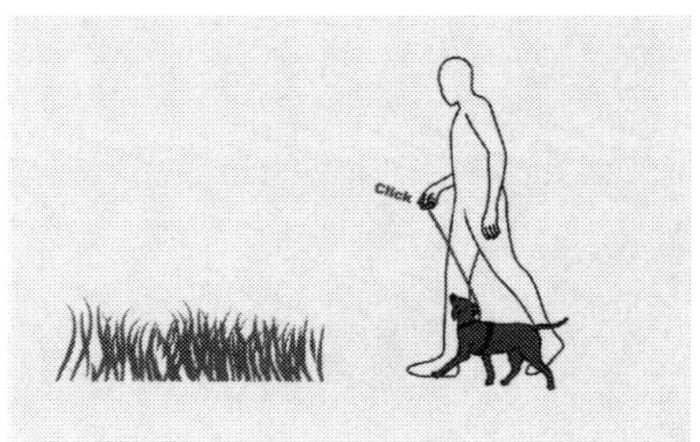

4 CLICK THE HEELWORK AFTER 1-2 STEPS.

5 DELIVER A TREAT FOR THAT CLICK, AS YOU USUALLY WOULD. (YOU CAN JACKPOT HERE IF YOUR DOG STILL NEEDS ADDITIONAL HELP TO KEEP LOOKING AT YOU WHEN YOU WITHDRAW THE TREATS AFTER REINFORCING.)

6 WHILST THE DOG IS STILL LOOKING AT YOU, GIVE YOUR 'GO SNIFF' CUE. AGAIN, IT IS IMPORTANT THE DOG IS LOOKING AT YOU WHEN YOU GIVE THE CUE – AND HAS NOT LOOKED AWAY YET, AFTER YOUR TREAT.

7 GESTURE DOWN TOWARDS THE GRASS TO ENCOURAGE THE DOG TO SNIFF. (YOU MAY FIND YOUR DOG STARTS TO UNDERSTAND THE CUE WITHOUT THIS HELP AFTER IT.)

8 AS BEFORE, STAND UP AND ALLOW THE DOG TO SNIFF FOR AS LONG AS SHE LIKES – AS LONG AS IT'S WITHIN THE REACH OF THE LEASH WITHOUT GIVING NEW GROUND. WATCH THE DOG CLOSELY AND BE READY WITH THE CLICKER.

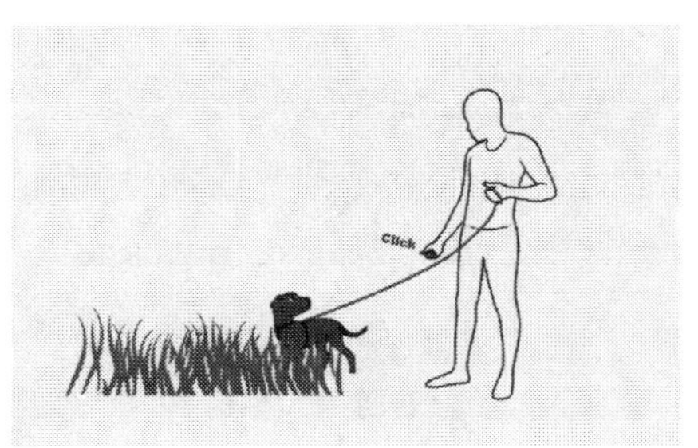

9 CLICK THE MOMENT THE DOG GLANCES AT YOU, EVEN MOMENTARILY.

10 DELIVER THE TREAT. AGAIN, JACKPOT IF YOU FEEL THE DOG NEEDS THIS.

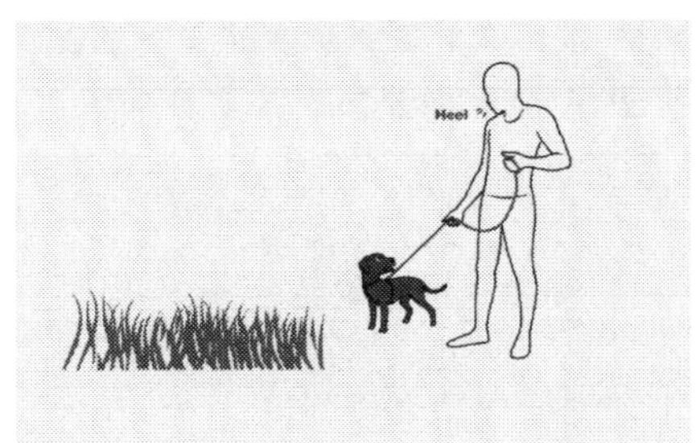

11 CUE 'HEEL' AGAIN, AS IN STEP 2. CONTINUE TO CYCLE AROUND STEPS 2-11.

STOP WHEN I STOP – A GAME TO CHECK YOUR CONNECTION WITH YOUR DOG

One critical point during heelwork occurs when the handler stops walking. Does the dog stop walking too? If so, where does she stop? (In front of the handler? In perfect heel position?)

In a retriever walk-up, when game is shot, the line of handlers stops walking — to mark the retrieve. It's vital that the dog stops in a good heel position at this moment. The dog should not move in front of you — even just a step or two — or you could be eliminated from competition for unsteadiness.

Heelwork is about a connection between the handler and the dog. This is a connection which has been developed through training and through your relationship. The dog has to remain in *relationship* with you, in the presence of high distractions. When a dog steps forwards two or three paces out of heel due to a temptation, she is momentarily not in relationship to you. Our sidecar has come adrift!

Here's something that happens quite often: A handler and her dog are doing the Hand Goes Up and Down. When the handler stops walking (for any reason), the dog just keeps walking forwards at a similar pace to before. It's as if the dog's body is on auto-pilot and just walking along at the same pace, with treats periodically descending through the air to her mouth. Like manna from heaven above! Although this dog looked like she was doing heelwork, she wasn't: There was no connection; no relationship there.

We've already established that the dog does not need to be visually staring at the handler all the time. But the dog must still be *aware* of the handler and her movements — through peripheral vision. The difficulty for us, as handlers, is — how can we know that the dog is connected and in relationship to us whilst we are doing heelwork? How can we tell? Especially if the dog does not need to be looking at us?

This is where the Stop When I Stop game comes in. It is a way of periodically checking whether your dog is connected to you. Each time you stop walking, imagine that you are asking your dog: '*Are we still connected?*'

1. Whilst walking forwards and doing the Hand Goes Up and Down, stop walking. I suggest you begin with just *one step forwards*, before stopping. So you might say 'heel', take a single step — and stop. If your dog also stops and maintains heel position — click and treat. (If your dog sits herself at heel, with a sit-at-my-side — great: Click the sit, and treat.)

2. If your dog keeps walking forwards after you've stopped, the lead may go tight — or she may just stop too far forwards and out of heel (without the lead going tight). Either way, it's not what we want. If your dog is very focussed on something in front of her, take several slow and deliberate steps backwards until she turns and re-engages with you. Click and treat as soon as you see that re-engagement from her. Taking deliberate steps backwards is necessary to *remove* the reinforcer she is sniffing. You are *not* yanking the dog back to your side as with traditional training. You are just slowly and gently walking backwards until the dog re-engages with you — and capturing that with a click, when it occurs.

3. Ask for a sit-at-my-side, click and treat that. If you find this difficult, return to Section 3.1, Sits (in the plural!), and the sit-at-my-side exercise — since you will need it functioning well as we move on with Stop When I Stop.

4. Repeat this, just taking *one step forwards at a time*, until you can easily take a step, stop, and have your dog maintain heel for a click and a treat. Consistently, over and over. At this point, increase criteria for a click and a treat, when you stop, to be a sit-at-my-side. Prompt or lure 'sit-at-my-side' when you stop, at first.

5. Now you can take *two to five steps* before stopping. Change it up a bit so your dog doesn't know when you will stop. But don't walk further than five paces yet.

6. The Stop When I Stop game is *easier when you stop more frequently*, because your dog is expecting the stopping more. She is anticipating that stopping is imminent, any time. The opposite end of the spectrum — making the exercise harder — is walking for quite some time before dropping in a sneaky stop, to see if you are still doing heelwork or your dog is on autopilot.

7. I like to make this exercise into a game: Can I catch the dog out? Will the dog notice I've stopped? Can I slowly sneak into a stop, and trick the dog? If the dog does drift ahead, I laugh in a playful way and say '*Haha — caught you, you cheeky poops!*' and make a game of it. (You don't need to call your dog 'cheeky poops' — that bit is optional!) This functions as engagement. You will find the dog is much more focussed and responsive on the next rep, after this brief spell of engagement.

The Stop When I Stop game will always be useful to you, no matter what stage your dog's training is at: You can always stop, and note how your dog responds to that. From that information, you know how securely you are connected in that moment.

'Should the dog sit?'

Yes. After your dog is able to stop at your side when you stop, you should increase the criteria to a sit-at-my-side. For a very long time, the dog should sit when you stop, as a default. In a trial, a dog is steady if they just stand without moving at your side — they are not required to sit. Still, a sit is one step further away from running in than a stand, and so it is a better position to uphold in training.

ENGAGEMENT BREAKS DURING HEELWORK

Trainers in other dog sports — like obedience, rally, schutzhund and other ring sports — expend huge effort in getting their dogs to do stylish and exciting heelwork. It's the dog equivalent of dressage: They want the dog moving beautifully with a lot of energy to the movement. To achieve this, they use high-energy reinforcers like tug toys or balls (or just food, used in creative ways — inspiring chase). The dog comes to anticipate these high-energy reinforcers when doing heelwork, and that results in a very *up* and high-energy heel behaviour. Since this high-energy reinforcer almost always comes from the handler, this translates into an intense focus on the handler during heelwork. Meanwhile, the actual period during which the dog is expected to heel is minutes.

So, in these other sports, heelwork: 1) is of short duration, 2) involves high-energy movement, and 3) inevitably involves intense focus on the handler.

In gundog heelwork, you won't score points for any trotting or fanciness. In fact, people would probably laugh! Meanwhile, gundogs — especially retrievers — must maintain heel position not for minutes, but for *hours*. Often all day.

Gundog heelwork is comparatively low energy. (Because we want the dog to conserve energy for hunting and retrieving.) And the concept of bursting-with-energy heelwork would be a bit risky to most gundog trainers: It hints at a lack of steadiness — a heinous crime. Instead, gundog trainers would rather see a lot of self-restraint at heel.

So, by comparison, gundog heelwork: 1) is of very long duration, 2) involves relatively low-energy movement, and 3) involves intense focus on the environment (to spot those retrieves) — whilst still maintaining a connection with the handler.

Since gundog heelwork goes on for a long time — and especially since it involves environmental reinforcers that are not on the handler's body — it's all too easy for the dog to become progressively less engaged with the handler. This lack of engagement is a major cause of the dog (for example) walking on a pace or two when you stop: After an hour of heeling, the dog falls out of relationship to you — and the attractions of the environment entice her off a step or two. After all, it's not like you are doing anything worth paying attention to...

To combat this, cycles of what we can call *engagement*, followed by heelwork, function really well for preventing boredom and disengagement. Engagement has become a bit of a buzzword, in recent years, and the next section of this book is dedicated to the subject.

Cycles of heelwork and engagement work really well for achieving a heel behaviour which maintains a connection between you and your dog. This is pretty simple to implement, too:

- Begin with the Hand Goes Up and Down.

- After a few steps of heelwork: Click and treat (as usual). Then cue 'gotcha' — and spring into what I call an engagement break (see below for an explanation).

- After about 30 seconds to a minute of engagement, resume heelwork by cuing 'heel'. Click and treat the heelwork as usual, for as long as feels appropriate for your dog.

- Then: Click, treat — and break into an engagement break again.

'What is an engagement break?'

An engagement break is a short spell during which you become amazingly exciting to your dog! For my own dogs, what works best is instantly becoming very excited with my voice, bending over to invite play, pushing them on the shoulder gently to encourage them to come back at me with enthusiasm (jumping up is permitted, during engagement!), 'fake' running away from them a few steps to get them to chase after me — essentially using body, voice, and personality to provide the dog with as much fun as possible for 30 seconds to a minute. You can give treats occasionally, during this — but must not use them continuously, nor as a lure. In short, an engagement break is a fun *break out* moment — where you stop the serious heelwork and are crazy fun to be with! At the moment I start an engagement break, I give the cue 'gotcha' as I gently push the dog on the shoulders. I recommend you use a cue because you don't want your dog anticipating an engagement break during heelwork, unless they hear a cue for it!

Engagement breaks during heelwork help the dog to pay attention to you, especially if you can use these when the dog is least expecting it. The dog learns:

FOOD BOWL GAME – HOW TO USE ENVIRONMENTAL REINFORCERS

THE MOST IMPORTANT MARKER POINT FOR RETRIEVER HEELWORK IS WHEN THE DOG IS LOOKING AT THE BOWL (MARKING THE RETRIEVE) WHILST ALSO MAINTAINING HEEL POSITION.

'*At any moment, my serious, slow-walking, predictable (boring) owner might suddenly burst into action and become incredibly exciting and fun.*' This tends to result in good attention during heelwork, and the dog remaining in relationship with you — waiting to spot your transformation into amazing fun!

Imagine a walk-up situation for a retriever: The dog has to maintain heel position, despite the perceived reinforcer (game, retrieves) being in front of her.

The dog is only to access that reinforcer when released to do so. Walk-ups involve the reinforcement being 'out there' in the environment, resulting in the dog looking forwards at what she wants — and not up at you. The more the dog wants something in front of her, the more she must maintain heel and not allow the reinforcer to tempt her forwards.

The Food Bowl game enables us to practise this. We use food bowls to simulate environmental reinforcers — something out there in the environment, which the dog wants to reach and has to approach at heel, to be released to.

Before I describe the way I use food bowls, it's important to take ownership of this concept as a general idea and to use it creatively: The food bowl is just a reinforcer which is off your person. You can really choose any behaviour you want to mark and release the dog to this reinforcer. Play around with this, as an idea, and you will find many uses in your training.

For this exercise, it is best to be on tarmac or paving, or very short grass — as you want the dog to be able to see the food bowls easily. You can also be indoors.

1. Have the dog on lead. Do not have treats or clicker on your person for this exercise.

2. Ask your dog to stay whilst you set out a food bowl in front of you (at 8-10 yds distance) and another behind you (at 8-10 yds), with a treat in each bowl. You are in the middle with the dog, between the two bowls, and the dog is aware of both.

3. When you release the dog from the stay after putting out the food bowls, be sure you are holding the leash: The dog will probably attempt to reach the bowl you're facing and strain on the lead. Restrain the dog and if necessary, take immediate steps backwards away from the bowl until the dog stops focussing on the treat and the leash is loose.

4. Give your 'heel' cue and take one step towards a bowl. You choose the criteria you are looking for, in order to mark and reinforce. Maybe you just want the *leash to be loose* and you want the dog to be *engaging with you*. This may be looking at you (at first), it may be stopping when you stop (even if looking at the bowl), or hanging back to be with you — but the absolute

minimum is that you want some sign of *self-control*: You need to feel that you and the dog have a connection and are in relationship in the presence of that environmental reinforcer, which is the food bowl. Just for a moment, not for any duration.

5. Mark that loose lead and moment of connection with a verbal marker (see below) and (for now) your release word ('ok'), and either run with the dog to the bowl — or drop the leash on the floor and allow the dog to run to the bowl.

6. Throw a few more treats in the bowl whilst restraining the dog with the other hand, turn around and do the same thing approaching the other bowl, behind you.

7. As the dog improves, you will be able to increase the criteria: You will be able to say 'heel' and take a step, then stopping — effectively doing the Stop When I Stop game towards the food bowl.

Tip: It is easier to take just one step before marking and releasing than it is to attempt continuous step after step, towards the bowl. Continuous steps getting ever-closer to the bowl will tempt the dog forwards out of heel. Of course, you need to be able to do continuous steps right up to the bowl — eventually — but you don't start with that. Begin with just one step, and do Stop When I Stop. When you can do this, you can try two steps and Stop When I Stop — and so on, until you are taking consecutive steps towards the bowl.

Tip: The 'art' to this exercise comes in deciding when to release the dog to the bowl. The closer you get to the bowl, the more suction the bowl has for her — and the harder the exercise will be. Therefore, when starting, release the dog from further away (dropping the lead if necessary): It is more important that the dog is in contact with you, when you release, than how close you are to the bowl. With practise, you will be able to get closer before releasing.

Tip: Beware the dog which makes a last-minute lunge for the food bowl before being released and manages to grab some food! Know the length of your lead at all times and ensure your dog is physically unable to reach the bowl. Remember the principles of prevention — as discussed in Section 1.2, Prevention.

Tip: Where should the dog be looking when released? If a retriever, ideally she should be looking at the food bowl. Remember this exercise is a rehearsal for the idea of a walk-up, where the dog needs to be walking at heel whilst looking forwards to mark the retrieves and birds. If the dog is looking at you, she is going to miss the retrieves and end up having to run blinds instead of marks. If your dog is a spaniel or HPR, it is less important where the dog is looking. (You won't be running marks with a dog walking at heel.)

Tip: Choose a specific word for your verbal marker — a word which will function like a click, but will mean 'Go and get the reinforcer from the bowl' (instead of 'I, your handler, am about to give you a reinforcer' — which is what the click means). I use 'cookies', but you can use any word you like. Since the word will be unfamiliar to the dog, add in the release word after the marker, at first — to help the dog understand she can go to the bowl at that point. You should phase out the release word and just use the verbal marker after a few reps.

This exercise is quite an important one, especially for retrievers.

BEGINNING WALK-UPS (RETRIEVERS ONLY)

This step is all about getting the dog used to the idea of walking forwards at heel, whilst there is a person in front — doing 'stuff' with dummies.

Before you can attempt this exercise, there are several other exercises you need to do. Some of them — such as the clicker retrieve, marking and steadiness — come later in this book. You will need to skip ahead to read these sections and cover that material before being able to undertake this exercise. Things will not go well, otherwise! In more detail, before this exercise, you should have covered:

- All earlier heelwork exercises in this section
- The sit-at-my-side (Section 3.1)
- The clicker retrieve (Section 3.6)
- Marked retrieves (Section 3.7; including steadiness and static marking work).

You've got all that covered? Then let's move on...

We are going to use exactly the same skills as outlined in the Food Bowl game. Instead of releasing the dog to a food reinforcer, there is now a dummy thrower and the prospect of a retrieve, out in front. (For any retrieves completed, you will still reinforce the delivery to hand, with food.)

In terms of making things easier or harder for the dog, there are two different variables to adjust, here: 1) What you are doing and 2) what the dummy thrower is doing.

Before we talk about the details, let's look at how we can dial these two variables up or down, to enable your dog to remain successful with this exercise. Imagine that we now have a dummy thrower out in front of us.

WHAT YOU ARE DOING – EASY TO HARD:

- Having the dog sitting static at your side and not walking forwards at all.
- Taking one step and then Stop When I Stop.

- Taking two steps and then Stop When I Stop.

- Taking multiple steps and then Stop When I Stop.

Remember that Stop When I Stop is easier the fewer steps you take before stopping (because it's more predictable and the dog is expecting the stop more).

To help your dog remain connected to you, occasionally snap out of serious heelwork into engagement breaks. It is hopefully starting to become obvious how all these skills we've been practising separately come together.

WHAT THE THROWER IS DOING – EASY TO HARD:

- Standing still and holding dummies, saying nothing.

- Swinging arms forwards and backwards holding dummies, saying nothing.

- Swinging arms forwards and backwards holding dummies, saying 'hey hey hey' (or whatever you usually call to get the dog's attention before a retrieve).

- Throwing quite a boring *small* throw, after saying 'hey hey hey'.

- Progressing up to throwing an exciting, *high* throw, after saying 'hey hey hey'.

- Using a bolting rabbit (a dummy on a piece of elastic, which imitates a rabbit bolting.) Bolting rabbits are extremely exciting for some dogs, and you are best starting with a good 50 yards between you and the rabbit. You also won't be able to send the dog for this one.

LET'S TALK ABOUT THIS EXERCISE IN MORE DETAIL:

- Remember that you want the dog to be successful (that is, gain a reinforcer) at least 85 per cent of the time.

- Start at the easiest level with both variables: The dog sitting at heel; the dummy thrower standing still and holding dummies. Progress through the handler's variables first, until you can walk for multiple steps towards the dummy thrower — doing Stop When I Stop. Then return to the dog static at heel, and move to the thrower swinging dummies. Progress again through the handler's variables, whilst the thrower swings dummies. Return to the dog static at heel, the thrower saying 'hey hey hey' and swinging dummies. Progress again through the handler's variables, whilst the thrower says 'hey hey hey' and swings dummies. And so on. Each time you increase a *thrower* variable, remain there until you can progress through all *handler* variables.

- For the steps where the thrower is not actually throwing retrieves (she is just standing there or swinging them about), of course the handler needs to give the dog a food reinforcer for maintaining heel. Being sent for the retrieve can't be part of the reinforcer, if we are not throwing retrieves yet!

- When retrieves start to be thrown, use sending the dog when steady at heel and marking well as part of the reinforcer. You should still give a food reinforcer when the dog delivers the retrieve to you. (The only times you will not give a food reinforcer for a retrieve is when you are under assessment.)

- If the dog starts to look at the handler excessively — because the handler is providing food reinforcers frequently — then you need to dial *up* what the thrower is doing and also send the dog for more retrieves. That means: If the thrower is waving the dummies about and saying 'hey hey hey', but the dog is looking at you because she's learnt that nothing good ever comes from the thrower — then the thrower should make more noise to attract the dog's attention, and start throwing the dummies. You should occasionally send the dog for a retrieve (provided the dog was looking at it fall). This should get the dog looking forwards next time. *The point isn't to teach the dog not to watch what's going on and just to ignore it and stare at you!* That would be counterproductive: We need the dog to mark and to remain locked-on to the fallen dummy. (To understand why this is important, be sure you have covered the material in Section 3.7, Marked retrieves, before this exercise.)

- On the other hand, if you send the dog for too *many* retrieves, the dog will start to anticipate being sent and you will lose your steadiness. So — once you start throwing retrieves, have the thrower pick most of them up and only send the dog for enough to keep the dog looking forwards. If you decide not to send the dog (because the dog was not steady), then wave at the thrower to pick up the dummy. When you do send the dog, remember that you are reinforcing what the dog was just doing. So make sure the dog is doing 'good' stuff you like(!): Meaning, that the dog is in a good heel position and showing self-control — *whilst also marking.*

- If you are walking forwards when a dummy is thrown, you should stop as soon as it goes up — doing Stop When I Stop. The dog should preferably go into an automatic sit-at-my-side — but should at least be steady and still in heel position and not stray forwards.

- Don't forget all the essentials on the subject of marking: Make sure you have read Section 3.7, Marked retrieves. Send whilst the dog is looking, not after the dog has looked away. Have a quiet 'leave' cue to tell the dog that a retrieve is not for her and she can look away now. (You will phase this out, but it's very useful for now.)

- On or off-lead? This exercise doesn't really work on a regular leash. When you need to send the dog for a retrieve, you then have to faff about taking the lead off. During this time, the dog looks away from the mark. If you then send the dog, you are reinforcing looking away. The faff of taking the lead off also becomes a big discriminatory cue for the dog, meaning 'you are about to be sent on a retrieve'. Then, when the lead is not taken off, it comes to mean 'you are not being sent'. All this is a bit counterproductive when you ultimately want the lead to be off always and the dog to rely on *your* cues to know if a retrieve is for her.

And, of course, we want to reinforce steadiness in this exercise and, if we are using sending the dog as part of the reinforcer, we don't want a big delay whilst we take the lead off.

Yet we also want some way of ensuring the dog doesn't run in. What to do? There are two options. One is to use a long-line, which can instantly be dropped on the floor when the dog is sent on a retrieve — yet can also be held shorter during the walk-up. The other is to use a training tab — a lead cut down to a short one-foot stub and clipped to the harness permanently. It's so short, it doesn't get in the way and can be left on whilst the dog runs the retrieve. Finally, you can also wave at the thrower to pick up the dummy if the dog isn't steady. (The thrower will need to ensure they can reach it before the dog.) These are all valid solutions, but don't fumble about with taking a regular lead off.

- Remember to throw in some engagement breaks once you start walking forwards — this will help to counter the suction the dummy thrower has for your dog.

3.5

FOCUS AND ENGAGEMENT

Many people struggle with getting their dog to respond to them when in outdoor environments — particularly environments with game scent present. Achieving focus outdoors can be especially problematic for the owners of 'questing' or hunting breeds (HPRs, spaniels, pointers, setters) — but can be a challenge for any gundog.

There is much you can do to avoid this problem by raising your gundog following the tenets outlined in this book. By far the biggest cause of a dog becoming excessively interested in the environment is too much free-running ('walking the dog'), *before* sufficient engagement with the handler has been established.

Your young dog's brain is learning what is reinforcing and is being shaped through these early experiences.

Focus and engagement are subjects which are not specific to gundog work — although gundog work is especially concerned with these subjects.

Do ensure that you have read the earlier Section 2.2, How to stop 'walking the dog!', before reading this section. If your difficulties with focus and engagement are more minor and occur during heelwork, take a look at the Go Sniff game and engagement breaks from Section 3.4, Heelwork.

THE AWOL DOG – A PROBLEM SCENARIO!

Frequently, on social media or internet forums, we see desperate owners of gundog breeds posting for advice. One common scenario is a dog which — in an outdoors environment — has zero interest in her handler, refuses food reinforcers, and just wants to hunt and run.

These owners want to know what they need to do to achieve some control and responsiveness outdoors.

We really have been covering this subject throughout this book. The answers are in these very pages — but they may not be immediately obvious to someone currently in this situation with a dog and needing a shortcut to advice. If you have a dog such as this, here are some tips:

- Read (and implement!) Section 2.1, Food motivation. Much as I am a fan of raw feeding, I would not recommend feeding raw (or wet cooked) food to a dog already struggling with food motivation. You need everything on your side — including food hierarchies — and you need to be training with all food that the dog gets, to increase her food motivation. If feeding raw is important to you, you could try feeding Ziwipeak — since it is an air-dried raw which you can still handle and train with. Or temporarily use a good quality kibble. Hopefully, once you've got things working in your favour, you can return to raw.

- AWOL dog problems are typically caused by allowing a dog to learn how reinforcing the environment is — by free-running or 'walking the dog' — before she has learnt to focus and work with you, outdoors. Consequently, you must think hard about how you can provide physical exercise.

  Getting the clicker retrieve working is a priority — since then you will be able to use retrieves outdoors to provide physical exercise. With retrieving, the dog is getting physical exercise, mental exercise, and a strengthened bond with you — *in an outdoor environment.* It is this combination of learning to work with you, outdoors, which will see you reap rewards — and, importantly, provides great physical exercise.

  Other ideas involve training your recall cues (verbal and whistle) with a long-line on and in one confined area, or even jogging or cycling with your dog on a leash to provide physical exercise in this way — whilst working hard to build the training up to the point where it can be taken outdoors, eventually replacing the jogging or cycling.

- Reduce criteria back down to the smallest of behaviours. If you want to work on your heelwork, but your dog won't even look at you — then forget about training heelwork. Instead, stand there with dog on leash and click any attention or focus your dog gives you — even accidentally. If you do that for five minutes, do you start to get better focus from your dog than you had to start with? Can you then move into some heelwork, just one step at a time?

  Perhaps you can do amazing clicker retrieves in the house — but in the field your dog can only *look* at the dummy at your feet, whilst being on-leash. That's fine — click and treat looking at the dummy, in the field. Have different criteria for more challenging environments. Your dog *will* be able to offer you more, if you keep building on this.

- Keep in mind the power of habituation. If you take a dog out to a distracting location and immediately try to do some training, you may get zero focus from her. Novelty has a huge part to play in this. On the other hand, you are much more likely to get focus from your dog if you hang out with her on-leash first — standing or sitting in one location — for five minutes. Don't ask for any behaviours or interact with your dog during this time. She is *habituating* to this new environment — so that it simply isn't so new anymore.

- When first taking the dog out to the field to train (on a long-line), don't use a vast and ever-changing terrain or a different location every day. Pick one field or location and work your training in that spot, daily. Return over and over, so that this one field becomes *familiar*. It's that habituation idea again, only this time it's occurring across days and weeks — instead of five minutes at the start of a session. Then add in another field or location. And a third. Rotate around these few locations, so now you have *some* degree of change and novelty — but only between these few familiar training locations. Expand these, gradually, to new locations. And soon you will be able to train anywhere you pitch up.

- Remember those human emotions we spoke about in Section 1.1? Reflect on your attitude and emotional response to the situation. Do you feel frustrated with your dog? Do you feel irritated or angry at the lack of focus your dog is giving you? These emotions (even if you try to hide them) are likely experienced by your dog — and only lead to more avoidance and less inclination to work with you. Do you believe it's impossible to train your particular dog to be well-controlled? This will only become a self-fulfilling prophecy, because you will label yourself a failure and give up without really trying. Do you believe that all this advice doesn't quite apply to *your* particular dog? ('*Yes, but...; no, but...*') — then you will not be able to learn. Do you want a well-trained dog but you're not really motivated, or finding it very reinforcing yourself, to achieve that? You, and your personality, have a part to play in your dog's progress (or lack of it) as well.

ATTENTION

Attention is a behaviour that is often overlooked as something that can be isolated and trained, in its own right. Too often, it is lumped into other behaviours and trained alongside these. This does not always lead to the best results. Moreover, a lack of attention (or focus) is behind most control issues.

There are some great resources available for isolating and training attention — including a DVD by Michelle Pouliot — *Performance Attention: Creating your Dream Team* — and a Puppy Culture DVD by Jane Killion — *Attention is the Mother of All Behaviours* — which can also be used with adult dogs. I strongly recommend you check these out.

UN-CUED ATTENTION

Attention can be cued or un-cued. That is, it can occur when we ask the dog for it — or the dog can *offer* attention to us, un-cued. Unlike most behaviours (which we don't particularly want the dog throwing at us, un-cued), attention is one behaviour which we love the dog to offer us, un-cued, in the vast majority of situations. Consequently, we should aim to reinforce it when it occurs. As Jane Killion's aptly titled DVD states: *Attention is the Mother of All Behaviours* — if the dog cannot give us any attention, then we cannot train the dog.

At its most basic level, training un-cued attention involves simply capturing it when it happens by clicking the moment the dog even briefly glances at you — and reinforcing.

We can then make this basic exercise easier or harder, by manipulating the distractions in the environment. Offering us attention in a dog training class is going to be harder than offering us attention in the house, for example. But we can also set up scenarios at home, through using food as a distraction, which the dog must look away from towards us. This way, we can practise *attention* around higher distractions — without going out to find them.

The more we reinforce the dog for paying attention to us, the more the dog will offer us that behaviour — even if we haven't cued it.

CUED ATTENTION

You might spot a distraction heading your way — such as another dog retrieving, or a horse passing by. You might decide to deal with this distraction by cuing your dog to focus on you, until the distraction has passed. (The other option, would be Look at That — the next exercise below.)

Cued attention is pretty simple to achieve:

We want the dog to learn that the pointed index finger is a cue to look at your face (see illustration 1). To achieve this, we initially hold a treat between middle finger and thumb, as shown.

You will soon find that you no longer need to hold the treat — the dog will give you focus when she sees the pointed index finger, in front of your face.

It doesn't matter what position the dog assumes for this exercise — but most dogs with a strong default sit, will assume the sit.

CUED ATTENTION

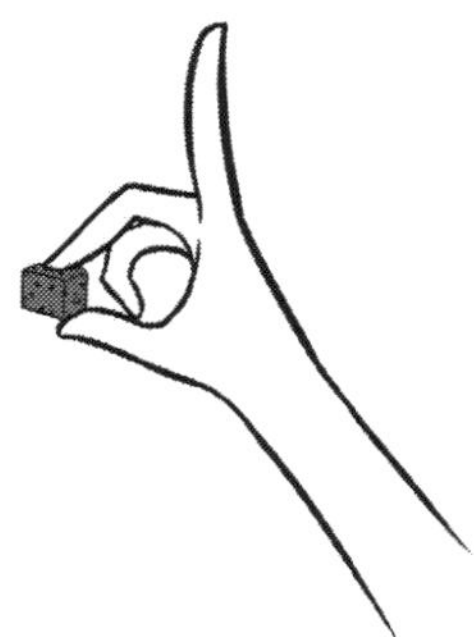

1 HOLD A TREAT BETWEEN YOUR THUMB AND MIDDLE FINGER. POINT YOUR INDEX FINGER UPWARDS. CURL YOUR OTHER FINGERS OUT OF THE WAY.

2 MAINTAINING THAT HAND POSITION WITH THE TREAT, LET THE DOG SNIFF IT. THEN HOLD YOUR HAND UP IN FRONT OF YOUR FACE. YOUR DOG WILL LOOK AT THE TREAT AND AT YOUR FACE.

3 CLICK WHEN THE DOG LOOKS AT THE TREAT. WHEN SHE CAN DO THE BASIC EXERCISE REPEATEDLY, YOU CAN DELAY THE CLICK SLIGHTLY TO WORK ON DURATION.

4 FEED THE DOG THE TREAT.

As you practise, delay the click and treat so that you get increasing duration on the behaviour up to three to five seconds. If your dog ever looks away before you have clicked, you waited too long on that rep and should click earlier next time and proceed more gradually.

LOOK AT THAT

'Look at That' is a key exercise for all dog owners and trainers. There isn't really a dog in existence which has never been distracted by anything, ever — and Look at That is *the* key exercise for working around distractions. (Remember that distractions, to us, are frequently environmental reinforcers to the dog — see Section 1.4, Generalisation and distraction management.)

Look at That is an exercise which has been around for a while and (confusingly!) has been given a few different names:

- the Engage-Disengage game (from an article by Alice Tong on the Karen Pryor website) (https://www.clickertraining.com/reducing-leash-reactivity-the-engage-disengage-game)
- BAT Stage 1 (in Grisha Stewart's original version of BAT it was known as Stage 1, whereas in BAT 2.0 it loses this specific name and is just part of Mark and Move)
- Look at That (from *Control Unleashed* material by Leslie McDevitt).

Whilst there are minor differences between these versions, they all involve the same core exercise. We'll go with 'Look at That', because it best describes what is happening. It's pretty simple, when it all goes well:

1. The dog looks at the distraction.
2. The handler clicks the split second the dog looks at the distraction.
3. The dog looks back at the handler, expecting a treat after the click.
4. The handler feeds a treat to the dog's mouth.

5. The dog looks back at the distraction.

6. The handler clicks, and so on... round and round.

The distraction can be something the dog is excited by (in a happy way), like another dog, people, livestock or game. Or it can be something the dog is scared of, or wary about — typically other dogs or people, but equally traffic, bicycles or skateboards. It is extremely effective when working with dog reactivity.

Look at That is most useful when the distraction is something animate. It isn't possible to play Look at That with scent, for example. So, if your dog gets distracted by scent and sniffing, Look at That isn't your game (but the Go Sniff game, in Section 3.4, would be).

For gundog work, the most useful applications are: Situations when there is a lot of game moving around on the ground — and the dog is not supposed to get it (i.e. when you're in a pen). The distraction could also be other dogs working in front of you, whilst your dog waits — at class or on a shoot.

'My dog doesn't look back at me when I click...'

If your dog doesn't look back when you click, don't click again! Put the treat on her nose and lure her just to turn her head away and disengage, then release the treat and let her eat it. She will likely look right back at the distraction again — be ready to click again.

If, again, she is unable to look away from the distraction when you click, it is likely that the dog is too close to the distraction to be able to disengage and turn back to you, by herself.

If this occurs, we would say that the dog is 'over-threshold'. This means she is too aroused to be able to focus on you, and work with you. The distraction has too much appeal or suction for the dog — we can say that she is not in her 'thinking brain'.

To reduce the appeal of the distraction, increase distance from it. Find a distance where the dog is able to disengage by herself at the click and keep working the exercise from that new distance. Over time, you will find that you can get closer — because there is an element of desensitisation involved in Look at That, which means your dog's emotional response to the distraction is also changing and so her thresholds will change accordingly.

'Aren't we just clicking the dog for doing what we don't want?'

Sometimes people don't understand why we are clicking the dog for looking at the distraction. This might seem to be reinforcing interest in the distraction.

There are a few important reasons why we want the dog to look at the distraction:

- We want the dog to become desensitised to the distraction, so that it loses some of its 'charge' and appeal for the dog. In order for the dog to become desensitised to the distraction, she must first be aware of it: It is not possible to desensitise a dog to something that she is ignoring! So, the dog must first *take in* the distraction, but at a distance or intensity which is manageable, for desensitisation to occur.

- In gundog work, what is sometimes a distraction (rabbit or bird running, dummies falling from the sky) is at other times a retrieve. Therefore, we really want a dog capable of looking at and *marking* these environmental reinforcers — yet remaining under control around them. It would not be much use for a gundog to learn to ignore all game! (As desirable as this might be in a pet dog!)

- We haven't really dealt with the underlying problem if we just teach a dog to ignore something they find it hard to be under control around. If we do that, we have papered over the cracks instead of fixing the problem at source. Whilst this is sometimes a valid solution (particularly when dealing with reactivity), it's not the ideal solution — especially with gundogs.

- With practice, your dog will become more interested in playing this game with you, than in the distraction itself. Distractions will become just an opportunity to play Look at That. So, not really distractions anymore!

'Should I use a cue for Look at That?'

Before we add in any cue, remember that we want to be sure we have the behaviour we like attached to it. If we say 'Look at That' and your dog lunges at a pheasant in a pen — because you misjudged the distance she needed — you are teaching your dog that 'Look at That' means: *'There's a really amazing thing out there which you should try to get!'* In fact, 'Look at That' is then well on the way to being a 'flush' cue!

As always: Be absolutely sure you have this behaviour functioning well without a cue, before you put one in.

With a cue, you can then cue your dog to expect a distraction *before she has even seen it herself*! For example: If you spot a rabbit eating grass ahead of you — which your own dog hasn't seen yet — you can say 'Look at That'. This tells your dog that something interesting is out there, at an earlier point — rather than being taken by surprise when she suddenly spots the rabbit, much closer than she can manage.

If you do add in a cue, be aware that your dog can still offer you this behaviour herself — un-cued — if she sees something distracting. It is not a behaviour which can *only* occur on cue. Think of 'Look at That' as a way your dog can communicate with you — the dog develops a way to let you know when she is distracted by something: You may be just walking along with your dog, and suddenly realise she is urgently looking at something and looking back at you — over and over. You look up and see she is telling you that she is distracted by a rabbit, running ahead. Then you play the Look at That game. This is one of the reasons we need the behaviour to be able to occur without a cue.

SOME EXAMPLES OF LOOK AT THAT IN ACTION

- During a drive, a dog is sitting at heel and resisting the temptation to run in, whilst watching other dogs working.

- In a rabbit pen, with dog at heel, looking at rabbits running about — trying to take some 'charge' out of how appealing they are.

- With a bolting rabbit, clicking as dog sees the rabbit 'bolt'. (A bolting rabbit is a dummy on a giant piece of elastic which simulates a rabbit running.)

Tip: It's important to teach Look at That around distractions which are less appealing to your dog before attempting them in scenarios such as those described above. If you go straight into distracting scenarios with this exercise, it won't work. You want the dog to realise: 'Ah, I know this exercise!'. Think of Look at That as a predictable framework for your dog, in times of stress (whether eustress or distress). Your dog can 'hold herself together' using this framework. But you need to build that framework, in advance, and import it into each scenario.

In training, use anything which is going to inspire your dog to look. Recruit other members of your household to provide distractions by:

- walking up and down at the other end of the room
- running up and down at the other end of the room
- making exciting noises whilst running up and down at the other end of the room
- bringing the distraction closer if it is no longer distracting
- bouncing a ball or squeaking a toy
- doing the funky chicken
- clicking your dog (on-leash, outside the house) for looking at other dogs/ people/bikes/skateboards/traffic/horses/livestock.

In all of these scenarios, you need distractions which are distracting enough that they cause the dog to look at them — but not so distracting that the dog can't re-focus (momentarily) back on you, at the click. If a particular distraction is too much, retreat further away to reduce the intensity of it.

Tip: It is important to have the dog on-leash when training this exercise, because otherwise you risk her learning to run to the distraction (the opposite of what we want!) if it is too distracting. Look ahead to what could go wrong and implement prevention to avoid this scenario — by using a leash. (See Section 1.2, Prevention.)

Tip: We are going to deliver the treats to the dog's mouth with Look at That — and not throw them around for the dog to get. The style and location of delivery influences training: If we throw treats for the dog to chase, we are arousing her further with that exciting chasing action — which makes calmness harder to achieve.

Tip: It doesn't matter if your dog is sitting or standing, as long as you deliver the treat to her mouth and she is relatively still and not lunging about. Focus on that, at first — and less on what position your dog is in.

Tip: If you continue using Look at That heavily and always, you may end up with a dog constantly looking at you and then away again — when she should be marking retrieves, for example. As with many things in gundog work, it's a balancing act: You need to maintain focus and interest in the distraction and not just build ever-increasing focus on your person.

CLOSE YOUR MOUTH

Signs of over-arousal in gundogs include panting, lack of focus on the owner, wide-eyed staring, and whining/squeaking. Over-arousal is closely associated with faults such as running in and noise-making. Training a dog to close her mouth, on cue, elicits an emotional state more typically associated with that closed mouth — which is a calmer emotional state. (Google 'the Superman pose' to see this idea in application to human psychology!)

'Close Your Mouth' is related to Leslie McDevitt's 'Take a Breath' behaviour — which can be found in her book *Control Unleashed: The Puppy Program.* Take a Breath involves marking and reinforcing the flaring of a dog's nostrils — which the dog then begins to do more consciously, resulting in deeper breathing and, consequently, relaxation.

The marker point for Close Your Mouth is, instead, the dog's mouth closing. Closing the mouth prevents panting and noise, whilst the (even partial) closing of a dog's mouth is a visually obvious behaviour for beginner handlers. A dog will visibly become calm and still when the mouth closes and you will witness your dog's supreme effort to get back into her operant and 'thinking brain' for a moment.

To achieve Close Your Mouth, we will merge a few different behaviours which should be familiar by now:

- cued attention (this section, above)
- Tempt the Dog sit-stay (Section 3.2)
- Close Your Mouth (the new bit!).

Assuming you have trained cued attention and Tempt the Dog sit-stay, you can move onto Close Your Mouth. Begin with cued attention for a couple of reps, as a warm-up. Then:

1. Get the dog to open her mouth (you can't close a mouth that is already closed!). The best way to achieve this is to do something which will cause your dog to pant lightly. An exercise like the 'elastic' recall would be ideal — since the dog will be chasing treats up and down.

2. Ensure you have a treat between middle finger and thumb — as with cued attention. Hold this treat about a foot from the dog's nose, and try to move it about very slightly and slowly. If your dog has done the Tempt the Dog sit-stay exercise, she should not attempt to get this treat (or, if she does, a quick reminder by snatching it away, should work). We are trying to get the dog into a state of focussed anticipatory stillness — think about the stillness of a point, or the still moment before you release a dog to get a reinforcer — the 'I'm about to get it' stillness. If you have trouble getting the dog to focus and anticipate, try higher value and/or smellier treats.

3. Observe your dog. When the dog becomes focussed in this anticipatory way, she will begin to close her mouth at least *slightly* and *momentarily* because she is preoccupied by the treat. (The focus on the treat is holding her together, at that moment.)

4. Click at the first sign of the mouth closing. Do not wait for the mouth to close fully, when you first begin this exercise.

5. As your dog becomes more fluent at this exercise, she will start to offer you a fully-closed mouth if you wait a little longer. You can quickly raise the criteria for a click, to a fully-closed mouth. You can begin to raise your hand slowly to your face as the dog's mouth closes - in the same way as the cued attention exercise. The dog will follow your hand up to your face with cued attention - and will now also close her mouth. Click!

6. Deliver the treat.

If your dog is prone to over-arousal, Close Your Mouth should now become merged with cued attention: Cued attention *requires* the dog to do Close Your Mouth, simultaneously. Not all dogs experience over-arousal and so not all will need to learn Close Your Mouth. For those that don't, maintain the previous cued attention alone — and forget about Close Your Mouth.

As your dog begins to understand this exercise, you can ask for Close Your Mouth whilst training other behaviours — any time you notice the mouth is open. You can also start to use this behaviour when you want to reduce your dog's arousal levels.

SNIFFING - OR THE 'FIND IT' CUE

Sniffing is clearly reinforcing for dogs. In fact, handlers often view sniffing as something they have to *fight against*, to retain their dog's focus. It's not necessary to view it in this way — take a look at the Go Sniff game in Section 3.4, for example.

We can use sniffing to reduce arousal levels, since it is a naturally stress-reducing and absorbing behaviour for the dog. It may be especially useful when you are waiting around for a drive to start on a shoot — or listening to an instructor

CLOSE YOUR MOUTH

1 BEGIN WITH A PANTING DOG. (DO SOME MORE PHYSICAL TRAINING TO ACHIWEVE THIS IF NECESSARY.) THE DOG SHOULD DO A DEFAULT SIT TO BEGIN AND YOU CAN REINFORCE THIS.

2 HOLDING A TREAT AS FOR CUED ATTENTION, SLOWLY MOVE IT RIGHT AND LEFT, ABOUT 1-2 FEET AWAY FROM THE DOG'S MOUTH.

3 AS YOU DO THIS, YOU SHOULD NOTICE THE DOG BECOMING MORE INTERESTED IN THE TREAT. HER AROUSAL LEVELS WILL BEGIN TO DECREASE AS THE TREAT ABSORBS HER FOCUS.

4 ALONG WITH REDUCED AROUSAL, THE DOG'S MOUTH WILL BEGIN TO CLOSE SLIGHTLY. AT FIRST, YOU WILL PROBABLY WANT TO CLICK THIS MOMENT – RATHER THAN WAITING FOR A FULLY CLOSED MOUTH.

5 WITH MORE PRACTICE, YOUR DOG WILL START TO OFFER A FULLY-CLOSED MOUTH – AND YOU CAN CLICK THIS.

6 FEED THE TREAT. BE READY FOR A NEW REP – IT MAY TAKE MULTIPLE REPS TO ACHIEVE A LASTING EFFECT ON YOUR DOG'S AROUSAL LEVELS.

talking to a class. It is great for preventing boredom or frustration in a waiting dog.

Simply cue 'find it' and then drop a treat on the floor in front of your dog. Whilst your dog is sniffing for that one, add another *behind her*. Keep adding them when she is not looking. Don't point them out for her! This will work best if you are on grass, since the grass will act as a real-life snuffle-mat for your dog.

3.6

THE CLICKER RETRIEVE

THE 'OTHER' TRAINED RETRIEVE

In North America, almost all working gundogs are put through a process called force-fetch. This is exactly what it sounds like: Forcing the dog to fetch.

There are a few variations on force-fetch, but the most commonly used version involves the trainer holding the dog's ear against their collar and digging the nail of their thumb into the cartilage of the dog's ear. When the dog opens her mouth to yelp, the trainer shoves the dummy in and simultaneously releases the pressure on the ear. The dog comes to learn: 'The quicker I get the dummy in my mouth, the quicker the pain stops.' The dog becomes very keen to get the object in her mouth, to turn off the pain. (This is negative reinforcement.) Usually, force-fetch is moved across to e-collar stimulation once it has been taught — so a dog can be 'forced' from a distance if she doesn't take a cast.

In most of Europe, force-fetch is not used — not even amongst traditional trainers.

I agree that the retrieve needs to be formalised for best results. And I agree that a trained retrieve is more reliable than a 'natural' retrieve - no matter how good that natural retrieve is.

I disagree that the method used to train a retrieve needs to involve causing a dog physical pain to achieve reliability. Because we have achieved reliability when it comes to training dogs to detect cancer, identify bombs, locate missing people, and predict seizures — without using any force. If the use of force and the achievement of reliability were correlated, we could expect all dogs working in ways that human lives depended on them to be trained using force. And the opposite is true.

CLICKER RETRIEVES – IN THE PLURAL?

The version of the clicker retrieve which I present here draws heavily from a version I learnt from the brilliant Anne Bussey about 15 years ago. Having largely worked with gundogs on the clicker retrieve since then, I've made changes specific to gundogs and added in some steps whilst removing a couple of others.

Which leads us onto the next point: It's important to keep in mind that there is not *one* 'clicker retrieve', since there are many different versions of the clicker retrieve available. The process can be adjusted in different directions, to suit different dogs — with more splitting of behaviours required for some dogs than others. People often say they did *the* clicker retrieve, as if everyone understands this to mean the same thing. But, for meaningful dialogue, it's important to dig a bit deeper and find out exactly what they did — with a clicker — to train their retrieve.

Whichever version has been used, a clicker retrieve is always more than just using a clicker at the end of the retrieve. Because the clicker retrieve involves breaking the behaviour down into a sequence of component parts — and training the parts separately — before building the sequence back up again.

'What do we mean by a sequence?'

A retrieve is not just one behaviour ('go and get something'), but a collection of behaviours: The go-out, the pick-up, the bring-back, and the delivery to hand. There may also be a sit and a wait, at the start.

At any stage in this, things can go wrong: The dog breaks the sit and runs in. Or the dog is uninterested in the retrieve and refuses to pick it up. Or the dog picks it up but then runs off with it and won't bring it back. Or the dog picks it up but then gets distracted by something and drops it — or even brings it back but dumps it on the floor instead of delivering it to hand. And there are probably many more ways things can go wrong!

To achieve a reliable retrieve, we need to isolate and train these component parts — before putting them together. We are not just going to try to mould them in some homogenous whole from the start.

'How old does a dog need to be to start the clicker retrieve?'

By the time a puppy is through the socialisation period, has mostly finished teething, has learnt clicker basics on a good puppy course, is toilet-trained and crate-trained and alone-trained and sleeping through the night — by the time your life is just about returning to normal — *that* is a good time to start. So, around the age of five to six months.

'Can I train an older dog?'

Of course, a dog of any age can be trained using the clicker retrieve. However, be aware that, the older the dog, the more time the dog has had to develop unwanted habits. Any time a dog has something in her mouth and she is relating to you, with it, habits are being formed. Whether you are taking your underwear off her which she has picked up or whether you are throwing balls she has dropped at your feet — if she is relating to you, and there is an object involved, it's likely that her feelings about retrieving are being shaped by your interaction with her — for better or for worse.

For example: Puppies commonly pick up everything — shoes and food wrappers and gravel and everything else besides. Owners are constantly removing things from the pup's mouth. And so the pup learns to dodge and run away from human hands, because they are coming to take the valuable stuff off the pup. And then you have more work to do, with your clicker retrieve. Because your pup has developed a desire to keep away from you — a 'keep-away' problem.

With an older dog, you are starting with even less of a clean slate. That dog will already have an attitude towards retrieving, for you to work with. (Good or bad.) Many dogs have learnt to spit out retrieves at the owner's feet, and the owner has often reinforced that by picking up the object and throwing it again.

So it is good to start young and before bad habits have had much time to set in, where possible. Around six months is also, by the way, the same age that US trainers recommend starting force-fetch. Presumably for the same reasons.

BEFORE THE CLICKER RETRIEVE: PRELIMINARY WORK FOR DEVELOPING GOOD MOUTH HABITS

There is quite a bit of time elapsing in a puppy's life between eight weeks and six months. During that time, the puppy is going to be... a puppy! That means she is going to pick things up which you don't want her to have. The way we respond to the puppy-with-an-item-in-her-mouth situation can have huge effects on the puppy's attitude towards retrieving — and working with you.

'Keep-away' refers to a dog's desire to, well, keep away from her handler, with the retrieve. Often these dogs want the handler to chase them, to get the item back — and they think this is a fantastic game. They may dodge around the handler at a distance, tempting the handler. They may want to flaunt the item and show it off.

To avoid enflaming keep-away issues, always try to resist the urge to remove whatever the item is from a pup's mouth by physically opening the mouth and taking it off her. Instead, have a pot of treats in your pocket and waft a treat in the air in front of the pup's nose when she picks something up. You can say 'drop' once, at the same time.

The pup will drop to get the treat. This is the important bit: Don't *instantly* give the dog the treat, just lure the pup away from the dropped object so it ends up behind her.

When you've lured the pup so her rear is towards the object, feed the pup the treat with one hand whilst simultaneously picking up the object behind her with the other hand. Why? Because, if the pup doesn't see you pick it up and doesn't witness you *in the act of reclaiming possession of it*, this will not trigger her resource guarding or keep-away tendencies — even if she then turns around and sees you actually holding it. It is the 'taking possession' which you don't want her to see. (Don't ask me why this is, as I have no idea. It just 'is'.)

DROP — Developing good mouth habits

1 WHEN THE DOG PICKS UP SOMETHING YOU DON'T WANT HER TO HAVE, GET A TASTY TREAT. WAVE THIS IN THE AIR ABOUT A FOOT IN FRONT OF HER NOSE, TRYING TO ATTRACT HER ATTENTION. YOU CAN SAY THE WORD 'DROP' ONCE, BEFORE PUTTING THE FOOD ON THE DOG'S NOSE.

2 THE DOG WILL DROP THE ITEM, BECAUSE SHE WANTS THE TREAT.

3 DO NOT ATTEMPT TO PICK UP THE ITEM YET. THROW THE TREAT AWAY FROM THE DROPPED ITEM. THE DOG WILL CHASE AFTER IT.

4 WHILST THE DOG'S BACK IS TURNED, RUNNING TOWARDS OR EATING THE TREAT, PICK UP THE ITEM.

5 THE DOG WILL TURN AROUND AND SEE YOU HOLDING THE ITEM. THIS IS FINE AND WILL NOT TRIGGER BIG POSSESSIVE FEELINGS IN THE DOG. (WHAT WILL DO THAT, IS SEEING YOU ACTUALLY PICK IT UP.)

If your dog doesn't deliver to hand, don't throw things repeatedly for her — allowing the dog to drop the retrieve on the floor before you pick it up each time. If you re-throw a dropped item, you are reinforcing the dropped delivery.

If your dog runs off with an object, don't chase her for it back. Go and get some really tasty treats and do the above drop protocol.

It is rare to start with a completely blank slate — but some slates are blanker than others!

'Tell me more about 'shaping' the clicker retrieve?'

Shaping is pretty treat-intensive. So you will be relieved to hear that all this initial training should be done at home, indoors, using your dog's kibble — or try Ziwipeak, if you feed raw.

With shaping, we are going to reinforce the dog for behaviours which *gradually* approach the end result we want.

The following general principles apply, regarding our own role in the process — but there are always exceptions to these:

- ***Don't ask for behaviours verbally.*** Don't give cues. Don't talk to the dog. Don't give verbal encouragement. Remain silent. People often jabber away at their dogs, thinking they are helping — when really the dog experiences this as pressure to *get it right*. And there is no faster thing to turn a dog off whatever you're doing together than putting pressure on her *when she doesn't know what she's supposed to do yet*. Besides, if you're doing this right, you (as handler) should be totally absorbed in observing your dog's smallest move in the direction of what you want. You shouldn't have a brain cell available to talk to your dog at the same time.

- ***Don't use body language.*** Don't point at things (pushing dummies with feet or otherwise physically encouraging the dog to do something). We might think this is *encouragement*, but — again — many dogs experience it as pressure to *get it right*. Occasionally, if you get stuck and you need to 'animate' the object for a few reps — by waggling it about and teasing the dog with it, before dropping it on the floor — you can. But don't get dependent on doing this every time. If you always need to animate the object, you have built that in as part of the cue for the dog to pick up: You animate the object and that communicates to the dog that you'd like it picked up.

Our main forms of communication with the dog are going to be 'I like that' = click. Or 'That's not in the right direction' = no click.

THE DOUBLE-EDGED SWORD OF FRUSTRATION

When I'm teaching the clicker retrieve, I tell (human) students to imagine that I have already trained them to touch their nose with their finger in order to earn a click and a reinforcer of a chocolate. And that we're going to practise this behaviour.

So, off we go: They touch their nose and I click. They touch their nose and I click. This continues for about eight nose-touches. It's all very predictable. Then I stop clicking. This is the pivotal moment: The person touches their nose and they don't get a click. What happens next, depends on the person. Some people touch their nose with two fingers. Some people touch their head. Some people stand up and touch their nose. And so on. People can be very creative. It can all go on for a long while.

Eventually, though — when nothing they try gets me to click again — they give up. (The behaviour of nose-touching is extinguished.) Everyone reaches the giving-up point sooner or later. Some people reach it sooner than others: Some people try just one thing, then give up. Other people try all kinds of things, for five minutes or more without reinforcement — and then give up.

Your dog, too, is an individual. When you withhold the click to move things on to the next criteria, your dog may try just one more thing — and then give up if there's no click. Giving up, for a dog, will look like sniffing around the room, chewing the dummy, or refusing to engage. When these types of behaviour occur indoors, this is not your dog getting *distracted* — this is your dog giving up. Alternatively, if you're lucky, your dog may keep trying all kinds of things for a while. It's most likely that your dog will fall somewhere between these two extremes.

Which dog is easier to train? The dog which tries one thing and gives up — or the dog which tries many different things, before giving up? The dog which keeps trying, of course. It is much more likely that the dog which perseveres in the face of failure and comes up with creative ideas is going to hit on something along the lines of what we're looking for. Then we can click that and establish it as the new criteria. A dog which gives up after just one 'failure', leaves us with nothing to work with — no behaviour to shape. Then we need to drop the criteria back to something easy, like the dog looking at the dummy. We need to reduce the criteria, to get the dog playing the training game again. We can progress with this type of dog — it will just take longer and require more of us, as trainers.

But, whilst dogs have different thresholds for feeling 'unsuccessful', if any dog doesn't get enough clicks — for that particular dog — she will give up. Dogs (like people) don't like to attempt to earn reinforcers and to fail. Being denied something you want is punishing.

So, what we are asking for, to earn a click, has to be easy enough for the dog to get it right *most* of the time. That is why we begin with a look at the dummy — and not a pick-up.

When a dog is getting something right many times in a row, we can say that the behaviour is *fluent*. This means that there is no delay between reps of the correct behaviour: The dog looks at the dummy, gets a click and treat — and *immediately* looks again. She doesn't try another behaviour or freeze, in thought. Before we raise the criteria and move on, we want to be sure that the current behaviour is fluent in this way.

Once the dog is fluently doing the behaviour, if you now withhold the click, she will become frustrated. '*Why is it not working any longer?*', the dog thinks. *Out of that frustration*, hopefully an exaggerated version of the behaviour will be born — something which is further in the direction of what we want. *This* then becomes our new criteria. (Just like the people who began touching their nose in creative ways when I stopped clicking them — they were also *exaggerating* the behaviour which was no longer working.) If a dog is touching the dummy fluently — and we withhold the click when she next touches it — she will become frustrated and may touch the dummy with more force. We can then click this firmer nose-touch, which shows even more intent towards the dummy and is more likely to evolve into an open-mouth and a pick-up.

So you can see that *frustration is a necessary part of the learning process — but it must be optimal frustration.* If you don't frustrate the dog at all — and keep clicking and treating just a look at the dummy — you will never get anything more than this. On the other hand, if the frustration is too much, the dog will give up. For each dog, we need to find and work in the sweet-spot, between these two.

Finally, a word about greed. Greed on your part, that is — not on the dog's part. As trainers, we always want to see progress. We have a tendency to withhold reinforcement because we want to see ever better results — higher jumps, longer blind retrieves, more duration on stays — and a full-pick up, instead of a nose-touch, for example. The problem with being a greedy trainer, is that the dog can only offer you more/longer/better if she *fully understands every step in the process to that point and is motivated by your reinforcers.* Otherwise, when you increase criteria — she will just give up. Many times, in class, I've seen dogs offer a really good nose-touch on the dummy — which handlers don't click. Because the dog can (at home) do a pick-up. When the dog doesn't get clicked for the nose-touch, instead of moving on to offer a pick-up — she gives up. The nose-touch isn't reliable enough yet to build on — or perhaps isn't reliable in a class environment, rather than at home.

So — don't be a greedy trainer! Remember: The wise man built his house on a rock. In dog training, a rock is a solid foundation, which a dog fully understands. The foolish man built his house on the sand. Sand is a foundation which will give way under any pressure and doesn't work to support further learning.

If this general overview doesn't make sense yet, don't worry. We're going to look at the clicker retrieve in more detail, next.

SETTING UP FOR A CLICKER RETRIEVE SESSION

I teach the clicker retrieve over a six-week course. I also have a five-week online course, which is taken by handlers all over the world. (Please do contact me if you'd like to enrol.) So I've seen a lot of different handlers and dogs going through the clicker retrieve process and I've seen the 'corners' of it which people find difficult.

All the details matter. There is no advice here which is optional (unless specified). You can't just 'do your own' version of these instructions and get the same results. I say this because I've had handlers come to class and say: '*Oh, I just decided to do X instead of Y, because I was having this problem.*' Often these changes only create more problems. Just like following a recipe in the kitchen, you won't get the same results if you substitute your own ingredients!

- When setting up for a clicker retrieve session, put the dummy on the floor only when you are ready to start and pick it up again when you are finished.

Do not leave it lying around for your dog to continue to interact with after the session.

- Do no other retrieving with your dog during the clicker retrieve process. Do not throw anything for her to fetch in a 'casual' way, otherwise you could be allowing all kinds of bad habits to continue to be reinforced — such as dropping balls at your feet, for example — whilst simultaneously trying to fix these issues with the clicker retrieve. This approach is unlikely to be successful.

- You are going to train the clicker retrieve indoors, and you need to be able to throw treats in different directions around the dummy (which will be at your feet). Try to have a good amount of space around you. Be aware of any furniture which may be crowding your area, reducing the directions you can throw treats.

- Think about the flooring in your training area: If your house has slippery floors, your dog is not going to be able to run enthusiastically at full speed for treats, without sliding about. You may lose some drive in the retrieve if your dog curbs her enthusiasm due to slippery floors. Can you put down runners or rugs — or vet bed with rubber backing — to give you a flooring with a secure purchase?

- Initially, you will be sitting in a chair. This will enable you to have a better vantage point on your dog's interactions with the dummy on the floor — you can lean over sideways if you need a better close-up view of things.

PHASE 1: LOOKING AT AND/OR APPROACHING THE DUMMY

1. Sit in a chair with your clicker and dummy in your hands and treats ready in a bowl on your lap. Sniff the dummy (yes, you, the handler!) — you can even pretend to eat it. Marvel at it, this amazing thing, and make sure the dog sees you enjoying it.

2. Place the dummy on the floor at your feet and fall silent. When you do this, be ready to click — the dog is going to look at it almost *as* you put it down.

3. Click the dog for looking at the dummy. Click *early*, when your dog is still at the stage of looking at, or moving towards, the dummy. Try not to click late, when the dog has already made contact with the dummy.

4. When you click, the dog should break off whatever she is doing — the click means 'behaviour over' — so the dog should now stop the behaviour of interacting with the dummy and look to you, for a treat. (Which you will throw — see Step 5.)

   Achieving this 'break-off-at-the-click' is an important goal for Phase 1. Some dogs might not break off when you click but instead continue right on and pick up the dummy — ignoring the click. If your dog does this, just put the treat right on her nose and she will drop the dummy. Once she has dropped it, continue with Step 5.

   Do not attempt to take the dummy from her, if she has picked it up. This only enflames keep-away issues.

   As you continue with this behavioural loop, you'll find that the dog starts to drop on the click. (Because she has learnt that you are about to put food on her nose.) The dogs which will need the most help to break-off at the click, will be enthusiastic dogs that immediately want to pick up the dummy — or dogs with keep-away issues. If you are having trouble achieving the break-off at the click, increase the tastiness of the treats — this will help 'sticky' dogs.

5. Throw the treat. We want to help the dog learn to approach the dummy from different directions and angles, so throw the treat to different positions around you each time you click and treat. The dog will eat the treat and then re-approach the dummy from a slightly new direction.

At the end of the session, you'll need to pick up the dummy somehow. *It is extremely important at this stage that the dog doesn't see you pick it up.* Seeing you pick up the dummy can trigger keep-away issues in many dogs, because the dog sees that you want possession of the dummy and are therefore a threat to *her* possession of it! So, to end a session, simply throw a treat a good distance from the dummy and pick it up quickly whilst the dog's back is turned, eating the treat. When the dog turns around, she just sees you holding the dummy. That's fine. That doesn't trigger keep-away or possessiveness — it's seeing you *take possession* which does.

NEVER TAKE THE ITEM FROM THE DOG. IT MAY BE TEMPTING, ESPECIALLY IF YOUR DOG SKIPS TO A PICK-UP. BUT DOGS OFTEN HAVE KEEP-AWAY TENDENCIES WHICH WILL BE MADE WORSE IF YOU TAKE THE DUMMY DIRECTLY FROM THE DOG.

PHASE 1 — Approaching the dummy

1 SITTING IN A CHAIR WITH TREATS AND CLICKER READY, SNIFF AND SHOW INTEREST IN THE DUMMY.

2 PLACE (DON'T THROW) THE DUMMY ON THE FLOOR AT YOUR FEET.

3 CLICK IF THE DOG LOOKS AT THE DUMMY OR APPROACHES THE DUMMY.

4 AT THE SOUND OF THE CLICK, THE DOG SHOULD BREAK OFF FROM APPROACHING THE DUMMY AND LOOK TO YOU FOR THE EXPECTED TREAT.

5 THROW THE TREAT A FEW METRES AWAY FROM THE DUMMY ON THE FLOOR. (EACH REP, THROW THE TREAT IN A DIFFERENT DIRECTION SO THE DOG GENERALISES ANGLES OF APPROACH.)

WATCH OUT!

1 A COMMON DIFFICULTY ARISES WHEN THE DOG DOESN'T BREAK OFF THE APPROACH, AT THE CLICK. THE DOG IGNORES THE CLICK.

2 HAVING IGNORED THE CLICK, THE DOG MAY EVEN PICK UP THE DUMMY.

3 IF THIS HAPPENS, SHOW THE DOG A TREAT – PUT IT RIGHT ON THE DOG'S NOSE. YOU MAY NEED TO USE HIGHER-VALUE TREATS FOR SOME DOGS WITH THIS ISSUE.

4 THE DOG WILL DROP THE DUMMY BECAUSE SHE WANTS THE TREAT.

5 WHEN THE DOG HAS DROPPED THE DUMMY, THROW THE TREAT AWAY FROM THE DUMMY ON THE FLOOR – AS USUAL.

HOW TO END A CLICKER RETRIEVE SESSION (all phases)

1 CLICK THE INTERACTION WITH THE DUMMY WHICH YOU WANT TO MARK..

2 THROW THE TREAT A GOOD DISTANCE FROM THE DUMMY FOR THE DOG TO CHASE.

3 WHILST THE DOG'S BACK IS TURNED, EATING THE TREAT OR RUNNING AFTER IT – PICK UP THE DUMMY. THE DOG SHOULD NOT SEE YOU.

4 THE DOG WILL TURN AROUND AND SEE YOU HOLDING THE DUMMY. THIS IS FINE AND WILL NOT TRIGGER OR ENFLAME 'KEEP-AWAY' OR POSSESSIVE FEELINGS IN THE DOG.

DO NOT PICK UP THE DUMMY IF THE DOG CAN SEE YOU TAKING POSSESSION OF IT. THIS WILL ENFLAME 'KEEP-AWAY' TENDENCIES. IF THE DOG IS TOO FAST FOR YOU, THROW ANOTHER FREEBIE TREAT OUT TO RE-DISTRACT AND TRY AGAIN.

OBJECTIVES:

- A dog that understands that if she looks at, or heads towards, the dummy, she gets clicked.
- A dog that breaks off the behaviour on hearing the click, and expects the treat.

EXTRA HELP:

People often want to progress too fast. They want to skip to clicking pick-ups straight away, because they think their dog can do these. Remember: The wise man built his house upon the rock, not the sand. Solid foundations will support later learning. Skipping ahead will give you a false illusion of progress — but the behaviour may fall apart, later on.

Make sure you are progressing only after the behaviour is secure, with multiple fluent reps — not just happening once or twice. Fluency means the dog is not hesitating between reps, sniffing around, or getting distracted. We want to see the dog eating the treat and then turning and making a beeline for the dummy immediately — because she knows heading for the dummy is the secret to getting another click.

Your click should be almost preventing the dog from making contact, because the dog keeps breaking off when she hears it. If your dog is not able to break-off at the click, you are not ready to move on from Phase 1 — even if your dog is continuing through the click to offer you (say) pick-ups. The dog *must* understand that the click ends the behaviour, and teaching this is part of our goal for Phase 1.

The stages we are looking at, in Phase 1, are:

- looking at the dummy
- heading towards the dummy.

And no further!

These steps may happen concurrently, especially if you have a fast and enthusiastic dog. That's fine. You just need to click at the earliest point of your dog's engagement with the dummy — and work on teaching the dog how to break off that engagement, on hearing the click (as per the instructions above).

PHASE 2: AT LEAST A TOUCH

After Phase 1, your dog should be targeting the dummy with drive — repeatedly. She should be eating each treat you throw, then turning and making a beeline for that dummy — understanding that targeting this dummy is what is making you click. Until now you have been clicking early, whilst the dog is looking at or heading for the dummy. And you have managed to teach the dog to break off at the click, to get the treat you throw.

1. Repeat as in Phase 1, placing the dummy at your feet.
2. *Delay the click.* When the dog is heading for the dummy, delay the click and see what happens when she reaches it. Some dogs might just touch it with their nose whereas some might pick it up straight away. Either is fine.
3. Click the contact with the dummy. From now on, 'at least a touch' is the new criteria. At least a touch means that if the dog picks it up, you will click, and if the dog returns to touching it on the next rep, you will still click. Everything from a touch upwards earns a click. Until this is fluent.

Do not click pawing at the dummy. Pawing the dummy will never lead to a pick-up. But watch closely: If the dog paws, and then moves her face down to investigate — click!

4. The dog should break off from the dummy and look at you at the click.

5. Deliver the treat by throwing away from the dummy. Continue until your dog can do multiple fluent reps in a row.

TOO LATE

IF THE DOG PAWS, WAIT FOR ANY FACE, MOUTH OR HEAD ORIENTATION TOWARDS THE DUMMY AND CLICK THAT. TIMING IS IMPORTANT, HERE.

Be aware that a dog can touch the dummy with different parts of her muzzle. Some dogs may 'nose' the dummy with the top of their nose — the same movement used to bury a bone or to roll something on the floor. Nosing the dummy with the top of the nose will not later lead to a pick-up. Click only front-of-muzzle touches.

Stay at this until your dog can do multiple fluent reps in a row, of 'at least a touch'.

OBJECTIVE:

- A dog that will at least touch the dummy, every single time. Sometimes she may offer more than a touch.

EXTRA HELP:

Remember to adjust to your individual dog. If your dog fails to earn a click a couple of times in a row, reduce your criteria back to just looking at the dummy.

PHASE 2 — At least a touch

1 PLACE THE DUMMY ON THE FLOOR AT YOUR FEET, AS BEFORE.

2 DO NOT CLICK THE DOG'S APPROACH, BUT WAIT TO SEE WHAT THE DOG WILL OFFER NEXT.

3 CLICK WHEN THE DOG PUTS HER NOSE DOWN TO SNIFF THE DUMMY.

4 THE DOG SHOULD BREAK OFF FROM THE DUMMY AND LOOK TO YOU AT THE CLICK. (IF SHE DOESN'T, DO AS PREVIOUSLY COVERED IN PHASE 1).

5 THROW THE TREAT AWAY FROM THE DUMMY ON THE GROUND.

Return to clicking that for a bit, before you withhold the click again, hoping for a touch. We need to keep the dog feeling successful.

Remember not to let the dog see you pick up the dummy, ever!

Remember never to try to take the dummy out of her mouth!

NEVER TAKE THE ITEM FROM THE DOG

PHASE 3: PICK-UPS

Within the clicker retrieve process, there are certain hurdles to overcome; tricky corners to be negotiated. A pick-up is the first hurdle in the process. If you find this step difficult, do not despair — this is very normal.

A reliable pick-up is the foundation of a good retrieve. Do not rush through this stage. Raising the criteria too fast — and before the dog thoroughly understands, rep after rep, and is fluent at picking up the object — is a major reason why the clicker retrieve can fall apart later.

1. Placing the dummy on the floor as before, warm the dog up with five fluent reps of the nose-touch behaviour — as in Phase 2 — to help her feel successful.

2. The dog will head to the dummy — but *don't* click when she next touches it. Be sure you are leaning over to one side so you have a good view of the dog's mouth and the dummy to know exactly what she is doing and what you are clicking. See what the dog offers you when you don't click the usual nose-touch.

3. Click if your dog picks up the dummy.

4. Ensure the dog drops the dummy immediately when you click the pick-up, as the click ends the behaviour. If she doesn't drop the dummy, put the treat on the dog's nose so she drops for the treat.

5. Throw the treat away from the dummy, as before.

If you don't get a pick-up, what *are* you getting? The dog may just touch the dummy harder — because she is frustrated that the previous touch didn't earn a click. Click that harder touch! We like insistence and intent — it tends to lead to pick-ups. Alternatively, the dog's mouth may open slightly on the dummy whilst it lies on the floor — click this! Don't be greedy and think 'maybe I'll get a whole pick-up' and hold out for that; click just that open mouth or harder touch. Why? Because, if you wait for a full-pick up, the dog might not offer you one. Meanwhile, you've also lost the opportunity to click the open mouth or harder touch.

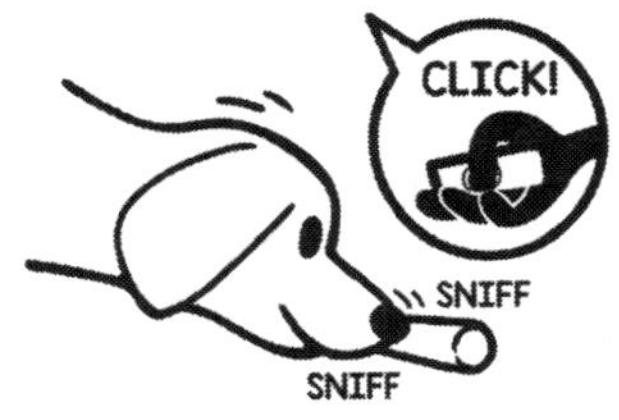

So, whatever the dog offers you — *if it lies on the continuum which is closer to a pick-up* — click it and try to make that the new criteria. That means you stop clicking everything 'less' than that. (Unless the dog struggles to repeat the new criteria and starts to feel a failure — in which case, go back to clicking a nose-touch again for a

PHASE 3 — Pick-ups

1 AS BEFORE, PLACE THE DUMMY ON THE FLOOR AT YOUR FEET.

2 THE DOG HEADS TOWARDS THE DUMMY.

3 AS SOON AS THE DOG'S MOUTH CLOSES AROUND THE DUMMY AND THERE IS AIR BENEATH THE DUMMY, CLICK. DO NOT WAIT FOR THE DOG'S HEAD TO RISE FULLY – SINCE THAT IS A RISKY MOMENT FOR A DROP. CLICK PICK-UPS EARLY SO YOU ARE CLICKING THE DECISION AND THE ACTION – NOT THE RESULT.

4 WHEN THE DOG HEARS THE CLICK, SHE SHOULD DROP THE DUMMY IN EXPECTATION OF THE TREAT. (YES, REALLY!) THE CLICK ENDS THE BEHAVIOUR.

5 THROW THE TREAT FOR THE DOG AS USUAL.

while — or even just a look at the dummy.) Note that not everything a dog does to the dummy is getting closer to a pick-up. If she nudges it with the top of her nose, or pounces or paws it — that is not going to lead to a pick-up. So, as in the later stages of Phase 2, try not to click these other types of contact. This is where the art of shaping comes in: You need to look at what your individual dog is offering you, and identify which interactions with the dummy are *slightly* more towards a pick-up than others. And click those — until you do start to get pick-ups.

The dog is now picking up the dummy and you're clicking that pick-up. *Do not be late with your click.* The marker-point is the *lifting up of the dummy from the floor*, the rising of the dog's head with the dummy. Not the dog standing there, holding it, looking at you. Why? Because dogs rarely drop the dummy whilst lifting it up. Dogs very, very frequently drop it once they have lifted it — since they are unlikely to stand there, holding it! So, one major mistake people make is clicking late — and *accidentally clicking the drop*. If this starts to happen often, you can end up with some quite weird behaviours: Like a dog which picks up the dummy and *throws* it immediately. (The only reason she is picking it up is to drop or throw it — because you've taught her, by clicking late, that letting go is what is earning the click.) So, be conservative on these early pick-ups and click the rising up of the dog's head from the floor whilst holding the dummy. Think about clicking the *intention* to pick-up — and not the end result of a completed pick-up.

HERE THE HANDLER HAS WAITED TOO LATE TO CLICK AND THE DOG'S HEAD IS FULLY UP WITH THE DUMMY. THE DOG IS LIKELY TO DROP WITH LITTLE WARNING, FROM THIS POSITION. THE HANDLER IS THEREFORE LIKELY TO CLICK DROPS ACCIDENTALLY.

If you're having to put the treat on the dog's nose in order for her to drop the dummy — and then throwing the treat away for her to eat — keep repeating this and she will begin to drop at the click. It might seem very counterintuitive and hard to get your head around that we want the dog to drop the dummy on the floor at the click — but we do! Remember that the click marks the end of the sequence for that rep. We only care about what happens up until the click. After the click, we want the dog to drop.

Keep repeating, rep after rep, once you start to get pick-ups — aim for about three minutes of fluent pick-ups per session. Pick-ups are one phase you can't get stuck at, or do for too long. You will only consolidate them further and lead to a real determination to *pick that thing up*!

Use a different dummy — or even other objects — if pick-ups start to get really fluent with the particular dummy you are using. (Anything the dog can safely pick up can become a pick-up item.) You may need to return to Phase 1 with a new object or dummy — but you should be able to progress through to this stage much more quickly than the first time. The reason to use other dummies and objects is to help *generalise* the retrieve. A gundog has to retrieve many different sizes and types of dummy, as well as game of all descriptions. To help her transfer these newly learnt skills to other items, generalise your pick-ups to other items, *now*. You don't need to use game or even dummies, you can use anything your dog can safely pick up. Like a plastic laundry detergent dispenser. Or half a clothes peg. Or a large metal bolt. Or your car keys. Your dog should learn that anything you put on the floor at your feet, in this game, is a pick-up item.

If you have a gundog which naturally likes to put the nearest available object in her mouth, then the pick-up stage might be relatively easy for you. If this is the case, you should still remain on it until it is deeply conditioned — preferably with several different dummies and objects. With these dogs, the focus is on achieving the drop at the click (and thereby reducing or eliminating keep-away).

WHAT TO DO IF THE DOG DOESN'T DROP AT THE CLICK?

1 THE DOG PICKS UP AND THE HANDLER CLICKS.

2 THE DOG DOESN'T DROP AT THE CLICK.

3 THE HANDLER SHOWS THE DOG A TREAT, WAFTING IT A FOOT IN FRONT OF HER NOSE.

4 THE DOG DROPS BECAUSE SHE WANTS THE TREAT.

5 THE HANDLER THROWS THE TREAT AWAY FROM THE DROPPED DUMMY. IF YOU REPEAT THIS SEQUENCE, THE DOG WILL START TO DROP AT THE CLICK.

OBJECTIVE:

- A dog that will pick up the object cleanly and clearly from the ground.

EXTRA HELP:

Sometimes people really do get quite stuck at the pick-up hurdle. This is usually because they have not broken down the pick-up sufficiently, and that particular dog is just not going to skip from a nose-touch straight to a pick-up. (The handler is not splitting the behaviour of a pick-up into small component parts — they are *lumping* behaviours together, for that particular dog.)

How to break down a pick-up? This requires skill: In deciding what to click and how to break down the behaviour — how to *shape* it into what you want it to be. Covering all the nuanced ways of achieving this is probably impossible. But, to time your clicks, you will need to be looking very closely at the interaction of the dog's mouth and dummy.

From the nose-touch, you could progress to:

- Clicking touches the dog offers which actually make the dummy move/ wobble (i.e. — harder touches), and not clicking if the dummy is still at the touch. When that is fluent, withhold the click again and see if the dog moves to a pick-up, or even opens her mouth at all.

- Clicking a mouth which is partially open when touching the dummy, and not clicking if the mouth is shut. When that is fluent, withhold the click again and see if the dog moves to a pick-up, or to opening the mouth wider.

- Clicking for teeth on the dummy — even if the dummy is still on the floor. When that is fluent, withhold the click again and see if the dog moves to a pick-up.

Which to choose? Hopefully your dog is sometimes offering you one of these already. That would be a good one to pick, to strengthen.

I'M STILL STUCK!

Fear not. We are going to abandon being shaping purists at this point. There's no shame in this, and frequently it leads to fast results.

Option One: Animating the dummy. Our goal here is just to get some mouth-around-the-dummy stuff happening. By 'animate' I mean: Tease the dog with the dummy — get the dog *into* it and wanting it (as if it's a toy), then drop it a metre away from you and click any resulting pick-up — letting the dog drop at the click, as above. (Again, here, you need to be extra sure to throw the treat away from the dropped dummy and to pick it up *before* the dog turns around to see you doing this — since you will be picking the dummy up for each rep. If you let the dog see you pick up the dummy, you can hugely encourage keep-away.) If you're going to use animation, this should be an *intermediate step*: You need to wean the dog off needing the animation, to do a pick-up. *A pick-up isn't properly/fully trained if it only happens when you animate the dummy*! You need to animate progressively less, until you have a reliable pick-up from the floor (without animation). Keep giving the dog a chance every now and again to offer you a pick-up without animation. Only step in, to animate, if you need to. If the dog won't pick up from the floor, see if you can just click mouth-around-the-dummy whilst it's in your hands.

IF YOU'RE REALLY STUCK WITH PICK-UPS, GET THE DOG ANIMATED. TEASE HER WITH THE DUMMY. CLICK WHEN HER MOUTH CLOSES AROUND IT. YOU WILL NEED TO REDUCE THE ANIMATION AND GET A PICK-UP FROM THE FLOOR FLUENTLY, BEFORE PROGRESSING.

Option Two: Shaping whilst you are holding the dummy. Hold the dummy at each end, with clicker in one hand as well. Present to the dog at head-height and see if she will open her mouth around the dummy, now that you are holding it. (Feel free to animate it to tempt the dog.) Click if the dog opens her mouth around the dummy, remove the dummy from the dog's reach and treat. Re-offer the dummy. Work on achieving an open mouth around the dummy whilst you hold it like this. (Keep animating each rep, like a toy, if needed — but try to phase that out.) Progressively lower the dummy to the floor — ensuring the dog is successful and able to put her mouth around the dummy at each new height. Start to click for feeling the dog pulling up against you — for attempts to pick-up, whilst you hold the dummy in this way. When you reach the floor, allow one end of the dummy to rest on the floor whilst you hold the other end. Gradually lower that to the floor. Can you now get a pick-up from the floor?

'My dog is picking the dummy up by the ends'

Many handlers are concerned about this, but the majority of the time it is not a problem in the long-term — because it sorts itself out as your dog gains experience with retrieves and learns the most secure way to carry the dummy. It is very common for inexperienced dogs to try to pick-up in this way. But I would not worry about it, at this point — wait and see if it is still occurring when you begin to run marks outdoors.

However, because it is so simple to do, I recommend that you remove throw-ropes from the dummy during the clicker retrieve — to reduce the risk of encouraging the dog to retrieve using these. On canvas dummies, you can also use a very large elastic band to strap the flap at one end tightly to the dummy — so dogs are not tempted to pick up using this.

PHASE 4: HAND TARGET

'Why the hand target delivery?'

The hand target is going to result in a 'standing' delivery, whereby the dog runs up to you and delivers directly to your *right* hand. This is the delivery which is used by almost all handlers in the UK, because it is seen as the fastest and most direct way of delivering game. There are other types of delivery — such as a dog which sits in front of you and 'presents' the dummy (common in mainland Europe). Or a dog which 'finishes' to your left side whilst holding the dummy (common in North America).

Whatever delivery you eventually want to have, I would highly recommend you teach the basic hand target delivery to begin with. Other deliveries are more complex behaviours, with many more criteria to them — like straightness and alignment, and holding whilst sitting. It is much easier to get your basic retrieve working to begin with, using a hand target — and then, separately, to train the more complex delivery you want — rather than try to train this type of delivery from the start.

The hand target gives the dog a target to aim for, on their return to you. No longer are they just heading generally for your entire body - they have a specific small target. This really helps with the delivery when we eventually add in the dummy.

HOW TO TRAIN THE HAND TARGET

There is no dummy involved in teaching this stage, so you can begin this alongside all the previous phases, even alongside Phase 1.

The hand target is a comparatively simple part of the retrieve to teach and most dogs get the basic hand target very quickly. But don't move on until your dog is really targeting your hand with drive, *from a distance* — fluently.

1. Standing up, look at your *right* hand — talk to your hand, sniff your hand and pretend to eat out of it!

2. Making a fist, move your hand down to the side of your right knee.

3. Slowly uncurl your fingers, timing the uncurling so that it occurs just at the moment the dog reaches your hand. If you open your hand too quickly, whilst the dog is still a distance away, she may think you have dropped food on the floor — and start sniffing the floor.

4. Click the second your dog's nose touches your hand. If your dog doesn't touch your hand, just remove it, pretend to eat out of it again — and then re-offer the hand. Don't leave it out there for the dog to ignore and choose to come back to: Remove and re-present it.

5. Throw a treat on the floor a couple of metres away. The distance you throw the treat will dictate the distance the dog approaches your hand target from, for the next rep.

6. Repeat, over and over. As the dog gets the hang of this, stop talking to your hand and pretending to eat out of it. Just place the hand down next to your knee-cap with the palm facing the dog.

PHASE 4 — The hand target

1 HOLDING YOUR RIGHT HAND UP TO YOUR MOUTH, SNIFF IT AND PRETEND TO BE AMAZED BY IT! DO THIS FOR AS MANY REPS AS YOU NEED UNTIL THE BEHAVIOUR IS ESTABLISHED.

2 PLACE YOUR RIGHT HAND IN A FIST DOWN AT THE SIDE OF YOUR RIGHT LEG, LEVEL WITH YOUR KNEE-CAP. THE DOG WILL HEAD TOWARDS IT.

3 JUST BEFORE THE DOG REACHES YOUR HAND, SLOWLY UNCURL YOUR FINGERS SO YOUR HAND IS FLAT BY THE TIME THE DOG REACHES IT. (IF YOU DO THIS TOO FAST OR TOO EARLY, YOUR DOG WILL SNIFF THE FLOOR.)

4 CLICK AS SOON AS YOU FEEL THE DOG'S NOSE ON YOUR HAND.

5 THROW THE TREAT AS FAR AWAY AS YOU CAN, INDOORS. (THIS WILL ENABLE THE BEHAVIOUR TO BE A SIMILAR OUT-AND-BACK TO A RETRIEVE.)

6 ONCE THE DOG HAS EATEN THE TREAT AND TURNED BACK TO YOU, IMMEDIATELY PLACE YOUR HAND TARGET OUT AGAIN FOR THE NEXT REP – SO THE DOG CAN TARGET FROM A DISTANCE.

EXTRA HELP:

'My dog licks my hand…'

We don't want the dog to lick the hand, so it's a good idea to make sure your hand doesn't smell of food too much. Try to hold and handle the food only in the other hand. If you do get some licking:

- If you feel your dog's tongue touch your palm, snatch your hand away quickly. Place it down again, and give the dog another try. Be aware that it is very difficult to know whether to click the second you feel something touch your palm — whilst also having analysed, in that split second, whether it is a nose or a lick first(!) — and so you can end up accidentally clicking licks with this approach. Therefore, this solution is fine for the occasional lick but, if you have a more determined licker, you'll need one of the following options…

- Angle your fingers back away so your dog's nose makes contact with your palm but the tongue can't reach your fingers, even if it comes out. With the fingers angled backwards, you prevent licking from being successful for a long while. When you have trained a strong nose-touch behaviour, the dog doesn't then usually try to lick even if you keep your fingers straight.

- If you have a really determined licker, *click early* for many reps — click *before* she has made contact with your palm and *before* she has licked. Try to think about clicking the targeting *intention*. Once the dog is really used to this and has done it for many sessions, then let her carry through to make contact with your hand and — since she won't be expecting to be allowed to reach the hand — you are likely to get a nose-touch. Then you can alternate between clicking intention (clicking early), and allowing the dog to carry through to a touch — until you get rid of the licking.

Don't push your hand onto your dog's nose

We want the *dog* to come to *your hand*. Not vice versa! Once you have placed your hand out, don't move it until you click. (Unless you withdraw it, if the dog fails to touch it.) Don't move your hand to 'bop' the dog on the nose!

GENERALISING THE HAND TARGET AND ADDING SOME DISTANCE

Once your dog is really fluent at this behaviour, you can start to change where you are holding your hand: Hold it to the side, hold it slightly above her — make her work a bit harder to target it and not just always see it in the same place by your side. You want to see drive and determination for that hand!

If your dog ever doesn't touch your hand because you've put it in a new position, just remove your hand and re-place it out in a new, easier place which isn't so strange — and gradually work back to the strange position.

To get the dog to approach your hand from a greater distance (as she will have to do, on a retrieve), throw your treats a good distance away across the room. Once your dog has eaten a treat, offer your hand for the next touch as soon as she looks up — so she races to your hand from across the room.

You should now have an 'out-and-back' behaviour, which is very similar to what a retrieve looks like — just without the dummy in it! This aspect of the hand target behaviour often goes unappreciated.

Imagine the retrieve *without a retrieve item*. What does it look like? A dog running out, pivoting on the spot, and returning directly and quickly back to you. Well, guess what? This is the same pattern we are conditioning in the dog, through the hand target exercise: The dog runs out, eats the treat, turns around quickly, and heads back directly to us. This *out-and-back behaviour* can therefore become deeply conditioned — *before we add a retrieve item to it.* And this is one reason why we really need to get some distance when we throw the treat for each rep.

The hand target is not just about the delivery, the bit at the end of the retrieve — it's also about conditioning the out-and-back pattern, without a retrieve item.

PHASE 5: INTRODUCING SLIGHT DISTANCE AND A MINI-HOLD

'Holding' as a conceptual leap: Don't click the drop!

Right now your dog believes that picking up the dummy earns a click. We need to make the transition to your dog believing that *holding* the dummy, earns a click. Another way to think about this is — putting *duration* on the pick-up to create a *hold.*

This can be quite a difficult transition. Why? When you don't pay a pick-up with an immediate click, the dog is highly likely to think that this picking up thing isn't working anymore: It must be the wrong thing now. So she gives up and drops the dummy. If this happens too many times, she will lose confidence and give up entirely.

In short: When training the hold, you are attempting to wait longer so that you can click duration. Meanwhile your dog is at *increasing risk of dropping, the longer you wait.*

The risk is that you end up clicking the drop, by trying to wait it out too long. What's so wrong with clicking the drop? It doesn't lead to a retrieve. A dog which believes the click is for dropping the dummy often results in a dog that is running out, picking up and then dropping (or throwing) the dummy: The only reason she picks up is to be able to drop. (Since that's what she has come to believe the click is for, because you have clicked too late - after it has left her mouth.)

So, it's imperative that you get a click in *before* a drop. That way, you are clicking the dummy being static in the dog's mouth. It is much better to click slightly early, than to wait too long and click a drop. If you do wait too long and your dog drops, don't rush to get a click in — you will only be clicking the drop — just do nothing. And resolve to click earlier next time.

You will make the odd mistake, and sometimes click a drop. Everyone does. As long as this is an occasional thing, it won't create huge problems. If you consistently click drops, you will create some big problems at this stage.

Let's look at what to do, in more detail:

1. Stand up — you can ditch the chair now — and place the dummy on the floor at your feet.

2. Immediately move yourself two to three metres away from the dummy. So, as the dog moves towards the dummy to pick it up, you are backing away to get a bit of distance between you and the dummy. Not too far, just two or three metres. The idea is: You don't stand right next to the dummy, but — for every rep now — you move to put distance between you and the dummy. IMPORTANT: *Don't throw the dummy to create this distance* — move yourself away from the static dummy on the floor.

3. Once you've moved away from it, the dog will pick up the dummy and automatically turn and begin to head back to you.

4. Click after the dog has taken just *one or two* steps back towards you, whilst carrying the dummy. Don't wait for her to carry the dummy all the way back to you before you click. You are clicking just a split second of walking and holding. For some reason, *moving and holding* tend to go together. And *stopping and dropping*, also go together. This means that the point of maximum risk (in terms of a drop happening) is when the dog stops moving because she has arrived in front of you — so you need to be sure you are clicking *before* this point. Try to click just one step towards you, whilst holding, at first.

Stopping goes with dropping

DON'T WAIT FOR THE DOG TO RETURN ALL THE WAY BACK TO YOU AND STOP BEFORE YOU CLICK. THIS IS TOO RISKY FOR A DROP.

5. The dog will drop the dummy on hearing the click, expecting a treat. The dummy will probably land a little distance from you — that's fine.

6. Deliver the treat, dropping it *at your feet*. IMPORTANT: We are no longer throwing treats out away from us. Over many reps, this is going to help the dog to get this carrying behaviour heading back towards us. If the treat is always delivered at your feet, that is where the dog will be heading. If you throw treats around everywhere, the dog will pick up the dummy but then not know where to head next — because the treats could appear anywhere. This results in a dog which picks up — and then stands, waiting at a distance from us. We lose the return. So — get the

Stop throwing treats now

DON'T THROW TREATS AWAY ANY LONGER. THIS WILL RESULT IN THE DOG STANDING AT A DISTANCE AND YOU WILL LOSE THE RETURN. ALWAYS DELIVER TREATS ON THE FLOOR AT YOUR FEET NOW.

dog into the habit of heading back to you for the treat at your feet. Remember that this out-and-back pattern of a retrieve is part of what we want to be conditioning.

7. Reposition yourself. When the dog has eaten the treat at your feet, look to see where the dummy fell and try to stand a little way from it again. It may already be a short distance away, but you may need to move away a bit further.

8. Repeat, repositioning yourself after each rep.

- ***Increase duration on the hold.*** As your dog becomes more familiar with this exercise, wait longer each time to click, letting her take more steps back towards you — until you are clicking just as she arrives back at you. Do not wait longer than this — because you will almost certainly start to get drops: Remember the connection between *stopping and dropping*!

- ***Increase distance from the dummy.*** Once your dog has this basic exercise working, move yourself further away from the dummy at the start of each rep. If the dog ever appears unaware of the dummy when you increase the distance, just walk up to it until the dog notices it. Then back away to where you started whilst the dog picks it up and approaches you.

- ***Increase drive back to you,*** by shuffling backwards when you see the dog approaching you with the dummy. Seeing you moving backwards away from her, the dog will want to catch up with you — so you get a bit more drive back to you. This will also help extend the duration and distance on the holding behaviour. At this stage, keep clicking the hold *before* the dog reaches you — before she stops moving.

PHASE 5 — Introducing slight distance and a mini-hold

1 STANDING UP, PLACE THE DUMMY ON THE FLOOR AT YOUR FEET.

2 BACK AWAY FROM THE DUMMY, AS THE DOG HEADS TOWARDS IT.

3 THE DOG WILL PICK UP THE DUMMY AND ORIENTATE TO YOU. (THIS IS A CLICKABLE MOMENT IF YOU NEED TO SPLIT FURTHER.)

4 CLICK AS THE DOG HEADS TOWARDS YOU, HOLDING THE DUMMY. CLICK AFTER JUST A STEP OR TWO TOWARDS YOU.

5 THE DOG WILL DROP THE DUMMY ON THE SPOT AT THE CLICK, EXPECTING A TREAT.

6 DELIVER THE TREAT ON THE FLOOR, RIGHT AT YOUR FEET.

7 WHILST THE DOG IS EATING THE TREAT, SLIP AWAY FROM HER AND THE DUMMY TO PUT SOME DISTANCE BETWEEN YOU AGAIN FOR THE NEXT REP.

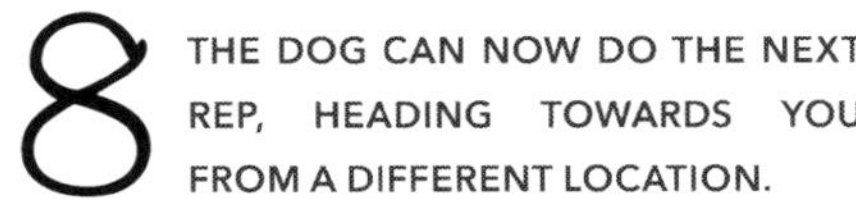

8 THE DOG CAN NOW DO THE NEXT REP, HEADING TOWARDS YOU FROM A DIFFERENT LOCATION.

OBJECTIVE:

- A dog that will pick up the dummy and then keep hold of it whilst taking multiple steps back towards you.

EXTRA HELP:

Remember, again, not to let the dog see you pick up the dummy, ever. You should only be touching the dummy at the very end of the session — when you still throw a treat away from it and pick it up whilst the dog's back is turned.

A word of warning: Seeing a dog coming back towards you, holding a dummy, might just tempt you just to try to take it off her at this stage. Especially if you have previously trained a retrieve in a more traditional way, by 'moulding' a dog's natural retrieve. Don't do this. Many dogs will still have residual keep-away tendencies at this point, which will be enflamed again if you start doing this — and we haven't taught the delivery or proofed the hold yet.

We need to communicate to the dog that you are totally uninterested in possessing the dummy, but that you do care about what the dog *does* with the dummy.

PHASE 6: PROOFING THE HOLD AGAINST FOOD

You need to have achieved Phase 5 before progressing to this step.

Before discussing how to achieve 'proofing the hold against food', let's first establish what it is and why we want it.

The goal of this exercise is for the dog to continue to hold the dummy, even when shown a treat. (Until the click.) Ultimately, we should be able to lure the dog around — following a treat — whilst she continues to hold the dummy until the click. At which point, she can drop and get that treat. But she should not drop until the click.

You might remember that, earlier in the clicker retrieve, we spent time ensuring that the dog dropped at the click. Dropping at the click is half of what we need to teach. The other half is *don't drop until the click*. Once a dog understands 'drop at the click' and also 'don't drop *until* the click', you will control the beginning and the end of this behaviour.

You might be wondering why we want to proof the hold against food. Is this some pretentious 'just because you can' trick, or is it actually a necessary step of the clicker retrieve?

You will have a pretty decent *basic* retrieve without this step. (So all is not lost if you really can't achieve it.) But your retrieve will not be as reliable or useful, without this step.

When we proof the hold against food, we are teaching the dog to keep holding, in the presence of a distraction. In the real world of a working gundog, no one is going to wave food around your dog's nose during a retrieve. But your dog will need to hold despite interesting scent and in the presence of other dogs and many, many other distractions. The dog will need to hold despite wanting to put the dummy down to shake, when exiting water. If you can proof your hold against food, you will have communicated the concept of 'don't let go, no matter what distraction occurs' to the dog. If you can get this working well in your house, now, you will be able to return to this method when, for example, working on water retrieves — to remind the dog to continue holding under those circumstances.

Although 'hold, even when food is around' is a difficult concept for your dog to get her head around, once the penny drops it will consolidate the meaning of 'hold' like nothing else. This step requires excellent timing on your part.

1. Place the dummy on the floor at your feet.

2. Wait as the dog heads towards the dummy.

3. As your dog picks the dummy, show your dog a treat whilst backing away or whilst luring the dog past the front of your body. In Phase 5, the dog was picking up the dummy and you were backing away from her. Now show her the treat whilst doing this. You can make this relatively easy at first, by holding the treat high up at about the height of your stomach — out of her reach — but be sure the dog sees it. Again, we do this whilst you are backing away because stopping results in dropping! Eventually we will be able to do it with you standing still, but we're going to help the dog make faster progress by keeping you both moving at this point.

Stopping goes with dropping

4. When the dog drops the dummy, instantly snatch the treat away. Clutch it up to your chest, so that the treat disappears — dropping the dummy loses the opportunity to earn a treat. The dog will, almost for sure, drop the dummy this first time. This is because she wants to put that treat in her mouth, instead. We don't want her to drop, but occasional drops (without clicks) are a useful learning curve for her: She will learn what doesn't work. Tip: Timing is really important, here. *As soon* as the dog drops, snatch that treat away! Don't be late or slow!

5. Wait for her to pick up the dummy again (as usual).

6. Show the dog the treat again. Click for just a *split second* of holding the dummy whilst the treat is being shown. We are talking micro-seconds. Don't expect her to hold for ages, gazing at the treat with adoring eyes! It won't happen (yet). You are trying to get a click in whilst 1) the dummy is in the dog's mouth and 2) the dog is aware of a treat available — it doesn't matter how briefly this occurs.

7. The dog will drop the dummy at the click. Remember: You get what you click for. If you click the dummy in the mouth, you will get more of that — if you wait too long and accidentally click whilst it is being dropped — several times in a row — you will get more of that. Try not to click the drop!

DON'T CLICK A DROP!

8. Deliver the treat at your feet.

PHASE 6 — Proofing the hold against food

1 PLACE THE DUMMY ON THE FLOOR AT YOUR FEET, AS BEFORE.

2 THE DOG WILL HEAD TOWARDS THE DUMMY. DON'T BACK-UP YET.

3 AS THE DOG PICKS THE DUMMY, BACK AWAY WHILST HOLDING A PIECE OF FOOD IN YOUR HAND. YOU ARE AIMING AT BEING ABLE TO HOLD THIS FOOD LEVEL WITH THE DOG'S MOUTH AND ABOUT 1-2 FEET AWAY. TO BEGIN WITH, YOU CAN HOLD THE FOOD CONSIDERABLY HIGHER – THIS MAKES IT EASIER FOR THE DOG. THEN PROGRESSIVELY HOLD IT LOWER IF SUCCESSFUL.

4 IF THE DOG DROPS THE DUMMY IN RESPONSE TO THE FOOD, SNATCH AWAY YOUR HAND WITH THE TREAT SO IT IS BEHIND YOUR BACK: DROPPING MEANS THAT THE DOG LOSES AN OPPORTUNITY TO EARN A TREAT.

5 WAIT FOR THE DOG TO RE-PICK UP THE DUMMY. THE HAND WITH THE TREAT REMAINS BEHIND YOUR BACK.

6 RESUME WALKING BACKWARDS AND PLACE THE FOOD OUT AGAIN. CLICK FOR JUST A SPLIT-SECOND OF THE DOG HOLDING THE DUMMY WHILST BEING AWARE OF THE FOOD.

(CONT...)

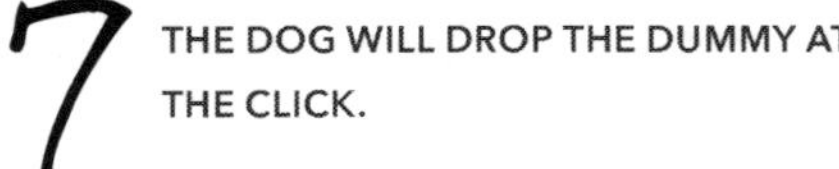

7 THE DOG WILL DROP THE DUMMY AT THE CLICK.

8 DELIVER THE TREAT AT YOUR FEET.

Next: increase the duration of the hold-in-the-presence-of-a-treat. And decrease the height of the treat — from out of reach and level with your stomach or chest, down to being level with the dog's eyes. Keep working on this until you have the dog holding the dummy and watching the treat — with the treat held level with her head (but still about 2 feet away in front of it), luring her around for a good five to six seconds — with the dog never dropping before the click. Through experimentation, the dog will learn that the treat disappears if she drops to get it before the click. And if she holds until the click, she then gets the treat. There is an initial learning hurdle for the dog to overcome here but, once the penny drops, she will swiftly grasp the concept and you will make fast progress with extending duration.

If you are familiar with the idea of 'reverse luring' or the 'Zen hand', that's pretty much what's happening here — if that reference point helps. If your dog has other reverse luring behaviours, you might want to warm up with those before trying this phase. Doing so might help the dog grasp the concept, here, faster.

OBJECTIVE:

- A dog that will pick up the dummy and keep hold of it whilst following a food lure around for several seconds — only dropping on the click and not before.

EXTRA HELP:

If your dog keeps dropping immediately, and you keep snatching the treat away — repeatedly — your dog is going to start to feel like a failure and become inclined to give up. Remember that we need the dog to feel successful, most of the time, to keep trying. So if you reach two or three 'no clicks', you should reduce criteria to earlier in the process, to rebuild some confidence. Build things back up and try the treat-showing again. Try to progress more gradually — are you really clicking a nano-second's worth of a hold? Are you waiting too long? Can you hold the treat higher to make it less tempting?

Sometimes people really want to reinforce their dog — and they find it hard to withhold a click. Don't be afraid of your dog getting it wrong *sometimes*. After all, your dog needs to learn what doesn't work — as well as what does. If your dog gets a click and a treat, whatever she does, then she's not learning anything. You're not failing as a trainer if the dog drops before the click. You just need to whip that treat up to your chest — and to ensure the dog feels successful enough to keep trying.

This exercise really is a 'penny-dropping' one and it's one that is a tricky corner. You will believe it is completely impossible and unachievable for you and your dog — until you suddenly start to be able to do it.

Once the dog has just a bit of duration on the behaviour, it is really very easy to increase that duration and to reach the impressive point of being able to lure the dog around, following the treat, without dropping: Progress will be very fast, once your dog has got the idea for just a second or two. So don't be too despondent if it looks like you're getting no where — the breakthrough will happen suddenly, *if* you can time that click right.

PHASE 7: PUTTING THE PICK-UP AND HAND TARGET TOGETHER

This step is not a particularly difficult one but, be warned, it can look a little messy at first.

We want to make sure that the dummy makes contact with our hand before it hits the floor. And we click only if we *could* have taken it. (Be honest with yourself here!) We don't actually take it off the dog — we still allow it to fall to the floor. This is to reduce the risk of keep-away developing — especially as we go on to generalise the clicker retrieve to new and different (more exciting) items.

In more detail:

1. Warm up with some regular hand-target touches, as you've been doing in the past and without the dummy. Then place the dummy at your feet again. (Don't move away.) This will give you maximum chance of getting your hand where it needs to be for contact with the dummy to occur. (Since you can be really quick to reach down when it's at your feet.)

2. There are two different options, at this point — since different things work for different dogs. Experiment and see which option works best for you and your dog. (Images show option one.)

   Option one: Once your dog has picked up the dummy, hold your hand-target out whilst *backing away with rapid little shuffles*. For many dogs, seeing you backing away will (as before) cause that acceleration towards you, and you can click the 'happy coincidence' of contact with your target hand. Click if you could have taken the dummy, *without actually taking it*, and allow it to fall to the floor.

Option two: Once your dog has picked up the dummy, hold your hand-target out right there on the spot — no backing away. If we could magic up a perfect response to this, it would be that the dog continues to hold the dummy whilst touching your hand with it — that is — she attempts to do a nose target to your hand, whilst holding the dummy. Click if you could have taken the dummy, *without actually taking it*, and allow it to fall to the floor.

3. Whichever option you take, at first your dog will probably drop the dummy to touch your hand. She doesn't realise that she can both hold the dummy *and* do the hand target at the same time. If she drops the dummy before the click, as always you should immediately snatch your hand away and wait for her to pick up the dummy again, then offer your hand back. (The dog should learn that dropping the dummy 'loses' her the hand — and the chance to touch the hand to earn a click and treat.)

4. After a few attempts, the dog should learn that dropping causes your hand to disappear. She should hopefully then continue holding the dummy whilst touching your palm with her nose.

5. Click the dummy touching your hand. It will probably be the case that the dog's nose itself can no longer quite reach your palm, because the dummy is there. So, when you feel the dummy touch your hand, click. You are clicking *the moment of connection between yourself, dummy and dog.*

6. Allow the dummy to fall on the floor and do not attempt to take it from the dog.

7. Deliver the treat.

PHASE 7 — Putting the pick-up and hand target together

1 PLACE THE DUMMY ON THE FLOOR AT YOUR FEET. THE DOG WILL APPROACH.

2 AS THE DOG PICKS THE DUMMY, BACK AWAY WHILST PLACING YOUR RIGHT HAND TARGET OUT NEXT TO YOUR RIGHT KNEE-CAP.

3 IF THE DOG DROPS EARLY AND BEFORE MAKING CONTACT WITH YOUR HAND, SNATCH YOUR HAND TARGET AWAY BEHIND YOUR BACK. DROPPING EARLY MEANS THE DOG LOSES THE OPPORTUNITY TO CARRY OUT THE HAND TARGET.

4 WHEN THE DOG RE-PICKS UP, BACK AWAY AGAIN WITH THE HAND TARGET OUT.

5 CLICK THE MOMENT THAT THE DUMMY MAKES CONTACT WITH YOUR HAND. THIS WILL ONLY BE A SPLIT-SECOND OF CONTACT.

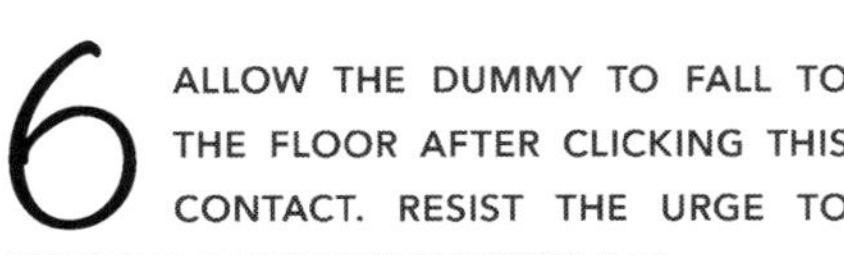

6 ALLOW THE DUMMY TO FALL TO THE FLOOR AFTER CLICKING THIS CONTACT. RESIST THE URGE TO TAKE THE DUMMY FROM THE DOG!

7 DELIVER THE TREAT ON THE FLOOR AT YOUR FEET.

Move away from the dropped dummy by a few feet as your dog gets more fluent at this. She should pick it up, and again target your hand with it. Progressively, as your dog is able, move further away from the dropped dummy each time — aim at getting this delivery-to-hand working, over increasing distances.

It's important to remember that, just because your dog is touching your hand with her nose, doesn't mean you can try to take the dummy from her mouth yet. If you do, this may enflame any keep-away tendencies she has. We want to drill the dog into not being possessive over this object and to teach her that you don't care about it and don't really want it. For this reason, click if you *could* have taken it — and then allow it to fall to the floor. Remember only to click that moment of connection between yourself, dummy and dog — click late, and you are clicking the drop rather than the connection.

DO NOT TAKE THE DUMMY DIRECTLY FROM THE DOG!

OBJECTIVE:

- A dog that will pick up the dummy, target your hand and make contact with it — as a hand target — whilst holding the dummy.

EXTRA HELP:

When this step goes wrong, it tends to be because the handler is expecting a perfect hand-touch, immediately — just as the dog does without the dummy. Although this *may* happen, most dogs will need more help, at first.

Why help? Remember that if your dog fails to get a click too many times, she will give up.

How to help? Here are some suggestions. Don't try them all at once(!):

- Kneel down in front of the dummy, so you are even closer to it to begin with — making this first step easier for your dog. This tends to work particularly well for small dogs, as you are more accessible. If your dog is excitable, you kneeling down with treats in one hand might prove a distraction and you may get mugged!

- Make sure you are backing away — fast — after your dog has picked the dummy.

- Once the dog has picked up from your feet, quickly reach out and touch the dummy yourself at first, still clicking that contact — that is: *You* make the effort and the contact, not the dog. You will need to be fast. Doing this should enable you to get enough clicks to keep your dog playing the game. Over time, you will progressively reach out less (help less), and you will expect the dog to make more of the effort to find your hand — until you reach the point where you *can* just stand there like a statue and have the dog determinedly target your hand with the dummy. If you help too much and continue to click everything — no matter how much the dog throws it at you — the delivery will never get any better, because you're teaching your dog that 'anything goes'. The secret is to juggle helping the dog enough that she feels successful and keeps going — versus letting the dog fail to get a click, so she learns to make more of an effort.

PHASE 8: THE FINISHING TOUCHES

1. Hold the dog by the harness on your *left* side.

2. Throw the dummy out in front of you with the other hand. (Do not ask the dog to sit or expect any steadiness just yet — you want lots of drive and desire for that dummy and no inhibitions yet. We also need to establish a 'retrieve' cue, first.)

3. Immediately release the dog's harness and allow her to run to the dummy and pick it up.

4. The dog should now want to return to you, and touch your flat, opened right palm with the dummy — for a click and treat. The dummy should still be falling on the floor when you click — you should not be taking it in your hand yet.

5. Start to deliver the food reinforcer directly to the dog's mouth now.

You can see that you have the beginnings of a reliable retrieve!

A CUE FOR THE RETRIEVE

When you reach the point of holding the dog by the harness and then releasing once the dummy hits the floor, you need to introduce a word to tell the dog to retrieve.

Many people use simply 'fetch'. Others use their dog's name in an excited tone of voice. Whatever you choose, make sure it is simple and short. (Not '*Go and get it*', as one of my students attempted to use!)

Conventionally, dogs are sent on their name for retrieves. This enables one handler to work several dogs at once, sending a specific dog from a group sitting together by verbal cue, for a retrieve. (If they were all taught to go on 'fetch', the result would be mayhem!)

New handlers are often worried about using their dog's name as a retrieve cue, believing the dog will be confused because the name is used on other occasions — to gain her attention, for example. In reality, dogs don't get confused by this if you start them out in this way from the beginning.

But if you only have one dog, or never plan to work more than one dog at a time, 'fetch' will do as well as any other word.

To add the cue, simply say it just *before* you release the dog to run to your thrown retrieve. (Not at the same time that you release the dog - but before!)

DELIVERY TO HAND

You should be in no rush to take the retrieve into your hand, even by this stage. We want to consolidate, in the dog's eyes, that this is not about *her* possession of the object versus *your* possession of it — so we are feigning complete disinterest in the possession of it.

However, you should be clicking when you *could* take the object into your hand — if you wanted to. This means that there is contact with your hand when you click, but you are then allowing the object to fall to the floor. And (importantly) you are then not letting the dog see you pick it up — you are feeding the treat to the dog's mouth in such a way that she is turned away, whilst you pick up the dummy.

If your dog has shown no keep-away tendencies, you can now start to take the dummy into your hand occasionally. If you don't see any evidence of keep-away developing, you can increase this until you are taking it in your hand every time. But at the first sign of any possessiveness developing, return to clicking and allowing it to fall — ensuring she doesn't see you pick it up by turning her away with a treat when you pick it up.

If your dog originally had some keep-away issues, you may not want to make this change for many more *months* — whilst you progress through more advanced exercises and training.

CONTINUING THE FOOD REINFORCERS

People often want to know when they can stop using food reinforcers for the retrieve. Do make sure you have read Section 1.4, Generalisation and distraction management, which covers the subject of variable reinforcement in detail.

Why keep reinforcing the retrieve, specifically? Not all dogs (or subtypes of gundog) find retrieving to be reinforcing by itself. Many dogs will show a deterioration in their retrieve if reinforcement stops completely. Environmental reinforcers may reclaim their attention. And the dogs which *do* find retrieving to be innately reinforcing are also often the dogs with keep-away issues — they love the retrieve slightly too much! With these dogs, continuing to provide a food reinforcer for delivering the valued dummy is really important.

Obviously in competition or tests you can't reinforce with food, but even (especially!) the most seasoned competitor spends more time training than competing — so it works out to be only the minority of time that a dog doesn't get a reinforcer.

My advice is: Don't even think about stopping the reinforcement except for *situations where you are not allowed to reinforce.* These would be competition or assessment situations.

THE CLICKER RETRIEVE ONLINE – A COURSE

I'm very aware that the clicker retrieve is a subtle and nuanced behaviour. Sometimes words are not the best medium for teaching complex behaviours, since it can take 500 words to say something which a video can show in 30 seconds.

I hope the illustrations in this chapter will help convey information. But, if you are a visual learner, particularly, trying to piece together the clicker retrieve on the basis of this section might be difficult.

Alternatively, you might have hit a problem training your clicker retrieve which you can't find the solution to, in the material above, and you might be looking for some help specific to your individual dog.

So, as previously mentioned, I run a five-week online clicker retrieve course — which has been taken by people around the world. As part of the course, you have access to a group where you can post videos of your training with the clicker retrieve and get individualised feedback from me.

Do get in touch if you would like to join us! Find me at Galody Gundogs (galodygundogs.com) or DogWorks (dogworks.org.uk), online.

3.7

MARKED RETRIEVES

A marked retrieve (or a *mark*) is also known as a seen retrieve (*a seen*): The dog has seen the retrieve in the air, and seen it land.

SOMEONE ELSE THROWING THE RETRIEVE

The clicker retrieve process involved only the handler, so the introduction of another person throwing retrieves can be confusing for dogs. Dogs can be distracted by the dummy thrower and want to investigate and greet this new person. Or they may try to take the retrieve to the dummy thrower, instead of the handler.

Here are some tips for first retrieves with a dummy thrower:

- Do these on short grass, where the dog can easily see and find the dummy.
- Don't worry about steadiness, and don't worry about a sit to begin with. Restrain the dog using a harness (no leash) on the left side of the handler.
- Have the dummy thrower stand about 20 yards away and make a 'whoop whoop' noise to attract the dog's attention, whilst waggling the dummy around temptingly.
- The dummy thrower should then throw the retrieve quite some way away from their own person. This makes them, the thrower, less interesting to the dog on her way out and back — reducing the chances of the dog being distracted by the thrower.
- As soon as the dummy hits the floor, the handler should release the dog on her retrieve cue.
- Once the thrower has thrown the dummy, she should be immediately silent and still. If the dog does approach the thrower, she should look away, fold her arms and not make eye contact with the dog. She has no more part to play in this retrieve.
- After the handler has said her retrieve cue, she should be still and silent until the dog reaches the dummy and picks it.
- The handler should then put out her hand target (see Section 3.6, The clicker retrieve) and talk to the dog in an encouraging and excited voice.
- If the dog needs a little extra help to return to the handler, the handler can also back away from the dog whilst showing the hand target.

- If the dog needs even more help, the handler can turn her back on the dog and jog away. The dog will usually come chasing after the retreating handler. The handler can then stop running away and show the hand target for a delivery to hand.

- The handler should still click and treat deliveries to hand, of course — still allowing the dummy to fall to the floor after the click on most reps to prevent keep-away.

If the dog is successfully running directly to the dummy on the ground, you can ask the thrower to stand slightly further away with each retrieve. This way, you are working on some distance too — but not further than about 30 yards (30 large strides!) on short grass, at this point.

If the dummy thrower is still way too exciting not to be investigated, she is going to need to practise being very boring. To do this, she speaks in a lower, slower and calmer voice ('whoop, whoop, whoop') — and then she spins the dummy in the air without letting go of the rope and places the dummy on the ground. (She may need to walk out to place it down, then walk back, to avoid throwing it.) She then folds her arms and looks away from the dog.

It will also help if the handler is using tastier treats to help the dog focus on the task and not on the distractions (dummy thrower).

Don't be in a rush to move on from this, until:

- The dog is bringing the retrieve back to the handler without investigating the dummy thrower.

- The dog is not hesitant or unsure of what to do or what is expected — the dog understands that this is a retrieve.

- The dog can do this basic retrieve at approximately 20 yards on very short cover.

This may take you one session. Or it may take you a few. It should not take more than that, because we don't want to practise loads of marked retrieves without any steadiness or control. That could create problems for us with steadiness, in the future.

So, once your basic retrieve is functioning with a dummy thrower, quickly move to introduce steadiness.

We will discuss steadiness more below. But first, the crucial point to understand is: *Steadiness and marking interact in such a way that improving one is often undoing the other. And yet we need both.*

We are going to come back to that conflict later in this section, but first let's explore marking and steadiness separately.

MARKING SKILLS

If a dog marks well, she will be able to run *directly* to where the dummy fell. Marking, for gundogs, is all about the eyes. Not the nose. The dog sees the dummy fall and, having seen it, is able to run directly to that spot. Speed is important to minimise the suffering of game and to ensure it is despatched quickly and humanely. Running directly to the location of fall results in a much faster retrieve than having a dog hunt up a large area using her nose. There is, of course, a role for the nose in finding retrieves — but the eyes should be leading things until the dog is in the location of fall, when the dog switches to hunting (nose!) mode.

You have probably seen many action movies where someone has a guided missile and needs to get a lock on a target. Once they have their missile locked onto the target, their screen goes red and there's a continuous 'beep' sound. They know they are locked on, so that's when they fire their missile. And it's pretty much guaranteed to hit the target. (That's why, in *Top Gun*, just getting a lock on another plane, in training, is sufficient to 'win'!)

Think of the dog as the missile, fired at the dummy. The dog's gaze is like a visual lock. If the dog gets a good visual lock on the target (dummy), she will go right to it when fired (sent). She won't need to use her nose to hunt-up the dummy too much when she gets to the area — because she will know almost exactly where it fell.

If a dog doesn't mark well, it's like firing that missile without a lock on the target. It's a gamble. (This happens once in *Top Gun* too, by the way — and the missile sails right on past the target without a hit!) The dog may run about everywhere and hunt up a large area, until she just happens to catch wind of the retrieve — using her nose to compensate for her eyes. She may even need help or handling — because it is taking too long, waiting for her to stumble across the retrieve. (In gundog tests and assessments, a dog should not need to be handled on a marked retrieve — if she does need handling, she will be severely penalised.)

Genetics plays a part here — some dogs seem, effortlessly, to be good markers, without much training. But marking is also a trainable behaviour, so let's look at what we can do to help.

WHY THE DOG SHOULD NOT LOOK AWAY FROM THE LOCATION OF FALL

If you are a responsible dog owner, you'll have been picking up your dog's poos for some time now! You might have noticed that the best way to find a poo easily (especially if it was produced at any distance from you!), is to stare at the spot where you saw the dog do it, as you approach — and never to take your eyes off that spot! If you have occasionally found yourself looking away (maybe to check what your dog is up to) and then looking back towards the poo again, you might have struggled to relocate it.

Well, guess what? This is exactly the same skillset that your dog needs, when marking retrieves. And, just as with you and the poo, if your dog looks away from the location of fall, she too will have less accurate marking.

This means:

- We don't want the dog to look up at the handler for permission to be sent.
- We want the handler to be as still as a statue when she sends the dog. We don't want her to thrust her arm or hand in some energising way as this movement can draw the dog's attention off the location of fall.
- We don't want to line the dog up for a single mark — we want to save pointing at retrieves with our arms for blinds or for complex situations when there are multiple marks down. Simple singles don't need lining.

INTRODUCING STEADINESS

Once you've got your basic retrieve with a dummy thrower going well, it's really important that the dog never 'runs in' on a retrieve. (Goes before she is sent by the handler.) If she does, she would be out of any trial and zero-ed on any test.

But remember that we've bred these dogs to be motivated by game and retrieves, so it's a dead cert that they are going to attempt to run in. They are not being disobedient if they try it. They are just trying to get to the good stuff — the reinforcers we have bred them to value — in the most direct and quickest way they know.

Just because we understand why it's happening, and just because we're not going to punish the dog for it, we are most definitely not going to allow this to occur — from now on. *Not even once.*

Novice handlers can sometimes be a bit lackadaisical when their dog runs in, with a relaxed attitude akin to '*Oops — oh well, there's always next time — ha ha.*' Well, no, there isn't actually — not in a trial or test or assessment. That's it. No next time. You may now drive all those hundreds of miles home again. Force-free training doesn't mean a free-for-all with no boundaries or rules and dogs accessing whatever they want, whenever they want.

Moreover, remember what we discussed in Section 1.3, Repetition: The more a dog does something reinforcing, the more likely they are to do it in future. The more they run in, the more they are going to attempt to run in. And think back also to Section 1.2, Prevention: A good trainer looks ahead to the future and puts things in place to prevent a dog from learning to do the things we don't want her to do. If a dog successfully runs in, we have failed to implement prevention adequately.

How do we prevent running in?

TEMPT THE DOG – WITH THE DUMMY

Back in Section 3.2, Sit-stays, we discussed the Tempt the Dog sit-stay exercise, using food as the temptation. You might want to revisit that exercise now, to remind yourself of it.

Now, we're going to repeat the Tempt the Dog exercise — but using a dummy in one hand as the temptation. We will still use food as the reinforcer.

- Hold the dummy out — just as you previously held out the food — about two or three feet away from the dog's face, for just one second.

- Give your verbal marker if the dog resists the temptation.
- Put the dummy behind your back.
- Reinforce the dog for not breaking.

Tip: If the dog tries to get the dummy, hold the dummy higher when you present it as a distraction — so it is less tempting — and progress downwards over many reps, more gradually. Just as you did with the food, in Tempt the Dog.

Tip: This exercise should be rapid-fire, with you holding out the dummy, quickly marking, reinforcing, holding out the dummy, verbally marking, reinforcing — the rate of reinforcement is so high, the dog has barely eaten one treat before you are marking the next behaviour. If you are slow and pedantic about holding out the dummy — waiting too long with it out, removing it slowly — the rate of reinforcement for the dog will be much lower and the dog will be more likely to break.

Tip: Be sure to retract the dummy, hiding it behind your back each time, before you reinforce. That way, we have a nice clean behavioural loop each time.

You will then repeat this basic exercise but developing it as follows:

- Hold the dummy out all around the dog to generalise to different angles and positions.
- Progressively get closer to the ground, until you can touch the ground with the dummy; pick it up and reinforce the dog.
- Drop the dummy to the ground from just a foot in the air, so it lands *at your feet.* Mark verbally if the dog resists this temptation. Pick the dummy up and reinforce. If the dog tries to get the dummy, *pick it up quickly before the dog*

can reach it. (This is why you should drop at your feet — so you can reach the dummy before the dog.)

- Progress to more exciting throws, but step away from the dog several metres before you do this — and try to keep these throws quite vertical — so they don't come down too far away from you. Again, this is so you can get the dummy before the dog, should she break.

- Introduce the noise a dummy-thrower makes to attract the dog's attention before they throw — since this can be a factor resulting in great excitement for dogs. (This noise will differ quite a lot depending on where you live — from 'hey hey hey' to high-pitched bird-like calls, to slapping the dummy with your spare hand!)

- Now that you have done all of the above with yourself acting as dummy thrower and your dog in a sit-stay, you need to borrow another person to be dummy thrower. You, as the handler, will now stand next to the dog and simply mark and reinforce. Adding in another person can immediately result in a more exciting scenario, so you need to return to earlier stages of the dummy thrower just dropping the dummy to the ground from a few feet high — and build up from there.

If the dog ever breaks for the dummy in this entire exercise, don't say 'no' or 'ah ah' or be physically intimidating by running at the dog — instead just focus on *getting that dummy before the dog does.* Once you are working with a thrower, the thrower should get the dummy if the dog breaks. Doing this removes the reinforcer, so the behaviour of breaking has not been reinforced. There is simply no need to use aversives and introduce confusion and conflict for the dog over whether she should go for the dummy or not.

You are done with this exercise when, repeatedly, you can:

- stand about five large strides away from the dog
- make the noise the dummy thrower makes
- throw a nice high dummy (which still lands near you)
- do the same with a dummy thrower, throwing the dummy.

Important: When you repeat these steps with a dummy thrower, your dog may start to ignore the dummy completely once it lands — just staring at you. She has learnt that she is never to get the dummy, so it has become irrelevant to her. Instead, she is focussed on where her reinforcers *are* coming from — you, her handler. Whilst we can accept her looking at us a bit more than usual during this exercise (marking is a balancing act with steadiness), we don't want this to become engrained as a habit — since, as discussed above, it will affect marking ability. The important thing to know at this point is that, if your dog shows a lack of interest in the dummy and has eyes only for you, her handler — then occasionally send her for the dummy with your retrieve cue as soon as the dummy lands and *before she has had a chance to look away.* Why? Because, if the dummy is occasionally the reinforcer, she will pay more attention to it. Experiment with how frequently you need to send her for the dummy to keep her interested in it on the ground.

THE TRAINING TAB

Given that we can be sure that novice gundogs are going to attempt to run in, we are going to do everything we can to 1) prevent that from happening in the first place and 2) prevent them from getting the retrieve (reinforcer), if 1) fails and they do get away from us.

To prevent running in, I recommend using a short training tab lead — (see Section 2.3, Equipment) — clipped onto the dog's harness. You need to be able to hold the tab whilst standing naturally next to your dog, and you need the tab to be slack — with no tension in it. When the dog is sent for the retrieve, you just release the tab — the dog runs the retrieve with the tab on.

The reason we need the tab to be slack is because we don't want the dog to know we are holding it — unless they try to run in. At which point, they get stopped. If you hold the tab so it has tension in it, the dog is going to know very easily when you are, and are not, holding the tab! You may end up with a dog which is steady when she knows you are holding it (because she knows she can't successfully run in then) and a dog which is unsteady when you are not holding it. (Your dog will become 'tab-wise'!)

Remember the training principle of *prevention to the point of extinction*: We use the training tab to prevent running in, until the behaviour of ever trying to run in has extinguished.

The difficulty, here, is that — as discussed in Section 1.4, Generalisation and distraction management — the variables involved in gundog training are infinite. And so we never do know — 100 per cent — that we have proofed steadiness against absolutely everything a dog might encounter in the field. And we don't even know exactly what is going to happen in the field, as we are working with game in a natural environment. (What about a pricked bird, landing three metres away and fluttering on the ground?) Since we don't know that we've proofed against everything we might ever possibly encounter, *why ever stop using the training tab (when training)*?

In my training classes, sometimes we see this scenario: Someone starts out with a training tab on the dog, they are diligent about holding onto it for retrieves, and their dog doesn't seem to be attempting to run in. Their marked retrieves are going well. They want to look and feel like a competent gundog handler who doesn't need such equipment and whose dog resembles those they've seen working on shoots — in other words — is 'naked'! So they ditch the tab. A few days or weeks or even a few months later, their dog runs in. It might be a retrieve which is more tempting than others. Or seeing another dog run right past them with a 'look what I have' glance at them. Whatever it is, it is something the handler hasn't proofed for. And the dog breaks and runs in.

There are situations where you can't use a training tab, of course. Maybe you are taking part in an assessment or test. Maybe you are attending a traditional class, where you know the organisers would not accept a dog with a harness and tab on. Maybe you have (in the future) reached the point of working your dog on a shoot, and it's important to fit in and be part of the team and wear the 'uniform' of a dog on a shoot. So, of course — there are legitimate situations when you will have to leave the training tab off. But *why stop using it, every other time as well*? My advice is — don't.

Remember that just one successful experience of running in can so powerfully reinforce a dog, it can be hard to get total reliability back again. Whereas it requires zero effort or planning to just stick a tab on your dog, and hold it slackly before a retrieve. Just get into the habit of doing that — always. It is not something your dog will grow out of and no longer need, because dogs at every stage of training run in. There are dogs in Open trials which occasionally run in. You are never 'above and beyond' that as a possibility, so why risk allowing your dog to learn how amazing it is to run in when you can easily and effortlessly prevent this?

The fall-back plan: If disaster strikes and the dog somehow runs in (maybe you forgot to hold the tab), the dummy thrower should immediately race to pick up the dummy before the dog gets to it. We can, at least, remove the reinforcer in these scenarios. Many dogs derive some reinforcement from movement and activity itself — so this solution isn't ideal except as a fall-back plan.

Lastly, some handlers prefer to keep a long-line on their dog instead of a training tab at first. In this case, the line would be trailing on the floor during heelwork — held slackly whilst marking, and then just dropped for the dog to trail when she is sent on a retrieve.

We do not want to be unclipping a regular leash from the dog after a mark has been thrown — nor taking a slip-lead off, over the dog's head. Either of these actions will be likely to take too long and/or to distract the dog from the mark. A training tab or a long-line enable us to prevent any attempts to run in, and yet do not need to be removed before the dog is sent — we just release with our hand and give the retrieve cue.

The handler keeps secure hold of the training tab with her left hand, whilst waving at the dummy thrower to indicate she is ready for a mark. The thrower attracts the dog's attention with noise before throwing the dummy.

SETTING THE DOG UP FOR A MARK

- To run a retrieve, we want the dog sitting *straight* at your left-hand side. This is where your sit-at-my-side behaviour comes in. Do check back over your left shoulder to be sure the rear of the dog is straight, since just looking at the front can be deceiving!

- When the dog is straight at your side, ensure you are holding the training tab slackly in your left hand. Wave with your right hand to the dummy thrower, to say you are ready.

- As the retrieve is thrown, keep hold of the training tab and, if the dog is unsteady, restrain the dog. Ask the dog to sit and wave at the dummy thrower to pick up the dummy and re-throw (in a more boring way).

- When the dog is steady to the fall of the dummy, say the retrieve cue after the dummy has hit the ground (*whilst the dog is still looking at it*) and drop the training tab to allow the dog to go.

Throw dummies in a boring way to help the dog achieve steadiness at first. We don't want the dog to fail (repeatedly) to get a retrieve, just because she keeps being unsteady. We want the dog to be successful, the majority of the time. So, the dummy thrower might just make the dummy throwing noise and almost place the dummy on the ground slowly. Then the handler sends the dog. If the dog is steady, you can gradually increase how exciting the thrower is until you are able to do a proper throw with the dog remaining in a sit.

Important: *Do <u>not</u> line a dog up for a single marked retrieve*! When the dog knows where the retrieve is, there is no need. We line the dog for blinds or for multiple marks — when there is a chance of confusion. For now: Do not point at anything when sending the dog for the marked retrieve. *Do not gesture, or throw your hands out in encouragement when you send the dog.* Why? Because all this only draws the dog's attention back to you, and we want her to remain visually locked onto the location of fall.

This is one of those points I have to repeat often, at class: People seem to be unaware of their own physical movements and gestures. And then there are those handlers with dogs lacking energy or drive, who try to energise their dog by throwing their own arm out enthusiastically when sending their dog. As if they can somehow pass their own energy into their dog and propel their dog forwards! It doesn't work. We need the retrieve and the dummy thrower — the stuff 'out in front' — to be doing all the energising and enthusing, here. We need that stuff out front to pull the dog out. So, if you need to dial up the excitement, dial it up with a more excited dummy thrower. Not with arm gestures or movement from the handler.

MARKING AND STEADINESS: THE CONFLICT!

I promised earlier that we would return to this conflict. And it's an important one to understand. Here it is, in a nutshell:

- What is best for developing *steadiness*? Not sending the dog immediately on retrieves — to prevent anticipation.

- What is best for developing good *marking*? Sending the dog immediately on retrieves — before she has looked away.

There's the conflict.

Novice handlers, wanting to instil steadiness in the dog, make her wait... and wait... and wait... to be sent for marks. Yet, the longer they wait, the more likely the dog is to look *away* from the mark — to look up at the handler, almost to ask permission to go. The novice handler, pleased with the self-control the dog is showing, then sends the dog for the retrieve. Thereby reinforcing the dog for looking up at the handler — for looking *away* from the retrieve. The dog will do this more and more — look away from the retrieve and up at the handler — because the handler is reinforcing this behaviour by sending the dog when she does this. The dog's marking ability is accordingly affected. (Remember how hard it is to find dog poos, if you look away!)

What we want, instead, is a very steady dog which visually locks onto the location of fall until either sent — *or* until told to quietly 'leave' with a word or a subtle body-language cue.

HOW DO WE ACHIEVE BOTH STEADINESS AND ACCURATE MARKING?

After the mark has been thrown, if we are going to send the dog, *we must send the dog before she has decided to look away. We must send her whilst she is still looking at the location of fall* — so that we reinforce that behaviour of being locked onto the target — like a heat-seeking missile before it is fired!

This means you may be sending the dog almost immediately, at first. Once we have established this habit of staring forwards at the dummy, we can gradually extend the amount of time the dog is looking before being sent. But if we extend this too suddenly, the dog will look at the handler for permission — so it needs to be extended incrementally and according to what each dog can manage.

If the dog looks up at the handler because the handler has waited too long, *the handler should not send the dog.* (That would only reinforce the undesirable behaviour.) The handler should wave at the dummy thrower to pick up the dummy and throw another retrieve, and the handler must send sooner this time — before the dog looks up.

Don't be in a rush to extend the time and to achieve prolonged steadiness: Handlers understandably want to move ahead with training, quickly. But putting too much emphasis on steadiness at the expense of marking can cause other problems. Instead, work on increasing the distance on your marks (more on this below) — and defer training duration on the steadiness until the dog has established a habit of staring forwards with that lock on the location of fall.

Think about this in terms of developing the right habit. The habit we want to develop, is staring fixedly at the location of fall until hearing the retrieve cue word. Don't worry about duration. Get that sequence working well, and then you can put duration on the staring!

WHAT HAPPENS WHEN THE DOG IS NOT TO BE SENT FOR THAT RETRIEVE?

If the dog is not going to get the retrieve — because there are multiple dogs working and it's another dog's retrieve, or for steadiness purposes — then the handler should have a cue which communicates to the dog: '*That is not a retrieve for you*'. Over time, this cue can become increasingly more subtle and minimal, to the point that it is a very subtle body-language cue that no-one but handler and dog are even aware of (your dog will come to read you very closely as you work together more) — but, to begin with, I do suggest using a word like 'leave'. You will then mark (click) the dog's decision to leave — and treat.

Importantly, you must say your 'leave' word *whilst the dog is still looking at the location of fall*. You don't want to wait for the dog to look away and then say it — because, to cue a behaviour, you must say the cue before the behaviour occurs. If we say 'leave' *after* the dog has already done this, we are not cuing the dog to look away. She is choosing for herself when to do this — we are reinforcing that, if we still give a treat — and this habit will affect her marking ability.

So, the correct sequence is:

- dummy is thrown and dog is looking at the dummy

- handler says 'leave'
- dog looks away
- handler clicks and treats the dog for the leave.

Whether the dog is to be sent, or the dog is to leave, she should be looking at the location of fall when she gets either cue.

Don't over-practise leaves. If you practise a lot of them, your dog will start to anticipate that you are about to say 'leave' and will begin to look up at you, un-cued. This is another one of those balancing acts so endemic to gundog training: Send your dog too many times, and you will start to lose steadiness. Not send your dog enough, and your dog will start to do auto-leaves — looking away before we have cued her to — and we will start to lose marking. So much of good dog training is learning how to confound anticipation!

'Leave' is not the only cue or behaviour you can use, at this moment. 'Heel' would be another — followed by walking backwards or away from the retrieve. Is your dog able to process a cue which involves movement — yet is not a retrieve — at this moment? Remember to keep hold of that training tab if your dog is not getting the retrieve, to prevent running in.

THE 6-POINT DRILL

The 6-point drill is a marking drill and ideal for developing marking ability in a young or inexperienced dog. You can start doing it at about *20 yards and on short grass or light cover* almost immediately after you've completed the clicker retrieve and got a basic retrieve to hand from a dummy thrower. It remains useful for dogs at all stages of training. (It can be made easier or harder, accordingly.)

The 6-point is so-called because the dummy thrower throws marks to six points around their person. The marks are singles — meaning that one dummy is thrown and retrieved before the next is thrown. Throw them in the order indicated below:

1. diagonally back (2:30pm)
2. diagonally forwards (7:30pm)
3. diagonally back (10:30pm)
4. diagonally forwards (4:30pm)
5. straight out to left (9:00pm)
6. straight out to right (3:00pm

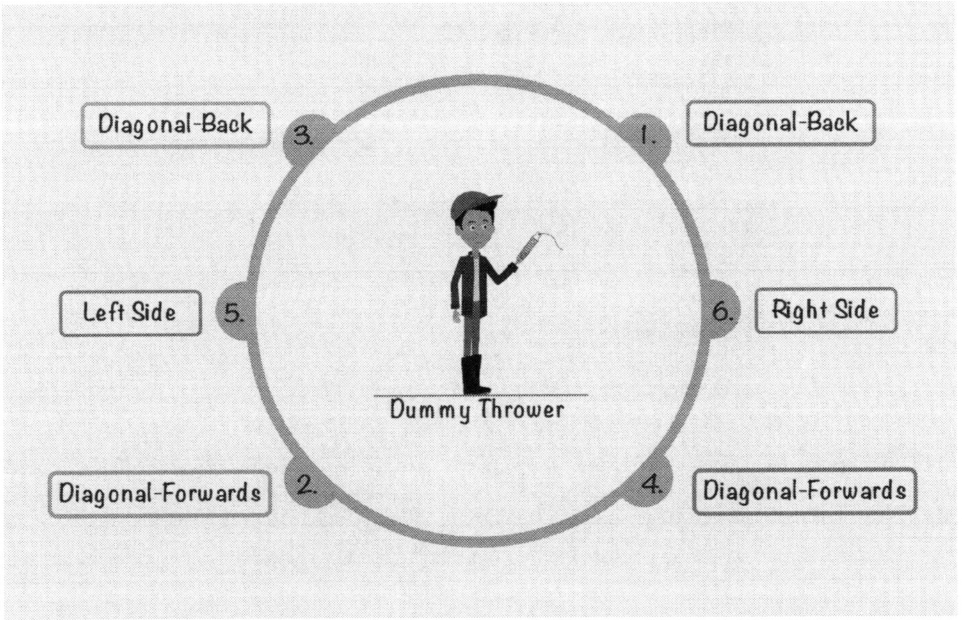

All six retrieves should be successfully performed before the distance is increased. The 6-point drill teaches depth-of-field, because the dog is learning to run through the location of old falls, to the current location of fall. She is learning how to judge what has landed closer to her, and what has landed further away — yet on the same visual line.

It also lets you assess your dog's marking ability in detail — across a range of marks at each distance — before you decide to increase the distance.

Begin the 6-point drill on *short grass, flat terrain, and at 20 yards.* Then move back to 30 yards and repeat. (Don't attempt to do all this in one session, of course!) Each time you move back, you are looking for almost perfect success on the drill at each distance, before increasing it.

Ensure that the dummy thrower is throwing the dummies a good distance away from their own person, since their own person will have suction for the dog running the retrieve.

Keep in mind that there are three *main* variables:

- cover (light, medium, heavy)
- distance (20yds up to 80-100yds)
- terrain (flat, sloping, undulating).

I think it is best to prioritise distance as the primary variable to increase. When you are making one variable harder, don't make the others harder at the same time: If you are increasing distance to 40 yards, for example, you wouldn't also introduce heavy cover. Instead, you would ensure the cover stays very light — so you are only adjusting one variable at a time.

When working in heavier cover or undulating terrain, keep in mind that the dog's view, from dog-height, can differ quite a bit from what you can see, at handler-height. Squat down sometimes and look at things from the dog's height — you will be surprised at how much harder it can be to mark from lower down, especially in cover or with undulating terrain. It's impossible to practise marking if your dog is unable to mark — you are putting the dog in a position where they will *have* to run out and hunt and use their nose, if you send them in these conditions. So, move yourself and your dog so that your dog can mark the location of fall.

The dog will need a larger and longer hunt-up in heavier cover than in light cover, but she should still be starting her hunt-up in pretty much the right spot.

Work at achieving distance, using the 6-point drill, until your dog can complete 80-yard retrieves on flat terrain and short grass. Then reduce the distance greatly — and increase the cover.

Provide your dog with experience of marks at a level of difficulty she finds challenging, but achievable:

- If your dog is getting 95-100 per cent of retrieves *marked accurately*, increase the level of difficulty (increased distances, heavier cover, more undulating terrain).

- If your dog is getting approx 80 per cent of retrieves *marked accurately*, remain at that level until you get to 95-100 per cent.

- If your dog is getting less than 80 per cent of retrieves *marked accurately*, decrease the level of difficulty (reduced distances, shorter cover, flatter terrain).

When it comes to marking, we are not concerned simply with whether the dog finds the retrieve (and that's all), but with *how* the dog finds the retrieve: Using eyes... or nose? If she finds the retrieves — but uses her nose to do this — it is not 'success'. If this occurs, we need to simplify and reduce the distance until we start to get the behaviour we want — dog's use of eyes!

If your dog struggles with using her eyes and has a tendency to use her nose to compensate, you might consider tying some black and white streamers or ribbons to your dummies. This will assist in attracting the dog's attention to them as they fly through the air.

3.8

MEMORY RETRIEVES

Having introduced you to marked retrieves and explained that these are retrieves which the dog has seen fall, we now turn to 'memory' retrieves. These fall halfway between marked retrieves and 'blind' retrieves — retrieves which the dog has not seen fall at all (and which are beyond the scope of this book).

So, at this halfway point — between the seen and the unseen — we find memory retrieves. They get their name because the dog has to *remember* where the retrieve was: Time passes between when the retrieve is seen falling, and the dog being sent. And other behaviours take place (like heelwork) during this time.

Memory retrieves are very popular in UK working tests and they are included in the Gundog Club's Grade 2 assessments for all the gundog subgroups. They are also very common in working tests.

A typical memory retrieve would be:

1. The dog is walked at heel in a *straight line* for (say) 30 yards, off-leash.

2. The handler stops walking and the dog does a Stop When I Stop — with a sit-at-my-side.

3. The handler throws the dummy out in front, a few metres.

4. The handler 'heels' the dog back to the start (say, 30 yards).

5. The handler lines the dog up.

6. The handler sends the dog for the retrieve.

There are many diverse, basic skills which are being called on here, at once. Which is why a really good memory retrieve is a great thing to behold. The skills involve:

- off-leash heelwork

- Stop When I Stop

- sit-at-my-side

- steadiness, when the handler throws the dummy (and during the 'heel' back)

- another Stop When I Stop and sit-at-my-side

- lining the dog up, for the retrieve (memory retrieves are the first time you will do this)

- accurate marking and remembering of the mark's location, by the dog

- delivery to hand.

You have all these component parts covered already, earlier in this book. The memory retrieve is an opportunity to put them all together into an impressive combo.

THE VALUE OF MEMORY RETRIEVES

Memory retrieves can sometimes be thought of as a 'puppy test' sort of exercise — which you can forget about once your dog progresses beyond that level. But the reality is that memory retrieves can be of immense value, even with an advanced dog.

Memories can be as easy (short) or as hard (long) as you need them to be, for your particular dog. Your very first memories will be only three paces away from the thrown retrieve. With an advanced dog, the memory might be 200 yards.

Along with increased distances, comes an increased passage of time before being sent. It will take you about three seconds to move three paces away before sending a dog, whereas it may take you 10 minutes or more to walk 200 yards away with the dog at heel, before turning to send her. With distance and time increasing in this way, you can see how a memory and a blind begin to blur into each other — and how memories can help pave the way for blinds.

MEMORY RETRIEVE

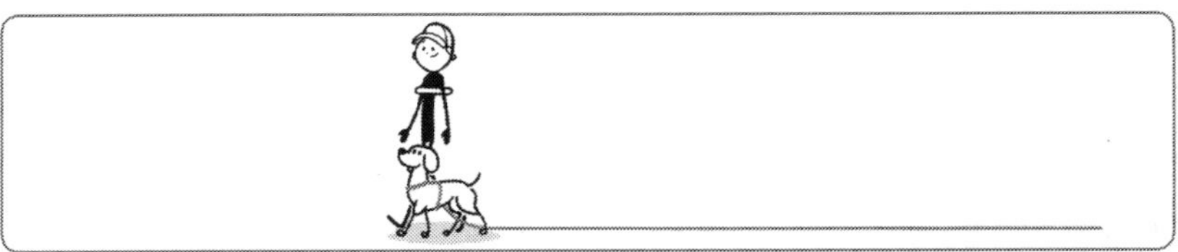

1 WALK IN A STRAIGHT LINE WITH THE DOG AT HEEL OFF-LEASH. CARRY A DUMMY. THE DOG IS TRAILING A 10M LONG-LINE OR WEARS A TRAINING TAB.

2 STOP WALKING. THE DOG SHOULD STOP AND OFFER A SIT-AT-MY-SIDE. ENSURE SHE SITS STRAIGHT.

3 TAKE HOLD OF THE HARNESS OR THE TRAINING TAB TO PREVENT RUNNING IN.

4 THROW THE DUMMY 2-3 METRES IN FRONT.

5 HEEL THE DOG AWAY FROM THE DUMMY, BACK THE WAY YOU CAME. KEEP HOLD OF THE LONG-LINE OR TRAINING TAB – SINCE THIS IS THE MOST TEMPTING MOMENT FOR THE DOG.

6 AT FIRST YOU WILL ONLY WALK AWAY 3-4 PACES BEFORE YOU TURN AND LINE THE DOG UP. THE DOG MUST BE VISUALLY LOCKED ONTO THE DUMMY WHEN LINED UP FOR IT. INCREASE THE DISTANCE ONLY VERY GRADUALLY TO ENSURE YOU ARE MAINTAINING THIS LOCK BEFORE SENDING.

7 YOU ARE LINING WITH YOUR LEFT ARM AND HOLDING THE BACK OF THE HARNESS OR TAB WITH YOUR RIGHT. TO SEND THE DOG, SIMPLY RELEASE THE HARNESS OR TAB WITH YOUR RIGHT HAND AND GIVE THE DOG HER 'RETRIEVE' CUE. DO NOT THRUST YOUR LINING HAND FORWARDS AS YOU SEND.

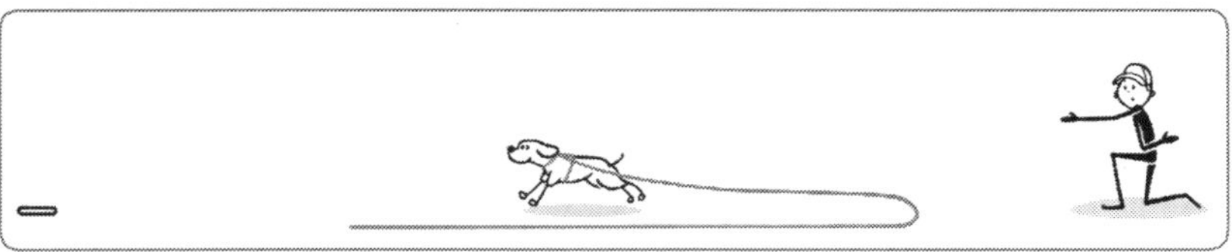

8 THE DOG RUNS OUT TO GET THE DUMMY. YOU CAN MOVE NOW! BUT NOTICE HOW STILL YOU ARE, UNTIL THIS POINT.

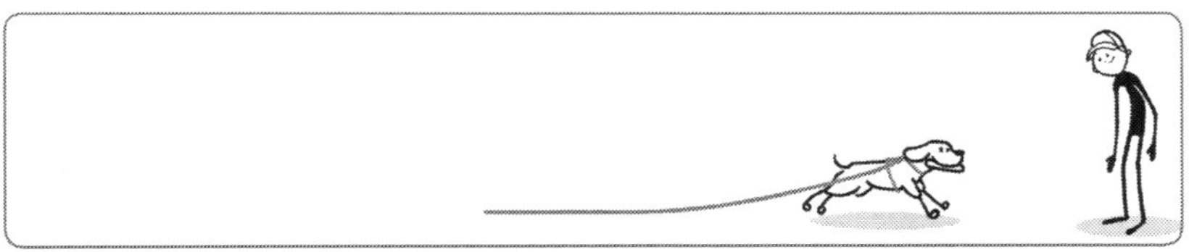

9 THE DOG BRINGS THE DUMMY TO HAND, AIMING FOR THE RIGHT HAND TARGET FROM THE CLICKER RETRIEVE.

Memories are an excellent way to develop a dog's confidence for running longer distances, because the dog *knows* there is a retrieve out there - she saw it thrown. This gives her the confidence to keep going - running hard, far and *straight*! She is becoming conditioned to running in this way when she didn't *just* see a retrieve fall. So, the running hard, far and straight when sent becomes a habit — which again, can transfer across to blinds.

Your dog won't *outgrow* memories —they can continue to be useful throughout her career.

BUILDING YOUR MEMORY RETRIEVE FROM COMPONENT PARTS

Off-leash heelwork: You will still be clicking and treating your dog frequently for maintaining the correct position.

Take care, after you have thrown the retrieve, when you ask the dog to 'heel' away from the dummy lying on the ground. This (literally) pivotal moment of moving from sit to heel, will see many dogs lunging and attempting to get the retrieve. Keep a secure hold of that training tab to *prevent* this, at this moment. Feel free to put a whole handful of treats on her nose, shovel them in her mouth liberally, and return to 'baby' heelwork 101, to help her in these first few reps.

If you are concerned your dog may run back to the dummy as you walk away, use your long-line instead of the training tab. The long-line will better enable you to prevent your dog from running to the retrieve, as you heel to the start.

Lastly, you will need to carry the dummy which you will throw, when walking out for a memory. In training, you can keep it in the dummy bag or in your coat pocket until you need to throw it. In a test you will probably be expected to carry it more visibly. Experiment with holding it in your armpit; this will free up both hands and, for dogs that are dummy-crazy, removes the dummy from temptation during heelwork!

Sit-at-my-side: You will need this behaviour three times in a memory — 1) before you start walking out with the dummy and dog, at the beginning of the heelwork; 2) when you stop walking, to throw the dummy; and then 3) once you have returned to the start, before you send the dog for the retrieve. You need to be able to achieve a straight sit-at-my-side, without attempting this many times. (Work on it by itself until fluent, if you don't yet have this behaviour.) Be aware that your dog may stand up when you throw the dummy out and/or may be unsteady at this moment. Have hold of the training tab or long-line to prevent running in. Re-cue the sit-at-my-side and reinforce.

GENERAL PRINCIPLES TO KEEP IN MIND WHILST WORKING ON MEMORIES

Your first memories will not be polished. They will be the equivalent of riding a bicycle with stabilisers on: There will be many preventatives (stabilisers!) implemented and a lot of generous clicking and treating, maybe luring — it will not look like the finished article, at first. It will look a bit wobbly! That's ok!

- Always practise memories in *very short* cover until your dog is really competent at them. The thicker the cover, the harder it is for the dog to maintain a straight line — so the more risk of 'hunting about everywhere' developing.

- Always walk in a *straight line* away from the dummy you have thrown. Memories are preparation for blind retrieves, and with blinds we are constantly working at maintaining straight lines. Don't run memories around twisty paths or bends. There should always be a straight and direct line between the dummy and you, which you have walked with the dog. If you reach the maximum distance available to you in a straight line, that's the furthest you can practise memories, in that location.

- Extend the distance very slowly and be guided by your dog. Do not extend distance until the dog is able to lock on to the dummy. (More on this really critical point below.)

- Make good use of hedgerows along the side of fields to assist the dog in holding a straight line, when you begin to extend the distance considerably. The hedgerow on one side of the dog will help guide her, keeping her straight.

GETTING A VISUAL LOCK ON THE DUMMY

At first, just walk *three to five steps* away from the thrown retrieve on the ground — repeatedly, for many sessions. I can't stress this enough: Keep it short.

Why? Because this is not just about getting the dog to run a really long way', it's about developing the right habits which will help us in the future. And the *habit we want to establish is a dog which is absolutely locked onto that dummy, visually, when we line her up for it.* Not a dog which will run out and hunt up the whole area, using her nose.

To achieve that intense forward-focus from the dog, we need her to be able to see the dummy as an object to fixate on, right in front of her. Many dogs simply will not be locked onto the dummy at this stage of their training, if you walk them away 30 yards on their first memory. Or even 15 yards. So — keep it very, very short. Have I stressed that enough, yet?!? Short!

This is not about achieving distance. It is about getting that visual lock, which is a component of lining the dog for blinds — later on. (Again - think about Tom Cruise in *Tom Gun*, trying to get that lock on a target!)

LINING THE DOG UP

This is one for you (the handler). It is really important to get this right — because we're laying the foundations for how you will set the dog up for a blind retrieve. When we start to run blinds, we want all this to be very familiar to the dog.

With the dog sitting at heel (straight!):

The view from behind when lining the dog up.

- Take hold of the dog's harness or training tab with your *right* hand. (This may be the opposite hand to the one you are used to holding it with.) We hold the tab for steadiness, to prevent the dog from going before we send her. We are holding it slackly, so she can't tell we are holding it — unless she attempts to go early.

- Bend over or crouch down. With your *left* arm, point towards the dummy with a flat palm (not a pointy finger). Try to get as much of your left arm as possible next to your dog's head, but take care not to crowd her or you will cause her to lean out away from you.

The handler uses her left arm to line the dog up. She holds the training tab slackly with her right hand, to prevent running in. The dog is sitting straight and aligned with the handler. The dog does not look up at the handler's face or at the hand itself, but straight ahead at the line given - this is the visual 'lock' on the dummy.

- Look left at your dog's head and facial expression. Is she visually locked onto that dummy on the ground? (Which she should be able to see, it should be so close.) If so...

- Send the dog. At this stage, use the dog's regular retrieve cue for marks — since we haven't taught a blind cue yet and the familiar cue will help her understand what we want.

- *If the dog is not visually locked on, don't send her*! Move up closer to the dummy, until the dog really is *locked on*.

  If your dog is unable to lock on, visually, to the dummy when your hand is extended, that's an indication you are too far away from it for that particular dog.

  If your dog still needs additional help to lock on, return to the dummy and be more exciting when you throw it — jiggle it around, saying 'Wow, what's this?', and hold onto the dog without asking for a sit when you throw it so she strains at the leash or harness to get it — all this will give the dummy more suction. Then don't walk as far away.

  Getting these habits right from this point on is why you need to be very conservative about the distance for memories, when starting to train them. When I show students how to train memories, often they just send the dog — whatever. But what we are doing here is not just getting through an exercise — no matter how. We are ensuring that certain learning outcomes are achieved. If your dog can't lock on, visually, to memory retrieves, there is no way she is going to start being able to do that, when lined for blind retrieves, later.

When the dog is sent, the handler does not thrust or jab her left arm, it remains absolutely still. She only releases the training tab in her right hand. Her whole body remains static.

- *Do not move your extended arm or hand when sending the dog*! You should not send the dog with a thrust of the hand or by moving the arm to propel her forwards. Your hand is not *sweeping* her out there, to the dummy! Or jabbing forwards as you say your retrieve cue. The movement may cause the dog to look at your hand. And that means she takes her eyes off the retrieve and we lose our visual lock.

Think of the guided missile and the lock on the target that we discussed earlier: Put your left arm out like a guidance device, to line the dog up to the retrieve. When the dog is lined up (locked on), we send ('fire') the dog ('missile'!). And the only thing that happens at the moment the dog goes, is that you say your retrieve cue! There is no movement from the handler, at all. *Except for your lips*!

THE LEFT ARM OR THE RIGHT ARM, FOR LINING THE DOG UP?

If you've done some training before, especially in the UK, you might be scratching your head at the suggestion that you should line the dog up with your *left* arm.

Because, in the UK, the convention is to line the dog up with your right arm. (In North America, dogs are conventionally lined up with the arm nearest the dog.)

I use my left arm to line a dog up for a retrieve because I believe this gives the dog the most accurate line to the retrieve.

If you want to test this: Get a friend and go and stand outdoors. Have your friend point at things on the horizon, whilst you stand on the left of her (where a dog would be). Can you accurately name the thing on the horizon which your friend is pointing to? Not just once, but many times over? Be sure your friend's arm is held out as we would hold it to line a dog (palm flat, not pointy-finger). Try a few times with the left arm, and then a few times with the right arm. Compare the difference between left and right arm-ed lines. What do you notice? *Which do you prefer*?

Here's what I observed: When using the right arm, it comes across the body and we are therefore making a triangle between dog, the right shoulder, and the tip of the right hand. Less of the arm is then available to give a *straight* line to the dog, because most of it is used up coming across the body diagonally — and it's not straight. Using the right arm also leads to handlers *crowding* the dog — bending over the dog or squatting and partially facing her — in an attempt to get the arm as straight as possible for the dog.

When using the left arm, because it is next to the dog, it is much easier to give a perfectly straight line to her. The arm is very close to the dog's eyes and also to the handler's eyes (being between the two!) so it is much easier to point at things accurately.

If you are going to attend traditional classes in the UK at any point in your gundog career, and you use your left arm to line the dog, you may find yourself criticised for this and told to use the other arm. I'm just putting that out there, so you know what to expect!

The left arrow here represents the dog's line of sight. When the right arm is used to line the dog, the line which the dog is given, cannot be given accurately. A triangle is formed between the dog; the handler's right shoulder and the tip of the handler's right hand.

The left arrow again represents the dog's line of sight. When the left arm is used to line the dog, the dog is given an entirely straight and accurate line to look along - from the shoulder to the tip of the fingers. The two lines are entirely parallel.

HOW MUCH TO BEND OVER, AND HOW MUCH ARM TO USE WHEN GIVING A LINE

If you watch US retriever trainers (you will find a lot of footage on YouTube), you will notice they almost always stand fully upright when lining up a dog. And they use just the hand itself, to give a line — usually held above the dog's head, rather than to the side.

In the UK, you will find handlers often using as much of their arms as they can get next to the dog's head — and holding that arm (whichever it is!) to the side of the dog's head. Sometimes, they may be doubled over or even squatting by the dog's side whilst giving the line.

Which approach is going to give the best lines? We need to think about this and make conscious decisions about what we want to do — rather than just unthinkingly doing what other people around us do. (Especially when this varies depending on which country you happen to be training in!)

Again — take a friend outside. For this one, to get the dog's perspective, you probably have to kneel with your friend standing on your right side — so you can take the height difference into account. Try having your friend hold a single hand out above your head, to point at objects on the horizon. Then try with her moving down to your level and using her entire left arm. Which gives you most accuracy, when identifying what she is pointing at?

What I observed with this exercise is that 1) having my friend more at my level — bending over or squatting if necessary — gave me more accuracy than having her stand upright. And 2) having my friend use as much of her arm as possible, so we were both looking together along the same line — gave me much more accuracy than just having her use a hand above my head.

So, that's what I advise, too. When a retrieve needs finesse on the lining and you want to give your dog as much of an accurate line as possible (all blinds — and splits which are close together), then get down to your dog's level and use as much of your arm as possible. If it's an easy split, with clearly one retrieve on the very obvious left and another on the definite right, then you will probably be just fine with less of an intense approach to lining — with a more casual half arm and less bending down.

Does it all matter? Is all this too pedantic? If in doubt, again take a friend outside and look at the horizon together and run through these exercises. Then decide whether this advice makes any significant difference.

However you decide to line your dog: Be consistent. She will learn how to work with you as you both gain more experience working together as a team. If you are constantly chopping and changing and trying out new ways of doing things, you will lose that consistency. (This is why I decided to continue lining with my right arm for my older two dogs — and to use my left arm for any new dogs I started.)

Bring some focus and attention to these issues: The most important thing is that you are thinking about all this and being mindful about your choices — whatever they are. And think about the dog's perspective in all this. Try to put yourself in her paws when you are deciding how to line.

Remember: However we line the dog, we are not moving anything except our lips when we send her!

INTRODUCING THE 'BACK' CUE

So far, we've been sending the dog on the cue you use for marked retrieves. This is a familiar cue for her, and is going to help build confidence in the early stages.

But, really, we want to be introducing the cue you will later use for blind retrieves. Which is, conventionally in the UK, the word 'back'.

This is very easy to achieve: Once your dog is confidently running out for memory retrieves, just say 'back' to send her, instead of her cue for marks. Say it in the same tone of voice you would usually say her mark cue. Almost all dogs will seamlessly transition in this way to the 'back' cue.

If your dog hesitates, add her cue for marks after saying 'back'. So you would say — 'back! Fido!' If you keep repeating this, you will find she soon goes on 'back' alone — because we have attached the new cue ('back') to the old cue (her cue for marks).

• • • • •

3.9

SWIMMING

Many pups take to water easily and with little encouragement — simply throwing something slightly desirable into the water soon sees their feet leaving the bottom and the beginning of swimming behaviour. You can then start to work on distance with the retrieves and, once you've finished the clicker retrieve process indoors and on land, you can use this to secure good hand deliveries. Ta da!

It's not always that easy, though. Let's take a look at some pitfalls and how to address them.

THE DOG THAT WON'T SWIM

Some dogs may wade, then reach out with their necks as far as they can for the retrieve — but they just don't have the confidence to allow their feet to leave the bottom. If you are faced with this scenario, here are some ideas:

- ***No steadiness or control required:*** When you are first introducing a dog to water — or if your dog is not yet confidently swimming — don't ask for any steadiness or control on water retrieves. We want the dog to feel as much desire for the retrieve object as she can (since it is that which will get her swimming!) — not to inhibit that desire through steadiness at this point. Don't even ask for a sit to begin with. Just throw and allow the dog to go.

- ***Use easy sloping entrances/exits:*** Dogs find it easier to start swimming when they can gradually descend into water. Don't expect them to leap off something to get into water, at first. A lot of otherwise great-looking water may not have suitable entrances for beginner dogs to use.

- ***Toys:*** Ensure you have an amazing collection of water toys, which float (of course!). These should be toys the dog doesn't have access to at any other time — so they are novel and desirable. I would highly recommend honking plastic ducks and oinking plastic pigs, as these have been a top hit in helping my gundog students to get their dogs swimming. Your dog has to want to get that retrieve object enough to overcome the slight worry she has about swimming, so dial up the incredibleness of your toys.

  If you are worried about toys floating away and being lost forever, tie a line to the toy before you throw it — so you can haul it back again if the dog won't swim for it.

At this point, we are not expecting a perfect delivery to hand with the toy — we don't mind too much what the dog does with it, after she gets it. We are just using it as an incentive to swim.

- ***Play and fun — no pressure:*** When humans want to get their dogs to *do* something, they tend to jabber manically at them in an excited way: '*Hey, Fido — want this? Want this duck? Go and get it…'. Where is it? Go on, you can do it, go on. Go and get it.'* And so on. Now, a certain amount of this can be considered part of just connecting with your dog and getting her interested, and I wouldn't suggest anyone does this training in complete silence — that would be weird. But there comes a point where this sort of jabbering constitutes *pressure* for the dog. The dog knows there is something she is supposed to be doing, and she knows she is not doing it. And dogs (like people) don't enjoy feeling they are failures: They don't like to see toys floating away which they want, but are too scared to get. So they start to tune out the handler and become avoidant, eating sticks, cocking their leg on things, sniffing about and becoming more interested in environmental reinforcers.

  Reverse psychology has a lot to offer here. The handler should just appear to enjoy herself in the shallows of the water, and feign zero interest in the dog and what the dog is doing. If you find yourself frequently 'encouraging' your dog, observe her response to that. Is she showing signs of avoidance or disengagement? If so, *you* might think it is encouragement — but to *your* dog, it is pressure.

- ***Lots of success at getting the toy:*** You might want to see your dog actually swim, but at this stage it is far more important to focus on *building the habit of retrieving fun stuff out of water.* Be happy about your dog retrieving something from the shallows which she has waded to get, and forget about actually swimming to start with. Once your dog learns that she goes in the wet stuff, and she comes out with an amazing fun toy — then you can gradually start to throw the toy a bit deeper until she would need to swim. But for the first many retrieves — sometimes for several sessions — just throw it in the shallows if she is reluctant. Don't be in too much of a rush to see actual swimming — give the dog time to gain confidence wading and retrieving fun stuff and be patient!

- ***Getting wet:*** Dogs are likely to feel better about water if they also see their handlers enjoying it and actually in it. After all, if you are dancing around on the shoreline, not even getting your toes wet, why should they want to go in the wet stuff? This may just mean wading up to your knees, but it could also mean donning a wet suit and playing around just out of reach of the dog — so the dog has to swim just a couple strokes to reach you. If there are two of you, you can both stand in the water and play catch with a tempting water toy, throwing it backwards and forwards between you.

- ***Lifejackets:*** Traditional gundog folks might crack up at the suggestion of a lifejacket, but I think lifejackets have much to offer. Firstly, they have a convenient handle on the back. This is much easier to get hold of than a collar, in the water. The handle also enables you to haul your dog up and out of the water easily if you need to (without choking them, as a collar would) — onto a pier, or onto a steep bank, or even into a boat.

I don't recommend the use of harnesses in the water — since there is the risk of the harness getting caught up on a hazard under the water — or (if too loose) the dog's front legs getting caught up in the harness. The handle on the lifejacket enables you to uphold steadiness, just like the training tab does on land.

The other use for lifejackets, is when you start to increase the distance on your water retrieves. Many handlers are quite nervous about sending the dog on an 80+ yard water retrieve and worry about their dog tiring in the middle of a large body of water, a long way from them or the shore. Whether or not this worry is justified, it exists — and can deter people. Lifejackets can give both dogs and handlers the confidence to run longer water retrieves at first, and they also give the dog some support so they are less likely to tire and get into trouble.

- ***Hydrotherapy:*** This is my top suggestion when people have real difficulties getting their dog to swim, and also as a routine puppy socialisation idea. Hydrotherapy involves someone being in the water with the dog (not you — the hydrotherapist!); it also involves warm water, loads of fun toys, and food — whichever the dog wants more. With such a great combo, the majority of dogs are going to love swimming after this. Be warned that, if you have a dog which won't swim, it's going to take more than one or two hydrotherapy sessions to address things. You will probably need to commit to going weekly for at least six to eight weeks to make decent progress in changing your dog's attitude to swimming. Puppies during the socialisation period will do well with just one or two positive sessions to make a lasting impact.

- ***Helping the dog:*** Should you ever *make* the dog swim? There are different degrees of 'help', here. There is picking the dog up and dumping her into water out of her depth, so she is forced to swim or drown. I do not recommend that, it will likely put a dog off water for life. And then there are lesser degrees: For example, when a fun toy has been thrown just out of the dog's reach, and the dog is teetering on the edge of swimming — having waded out as far as she can and obviously wanting the toy, and reaching for it — but just not committing to letting her feet leave the bottom. In these cases, with the handler in the water by the dog's side, it would take just a gentle pull on the handle of a lifejacket to enable her to swim and get that toy. I think that is an acceptable amount of 'help' and usually the success of getting the toy will mean the dog is more willing to do this by herself next time. I would recommend trying most of the above ideas before this one.

- ***Puppies:*** It is advisable to introduce your puppy to water as early as possible in her life, bearing in mind the seasons — taking a pup swimming in the middle of winter might not be a pleasant experience, so you may want to wait for warmer weather — or try a hydrotherapy pool if you want to get a swimming experience in, during the socialisation period.

AFTER THE DOG IS SWIMMING: THE DELIVERY TO HAND

Once you've got the dog swimming for toys, the next stage is the delivery to hand.

Deliveries to hand are especially challenging around water, because dogs — left to their own devices — will choose to put retrieves down, to shake. They will then pick up the retrieve again, and deliver to hand. This is not acceptable in any assessment and would see you heavily penalised in competition. If the retrieve were game, and if it were lightly pricked (not dead), it could well escape when the dog puts it down. Once the dog has picked a retrieve (on land or water), that item must never be put down until it is delivered to the handler.

To be able to train this, you absolutely must have done the clicker retrieve — see Section 3.6, specifically Phase 6: Proofing the hold against food. Whilst it is very possible to have an acceptable retrieve *on land* without having gotten to grips with proofing the hold against food, we really need the dog to understand this concept thoroughly to be able to deliver to hand out of *water*. (This is because the addition of water to the retrieve makes dropping the retrieve item extra-appealing.)

So, as a recap: The dog needs to be able to keep holding onto the dummy in the presence of the temptation of the treat.

If you can do this on land, then to achieve a good water delivery:

- First, remind the dog of proofing the hold against food on land — before you do the water retrieve. Put the item at your feet on the shore, let the dog do a pick-up, and then tempt her with food. Don't throw a water retrieve until you have this working well on the shore, with a dry dog.

- Then throw a pretty short and easy water retrieve which involves swimming. As the dog emerges from the water, *immediately* put the treat on her nose just as you did before. If the dog holds on, click and *allow the dummy to fall to the floor*. Because you just don't have enough hands to hold the clicker, put food on the dog's nose to tempt her, and also take delivery of the dummy. And we don't need to: We clicked, so that ends the rep and the dog is permitted to drop on the floor — as with the clicker retrieve. Don't worry about getting the dummy in your hand, that is the easy part. Getting the dog to hold on until the click is the tricky corner.

- If the dog drops before you click, probably to shake, you can't then allow her to re-pick the dummy up and continue. Because we will just end up training a behaviour chain: The dog will drop and shake, and then pick-up and do a lovely 'proofing the hold against food' — and we will never move on from that to eliminate the shake. So, if the dog drops before you click, pick up the retrieve. That rep is now over and has failed. You can't recover it. Hold the retrieve and feel and be a bit sad about what's happened for a good five seconds — to give the dog a chance to learn that no reinforcement is coming for that rep. Then throw the retrieve back into the shallows just a few metres again. We want the dog to get a bit wet again and to re-emerge from the water with the item in order to have another chance.

- Make this exercise easy to start with, standing right at the water's edge to put the food on the dog's nose as she emerges. Once your dog really is getting the idea, you can stand further away from the water so she has to carry the retrieve across more land before reaching you. You will often find that the first retrieve of the day, when the dog gets wet for the first time, is the most tempting for the dog to drop on. Unfortunately you will probably only get one chance to get your dog wet at a test or assessment. So you're not done with this until you're getting it right, the first time the dog gets wet that day.

STEADINESS ON WATER MARKS

It is much harder (if not impossible) to pick up the retrieve from water, should the dog run in before being sent. This means that, if your dog runs in, she will very likely get the retrieve. That will be a powerful reinforcer for running in. So a training tab to prevent running in becomes even more essential — and you need to be holding the end of it before each retrieve is thrown.

DISTANCE ON WATER MARKS

To give the dog more confidence, it helps if what we are throwing is very visible from land and whilst the dog is swimming out. When the dog starts to falter, being able to see something bobbing around out there will encourage her to keep going and not to give up and turn back.

So, at this point, discontinue using the amazing water toys and switch to items that float tall in the water and that can be thrown far. I recommend:

- the red and white striped Lighthouse toy made by Rogz. This floats really high (vertically) in the water and is very visible from a good distance. It's my favourite water toy for throwing far, and for visibility in the water.

- a ChuckIt ball chucker, using the ChuckIt ball which resembles a duck's tail — it sticks up more than a tennis ball and is mostly white.

Remember too, that using a lifejacket when starting out with these distances can really help give a dog (and handler!) confidence.

USING A DUMMY THROWER FOR WATER MARKS

There are a few extra considerations when it comes to using a dummy thrower for water retrieves. Most importantly, the dummy thrower must stand somewhere that is not going to encourage the dog to run around the shore.

What do I mean by that? If you simply position the thrower further along the shore from the handler, when the dog is sent, the dog will simply run along the shoreline towards the thrower and then get into the water at the closest point to the retrieve. Although this might be faster from the dog's perspective, we don't want this. We always want a *straight line* between the dog's starting position with the handler and the location of the (thrown) dummy. If that straight line involves more swimming, that's what we want the dog to do. Even if it takes longer. (This is partly about safety: The dog should get in the water where they are asked to get in — which is a location selected by the handler, and not the dog.)

'Water-cheating' is a whole advanced topic in itself, which we won't be getting into at this point. But we do need to set things up to discourage the wrong habits from developing.

Wherever possible, position the thrower so that running around the shore simply isn't possible. The thrower could be on an island in the water, in a kayak or boat, on the other side of a very long but thin channel (it's quicker to go across than around that shape of water), or even at the end of a long (but tall) pier, with the dog and handler below on a slipway.

However you set things up with a thrower, give some thought to discouraging and *preventing* the dog from running along the side of the water to get in, closer to the dummy.

3.10

HUNTING OR QUARTERING (FOR HPRS AND SPANIELS)

Hunting or quartering is the behaviour a dog must perform in order to find live game — before the shot. The dog must use her nose to locate the game and she must then enable us to get the game into the air — so we can shoot it.

Although we haven't directly talked yet about how to train quartering (hunting) for spaniels or HPRs — we have touched on this subject, in discussing many others.

- We've talked about the risks of free-running and how important it is to avoid 'walking the dog'.

- We've discussed how we want to associate being in a rural environment with the type of behaviour we want from our dogs there (hunting or quartering).

- And we've mentioned some types of physical exercise which can replace free-running (running retrieves, recalls, or even jogging with a dog on leash).

If you've skipped these previous sections, do make sure to go back to this material before continuing with this section. You will find it in Section 2.2, How to stop 'walking the dog'!), Section 3.5, Focus and engagement, and Section 1.2, Prevention.

THE IMPORTANCE OF HUNTING

A dog which hunts beautifully and stylishly with pace and intent is going to make a great first impression. Most judges would *want* to see that dog complete a retrieve — any sort of retrieve — to enable them to put her in the awards. On the other hand, a dog which pootles around just isn't going to make a good impression — and no one will really care to see what that dog's retrieve is like.

Both spaniels and HPRs must, first and foremost, be hunters. Their handlers are relying on them to find game, to put it on the table. It doesn't matter if they are brilliant retrievers, if they can't find the game in the first place. They will never get to retrieve anything, if they can't find it.

Unfortunately, the value and importance of hunting isn't always obvious to people starting out in gundog training — at least, not in the UK. Most beginners in the UK start with working tests, and the hunting test at a working test can appear to be the test where you just have to let your dog run about everywhere. (Which is what most young dogs want to do anyway!) When compared to the retrieving tests — where your dog is expected to handle and to be steady and obedient — the hunting test can seem easy, or at least just down to the dog's natural ability. And beginners can then often assume that hunting needs less work or training.

TWO (OPPOSING) WAYS THE WHEELS CAN COME OFF – 'OUT-OF-CONTROL DOG' AND 'BOOT-LICKER DOG'

The ideal is that the dog's strong hunting desire co-exists with an equally strong desire to work with her handler.

This is another one of those tightropes to walk in gundog training — and many dogs fall off the tightrope on one side or the other. If we fall off one side of the tightrope, we have the *out-of-control dog*, and if we fall off the other side, we have the *boot-licker dog*. It's likely that not many dogs fall entirely into either of these categories: Consider these terms shorthand for the extremes, and for the purposes of easy communication.

OUT-OF-CONTROL DOG

One common way that the wheels come off questing breeds (spaniels and HPRs), is through the dog learning that the environment is the most amazingly reinforcing thing, ever — whilst you are relatively boring. She learns this through repeatedly being allowed 'free-running' — exploring scent and game, whilst you plod along behind her. (Otherwise called 'walking the dog', in common parlance.) They can learn this lesson from a young age. We have discussed this in Section 2.2, How to stop 'walking the dog'!

The *out-of-control dog* can be a dog that just bogs off as soon as you take the lead off. She can be the AWOL dog which ignores recalls and 'sit' whistles, and is off on a mission to find game — whether you trail along or not.

Clearly, part of this is down to genetics: Hunting breeds have been deliberately bred to be interested in game, and to find hunting for game inherently reinforcing. So it *is* about 'nature'. But it's also about what the pup is allowed to *learn* is reinforcing — about 'nurture': If the pup is not given opportunities to learn how amazing the environment is, but instead learns to find her handler reinforcing from a young age, then, when it is time to venture into the field, there would be a history of reinforcement from the handler to counterbalance the interest in environmental reinforcers.

The out-of-control dog is a welfare issue. Dogs which behave like this will frequently end up being re-homed — the owners in utter despair. These dogs may eventually spend the rest of their lives on lead: An awful fate for active dogs bred to hunt, which truly need off-leash exercise.

The out-of-control dog is very common, especially amongst breeds with strong hunting drive — pretty much all working lines of spaniel and many of the HPR breeds. Moreover, the challenges posed by the out-of-control dog — for fitting into human society — are far more difficult than those presented by the boot-licker dog. By the time a dog has become an out-of-control dog, there is often no coming back from this: She has deeply embedded into her psyche, how amazing independent hunting is. Once that lesson has been learned — typically at a young age — it is so hard to unlearn, or to replace with anything else.

(If you are reading this and you have an out-of-control dog, don't give up. Whilst I want to put the emphasis on how much easier it is (as always) to prevent this problem in the first place, it is still possible to make some headway. You have an uphill struggle ahead of you, but there is hope. Be sure to read Section 3.5, Focus and engagement.)

BOOT-LICKER DOG

The *boot-licker dog* is pretty much the opposite of the out-of-control dog. The clue is in the name — the boot-licker does not want to move away from your boots. Tripping along, almost at heel, maybe a few metres away, the boot-licker is never going to put much food on your table because she is not looking hard enough to find it. *You* might be as likely to put game up, walking around, as a boot-licker. (Why, then, have a dog?)

No amount of urging or encouragement from the handler can propel some boot-lickers to leave the handler and hunt. If anything, talking to the dog just results in the dog being *more* engaged with her handler and even less inclined to explore.

As a gundog, a boot-licker is pretty ineffective. But she is not going to get herself into trouble, and boot-lickers can be ideal pet dogs. They can also turn their paws to other dog sports — focussed on the handler, as much as they are. As a result, if you had to choose one side to fall off the tightrope, it would be best for most people to fall off with a boot-licker, rather than an out-of-control dog.

Note that being a boot-licker does not equate to being low-energy. Many lack-lustre hunting dogs can be speedy bullets on retrieves. On a retrieve, the dog is working for a reinforcer relating to the handler — bringing the retrieve back for the food reinforcer afterwards — retrieves of any sort are an excellent way to develop more handler-focus. Hunting instead requires the dog to look for environmental reinforcers — and the boot-licker's motivation for that type of reinforcer can be low. Don't look at your high-energy puppy and assume that this is going to translate to 'run' when hunting — it may not.

Is the boot-licker born or made, then? Again, both: Genetics and how much run a dog has, plays a large role. But handlers also shape what a dog finds reinforcing. If a dog already lacks run or hunting initiative (genetically) and then is paired with a handler who spends a lot of time training behaviours outdoors which foster even more focus on the handler (retrieves, recalls, 'sit' whistles, etc.), the result can be a boot-licker.

WHAT ABOUT DOGS IN BETWEEN?

These two categories are extreme and over-simplistic: The out-of-control dog and the boot-licker dog are at opposite ends of the spectrum. But the categories are still useful for understanding that spectrum — so you can try to steer a path through the middle and avoid falling off either side of this tightrope.

Sometimes it's more about tendencies which dogs have: Perhaps, when the wind is strong, or with game scent in the air, we see a sluggish dog start to hunt with intensity and purpose. But, lacking these factors, *usually* the dog tends towards the boot-licker. On the other hand, when there is not much game around, perhaps a 'hot' dog demonstrates keenness and enthusiasm but is able to remain under control. But then, at the third or fourth flush, the dog loses her mind and chases — ignoring whistles — becoming an out-of-control dog.

The majority of dogs will have a tendency one way or the other (or both ways!), and thinking about which direction your own dog tends will help you plan your training.

ASSESSING A DOG'S TENDENCIES

If you have a puppy, you will want to think ahead about how you will approach training and what *sort* of dog you likely have.

- ***Look at your dog's pedigree.*** Pedigrees with a lot of field trial titles (FTCh — field trial champion, or FTW — field trial winner), denote a dog which has been bred to hunt and which will have strong hunting drive. There may, though, be strong-hunting dogs which don't have field titles — many people don't compete with their gundogs, but this doesn't mean they are not worked in the field. Some HPR breeds have been imported from Europe and assessed under European systems which are not recognised by the UK Kennel Club, and so their qualifications won't appear on their pedigree. (Even the title FTW (field trial winner) is not recognised by the Kennel Club, but many breeders and handlers add it to their dogs' pedigrees because it communicates valuable information. It will not appear on a dog's official Kennel Club pedigree.)

The more you can know what's 'behind' your puppy, the more you will know what she will become. How much run or hunting drive did her parents have? Are there videos you can watch of them? Look back five generations — what names or titles appear there? Are they show or working? If you know people in the breed, ask them to take a look at your puppy's pedigree and tell you what they think you can expect. Ask for their honest opinion. And ask a few different experienced people, not just one. Feel free to email people out of the blue: Most people are only too happy to talk about their beloved breeds and enjoy scouring pedigrees.

- ***Do you have a HPR/bird dog or a spaniel?*** Spaniels need to hunt within shotgun range, since they will instantly put up game with no warning. If you can't shoot the game (because the dog is too far away), it will be lost to you. Spaniels therefore don't need to run far and they should have a tight quartering pattern. HPRs should range *much* further — because they can point and give you time to walk up and position yourself for the flush and shot.

It is very rare to find a well-bred working spaniel which lacks hunting drive — if the wheels come off a spaniel, they typically come off towards the out-of-control dog. If you have a spaniel and the pedigree shows a decent amount of working blood, assume you have a dog naturally tending towards an out-of-control dog until proven otherwise!

On the other hand, if you have a HPR, you will need to think more carefully about the type of dog you have — since there can be a lot of variety between the different HPR breeds, with some showing more consistent hunting drive than others. Many HPR breeds these days are bred mainly for show purposes. In addition, many HPR breeds have historically produced very few FTChs, making it harder for newcomers to look at a pedigree and be able to predict what they will get — the pedigree may not give much away. (Hence the importance of showing it to someone experienced in working the breed for an opinion.)

- ***Assess your dog's natural 'run'.*** If you were to go to a wide-open space with your dog — a field with shortish grass, a beach — and there were no other dogs or people around and you let her off the leash: How far from you would your dog range? Would she take off for whatever boundary exists, immediately? Would she hang around, near you, and not 'get out'? Would she be confident running about at a distance from you? What is her general activity level like in this environment? Is she moving constantly, does she enjoy running for the sake of running, or movement for the pure sake of moving? Or is she more stop-and-start, stopping to investigate things and moving on? Is her nose up in the air, to air-scent (usually faster running dogs), or down on the ground, ground-scenting (slower running)?

- ***Assess your dog's ability to offer you attention, in rural environments.*** If you were to go to a rural location with your dog — and there were no other dogs or people around — but there was game scent: How much focus or attention would she offer you, *without you asking for any*? What is that invisible connection between you like? How much *in tune* with your own movements and direction of walking is your dog?

- ***Continue to reassess all of the above, always.*** Dogs do change, especially when young — especially as their training progresses and as they mature through adolescence, and have many first-time experiences of hunting and game. You might start out believing you have a boot-licker, so you expose her at a young age to game — only to realise that you've awakened more hunting drive than you can deal with right now. If that's the case, you'll need to change up what you are doing.

Don't categorise your dog and sit back and think you're done with it. These qualities are not immovable genetic traits. We are into the realm of epigenetics: These are influenceable tendencies. Continually reassess your dog, your dog's interest in scent and game, and your dog's responsiveness to you. Be flexible and thoughtful and ready to switch up what you are doing and to change your training plans, accordingly.

WHEN AND HOW TO START TRAINING HUNTING?

Let's assume that you have a dog with a strong hunting drive, a good amount of run, and a field-bred pedigree. In other words, you are starting with, genetically, a dog which wants to hunt. A dog which, raised in a different way, could well become an out-of-control dog. This will include most field-bred spaniels and many breeds of HPR.

When training without the use of aversives, it is best to get your basic obedience proofed to outdoors before beginning any hunting training. This means, essentially, the contents of this book are all started and progressing outdoors: Heelwork, recall whistle, 'sit' whistle, sit-at-my-side, 'Look at That', sit-stays, the clicker retrieve, basic marked retrieves, and memory retrieves.

Before beginning your hunting training, you should feel as if you generally have a biddable pup which is well-focussed on you outdoors. And why shouldn't your dog be? She has grown up learning that it pays to give you attention in outdoors environments. She hasn't been given much of a chance to learn anything else. You haven't been 'walking the dog' and running into game, which your dog flushes and learns to chase!

HUNTING 101: BASIC QUARTERING AWAY FROM GAME

With the written word, I can only convey so much of what good hunting looks like. I can't stress enough how important it is to learn by watching experienced dogs and handlers. *They don't need to be force-free — good hunting, is good hunting*! This is one area force-free handlers can learn much from traditional handlers. Ignore any well-intentioned tips about corrections for the purposes of steadiness — and focus instead on what is happening before the flush or shot: The style, pace and range of the dog — and what the handler is doing. It is a great idea to spectate at some trials — email the field trial secretary and ask if you can watch. Try to find some moments during the day to ask all and sundry about hunting and what is desirable and undesirable. Competitors will be unlikely to want to critique each other's hunting on the day, but they will probably be happy to talk generally about hunting — and to point out good work when it occurs.

If all else fails, purchase some DVDs of field trials from Paul French at paulfrenchvideo.com — so you can watch dogs working. It is so much easier to train this material, if you have — in your mind — an idea of what you are aiming for.

Remember that these directions are assuming you have a potentially hard-hunting dog — a dog which may end up being an out-of-control dog without optimal raising. (We will get onto how to adjust things for potential boot-lickers later.)

SETTING UP THE SESSION

- As far as possible, pick an area which doesn't have game in it whenever you practise hunting at this stage. If you will be hunting quite a small area (because you have a spaniel), it would be advisable to walk out the area yourself, first, to be sure there is no game there.

- Hunt your dog with the 10m long-line trailing. This will get her used to the line from an early stage — it will be essential later, when we are working on 'sit-to-flush' and 'fall'. In addition, if you do happen to put up game which somehow has remained in the area, you have a chance of grabbing the line and preventing a chase.

- Choose cover which is neither really dense and impenetrable, nor a golf course. Ideally ankle-to-knee high light cover. Light grass or a cover crop is ideal.

- Don't pick a dog-walking area, or an area that many people have walked through — or a location where other dogs are likely to have cocked their legs or defecated: That is likely to get the dog into a whole other frame of mind, and will only encourage marking behaviours whilst hunting. (Which is penalised.)

- Think about the width and extent of the area you are going to hunt — your 'beat'. If you have a HPR, you might choose an entire field for the dog to cover. If you have a spaniel, you might want to define a smaller area in your head. If you have a field to hunt, perhaps decide you will work a hedgerow and then out into the field some ways, and then back into the hedgerow again. (A lot of game hides in hedgerows.)

  Be really clear in your mind, before you start, what your self-designated area is. Not covering ground adequately, or missing game, is a heinous sin and will see your dog put out of trials or tests. If you just set out to follow your dog in a casual way, without thinking about your beat to start with, you will almost certainly miss ground. In a test or trial, a judge will tell you the area they want to see your dog cover. In training, you don't have someone else to tell you this — but you must tell yourself, instead. Look at likely hiding places for game in the area: Hedgerows, clumps of cover, bushes. These are the areas you want to be sure you cover with your dog.

- Conventionally, when training *spaniels* to quarter, retrieve objects are hidden for them to hunt up within the area you are quartering. Most often, these are tennis balls or puppy dummies. Hiding objects to discover whilst quartering is not conventionally done with HPRs. This may be due to the differing ranges for these two subgroups: It would be very hard to hide a sufficient number of tennis balls all over the area that a HPR needs to hunt, since this can be hundreds of yards either side of you! Spaniels, on the other hand, need to be kept close and the battle is usually keeping them in and not allowing them to pull out, either side or ahead. Teaching a spaniel that there is a high density of reinforcing finds near you, is one great way to keep her tight when quartering.

  This difference in training HPRs and spaniels may also be due to the desired behaviour from the dog, when the dog makes a find: Spaniels will just bustle right in and flush the game — that is, they will immediately attempt to get the game in their mouths. In training, it doesn't matter if this is what they actually do — get the dummy or ball. Whereas for HPRs, there is a difference in their treatment of shot and un-shot game: They must point when finding un-shot game. They can't just bustle in, right away, on it. So there may be concerns about associating quartering (for un-shot game) with finding what effectively represents shot game (dummies/balls) and then attempting to get it immediately - without pointing.

  Anyway, whatever the reasoning behind it: If you have a spaniel, you will need 5-10 tennis balls or green/orange puppy dummies, and a functioning basic clicker retrieve with delivery to hand. If you have a HPR, you don't need these to get started with your hunting.

- Try to pay attention to wind direction at all times — learn to be more aware of it. Where you just feel a light breeze on your face and think nothing of it, to your dog it carries a load of information about game — where it has been, how long ago, what type of game, and what direction it went in. There is a whole world of scent — a whole fifth dimension — which we humans have no access to. But we can learn to pay more attention to air movement, to help us read and handle our dogs. Be aware that wind can move differently at the edges of fields, when it eddies in cover, to out in the open.

WHAT TO DO IN THE FIELD

- *Tennis balls/puppy dummies*: If you have a *spaniel* (not a HPR), for your first couple of sessions leave your dog in a sit-stay and — with your dog watching — go out in front and hide some dummies and balls within the area you plan to hunt your dog over. Experiment with how many balls or dummies works best for your particular dog: Too few and your dog may not be encouraged to continue hunting or may become too focussed on you because there is nothing much to find out there; too many and your hunting will be interrupted every few seconds with a retrieve and you might not get enough flow to it. Some dogs will be happy to look for tennis balls and puppy dummies, whereas others might prefer tennis balls covered in rabbit fur (more reinforcing) — which you can purchase online from many gundog stores.

  After the first couple of sessions, try not to let your dog see you hide the dummies/balls — toss them out when she isn't looking or leave her in the car or house whilst you prep the area. Your dog should start to learn that the cue 'get on' means there is 'stuff out there to find' — even if she has not seen you put it there.

- *Hunt into the wind*, with beginner dogs — where possible. Hunting into the wind doesn't mean with the dog running *directly* straight into the wind — that would be considered 'boring on', and it's undesirable as it leads to game being missed left and right of the beat. So, hunting into the wind means with the dog zig-zagging *across* the wind — as in this diagram: This way, your dog will get to sample what lies in front, across a wider area than if she is boring directly into the wind.

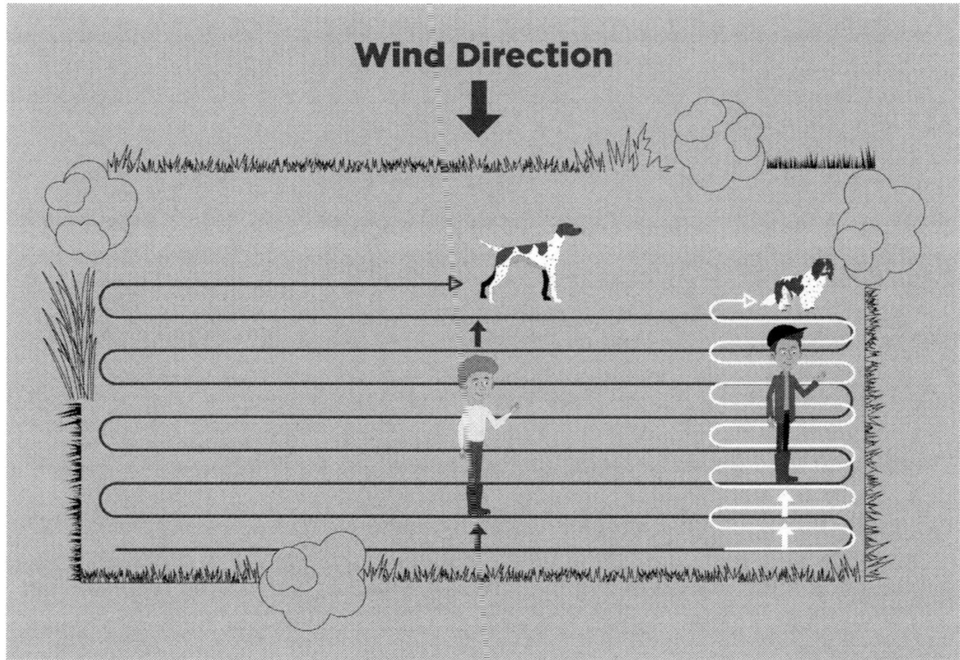

A SPANIEL SHOULD HUNT WITHIN SHOTGUN RANGE, WHICH WILL BE MUCH TIGHTER TO THE HANDLER THAN A HPR. ALWAYS HUNT INEXPERIENCED DOGS INTO THE WIND. YOU WILL NEED TO WALK THE ZIG-ZAG WITH THE DOG AT FIRST, SLIPPING AWAY WHEN THE DOG OVERTAKES YOU – BUT YOU WILL GRADUALLY NEED TO WALK LESS OF EACH ZIG AND ZAG – UNTIL YOU CAN JUST WALK DOWN THE CENTRE WHILST THE DOG CONTINUES TO QUARTER.

Once you see that your dog understands what hunting is about (which may not be long, depending on the dog), you can start to expose her to wind coming from other directions and you can allow the wind itself and the environment to teach the dog how best to cover the ground. But, when starting out, it helps your task if you are hunting into the wind — because you then have the wind bringing interesting scent towards your dog, and enticing your dog out to explore.

If you can't tell where the wind is coming from, pluck a few blades of grass, drop them in the air and see how they fall.

- Our ultimate goal, here — when the dog is fully trained — is that *you* are walking in a straight line down the middle of the area to be hunted. (That is — you are walking directly into the wind, in this case.) Whilst your dog quarters backwards and forwards, like a windscreen wiper, from one side of you to the other. (Dog runs across the wind.)

- But that comes after a lot of training, for most dogs. So, at first, you will need to walk the zig-zag *with* your dog. But ideally not the whole zig-zag, just the first part of each leg — with your dog over-taking you to run the whole leg — and you slipping away towards the other direction. (See the diagram.)

- Cast your dog out to one side of you, with a casual *underarm* gesture, giving your hunting cue — typically 'get on', but you can use any cue or phrase you like. Use this casual underarm gesture to differentiate it from a trained cast you might use during a retrieve. Think of this more as a releasing gesture and a *suggestion* of a direction, which your dog may or may not take (dependent on what they can smell). Your dog will start forwards, having been released. Follow your dog, walking across the wind.

- If the dog independently runs out a good distance away from you (ideal), slip away and walk towards the other side of the area you are hunting — walking the *zag* of your *zig*! The dog will spot you walking in the opposite direction, and will turn and run after you and past you... again, hopefully, independently a good distance past you. And again, you slip away when she isn't focussed on you and walk the other way. And so on. What a 'good distance' away from you is, will vary depending on whether you are hunting a spaniel or HPR, of course.

- If your HPR doesn't independently run out as far as you would like, you are just going to have to follow her towards the edge of the designated area, until the environment appeals to her enough to draw her out away from you, so you can slip away in the opposite direction. If this happens repeatedly or is a tendency that your dog has, she is tending towards a boot-licker — and needs some remedial work early on. See below for more info.

- *Distances*: The goal with a spaniel is to have high energy quartering — but to keep this close on either side of us. Think of a *storm in a teacup* — a small area with a lot of activity in it, from your dog! Whilst you definitely want a spaniel to be always within shotgun range, it is probably advisable to reduce that slightly in training — since a hard-running dog will tend to push the boundaries and always want to pull out further — you can compensate slightly for that, in training, by keeping the dog in slightly more. In your early days, if you have a fast-moving spaniel, you may only take a few steps yourself before you are turning in the other direction — in order to prevent the dog pressing on too far and thus quartering a beat which is too wide for a spaniel.

  To help the dog notice that you have turned, you may need to be encouraging the dog with your voice (not a trained cue, but just 'pup-pup-pup' or similar) and even hands clapping, to turn and follow you. (As soon as she turns towards you, stop the voice and hands clapping — we don't actually want her to come right up to you, just to turn.)

  On the other hand, if you are hunting a HPR, you typically want the dog to run on as far as she can or until she hits a boundary — so you will, most of the time, be trying to *quietly* turn and slip away without the dog realising, to enable her to run on as far as possible before she notices you have changed direction.

- *When the dog stays too close or too focussed on you*: The more you talk to your dog, engage your dog, and respond to your dog, the more you attract her focus and attention onto *you*. This is not what hunting is about — it's about the dog engaging with the environment. When handlers find themselves with a dog that is sticking too close, they often try to get the dog to go and explore by saying things like '*Off you go, then*' or '*go on*' or '*get on*' or similar — over and over and over again. All of this talk only further encourages the dog to focus on *you*. Stop jabbering to your dog!

In a nutshell: Ignore your dog. Give the environment time to draw her out; time to teach the dog that it is reinforcing. Remember how the out-of-control dog is created in a lot of pet gundogs? By owners taking them out for a walk — which means not engaging with them, or training them — so the dog learns how reinforcing the environment is. We don't want an out-of-control dog, but we do need to give the environment a chance to teach her it is reinforcing. We have done our best to ensure the area has no game in it, remember, so it is safe for us to allow the environment to teach the dog.

- *'Turn' whistle*: I suggest not using the 'turn' whistle at this early stage of training. I find dogs get confused if they are taught too many whistle cues, too close together. They can start to respond to the 'turn' whistle like a recall whistle or 'sit' whistle. When we then don't reinforce this response, it can in turn weaken our recall and 'sit' whistles — and lead to the dog ignoring those whistles. Everything can end up in a muddle. I find it is better to focus on teaching a very reliable recall whistle and 'sit' whistle first — and the 'turn' whistle can be added in later, once the dog has the gist of hunting.

  In addition, I reckon that the 'turn' whistle is best taught using classical conditioning rather than operant — unlike the recall and 'sit' whistles. That is: The turn whistle is taught through being associated with *something which is already occurring* (a turn), rather than taught through a conditioned response which is reinforced. But the 'turn' whistle is a subject we will need to get to in the sequel to this book!

- *Length of time*: You don't want to keep hunting until your dog's energy starts to flag, or to the point that she starts to pace herself for an endurance exercise. On average and for most dogs: Keep sessions relatively short and stop before your dog slows or tires. This is especially important if you want to compete with your dog (rather than work on a shoot), since style and pace and drive are all highly valued in competition — think of your dog as more of a sprinter than a marathon runner. Perhaps keep it to 10 minutes for each hunting session.

There are some exceptions to this, though: Some dogs (especially HPRs) take a while to settle into their stride — they are just running about like loons and not really hunting, at first. Then they start to concentrate and focus on the task at hand (or paw!). These dogs might need longer.

And some dogs which border on the out-of-control dog, need very brief sessions that stop before she gets herself into deep water — stopping whilst the dog is still able to focus on you, and doesn't get too into the environmental reinforcers. These dogs might need just 3-5 minute bursts, at first — interspersed with static training that involves focussing on you a lot.

- Continually monitor and assess 1) your dog's interest in environmental reinforcers and 2) your dog's interest in your own reinforcers (in a rural environment). If you notice your dog becoming increasingly addicted to running, hunting, scent — and out of relationship to you — that is a sign you need to adjust your training in the direction of teaching her that you are reinforcing, and not the environment. If you notice your dog becoming excessively interested in you and your reinforcers, to the point that it is hard to get her to engage enough with the environment to hunt adequately — that is a sign you need to adjust your training in the direction of teaching the dog that the environment carries reinforcement too — and perhaps to introduce some game. Getting the balance right between focussing on you and focussing on the environment is a fine line to tread and for some dogs requires constant adjustments in training.

- Many dogs don't put two and two together and figure out exactly what is expected of them until they are onto game. Nothing will teach your dog like game itself. Your dog will go up several gears when on game.

Consider all of this to be the preliminaries to enable you and your dog to approach those first encounters with game in a productive way.

PROBLEM SOLVING – THE BOOT-LICKER DOG

If your dog is not 'getting out' and hunting adequately, be sure you are not engaging her when you want her to hunt. As mentioned above: The more you talk to your dog, engage your dog, or respond to your dog, the more you attract your dog's focus and attention onto you.

What is *encouragement* to a handler, is *pressure* to most dogs. Imagine sitting behind the wheel of a strange vehicle, unsure how to drive it, whilst the person next to you is talking at you in a foreign language — more and more intensely as time goes on, gesturing and pointing all over the place. You know there is something you are not doing right, something you should be doing — but you have no idea how to drive the vehicle. So you fall quiet and subdued. This is what happens to dogs whose owners 'encourage' them excessively (in any situation). So — instead — *be quiet*! Give the environment time to draw the dog out, and give her time to gain confidence.

With a dog which is finding it difficult to leave your side, you might also choose locations carefully and weather conditions that come with a strong wind, since many dogs run better in these conditions and the wind will have more of a chance to entice the dog out to explore, if it is stronger and carrying more scent to her.

You can pick locations which are 'gamey' in terms of scent — but make sure you walk the area out beforehand, so there is unlikely to be game still there.

If you have a spaniel, ensure that the retrieve objects you are hiding for your dog to hunt up are reinforcing for your particular dog. If you have a dog which doesn't like tennis balls or dummies — or a dog which just does them as a functional retrieve for a food reinforcement afterwards (not seeing them as especially great things, in themselves) — then try hiding fur dummies.

Finally: If you've done all the above and you still need more drive and hunt in the dog, get her on game early — and don't worry about control for now. Allow some chasing of birds at the flush (they will fly away and the chase will end). Try to avoid flushing and chasing of ground game (this can go on for some time and is so reinforcing for a dog, it will be hard to stop later). We will talk about introductions to game in the sequel to this book. But you don't need to know much, at this point, to implement it — because the teaching is happening between the game and the dog. Not *you* — *you* are just providing the opportunities for the game to teach the dog.

If you are going to attempt what is described in this last paragraph, or if you live in North America, do have a read of the next section. This illustrates the idea of an early introduction to game, taken to an extreme — and the pitfalls of this approach, if you want to train without force.

EARLY INTRODUCTION TO GAME – A WARNING!

In some countries (including North America), the approach is to prioritise the dog's hunting ability above all else. The dog is introduced to game from day one (even as a little puppy) and is encouraged to chase dizzied pigeons and even to catch them, after their wings have been clipped. All this is seen as part of developing drive. Independence is prized, because it is seen to be related to hunting confidently and far with drive — covering the vast expanses of land that are involved in North American tests and trials.

Dogs are not involved in much training that includes the handler, other than some simple puppy retrieves — perhaps. They are not even taught to sit. They are just exposed to birds and their pointing instinct is developed.

Then, suddenly — usually towards the end of the dog's first year — the dog is 'broke'. These days, this means they are introduced to the e-collar and conditioned to it. They are taught to 'whoa' on point (to hold a point until told). They are also force-fetched, and the recall is conditioned using the e-collar.

Since the aversive nature of the e-collar means it can be dialled up in intensity to the point where it reaches even the most hunting-crazy dog, it can be relied upon to force any dog to respond to commands (they are not 'cues', in this world).

It is almost impossible to imagine this approach working without an e-collar: Installing such an over-whelming desire to run and hunt in a young dog, getting her addicted to finding game, not being particularly bothered about teaching her to pay attention to her handler — and then *not* having an e-collar to force her to comply with commands, is a surefire way to create an out-of-control dog. In fact, if we were told to come up with a training recipe for creating an out-of-control dog, we couldn't do a better job than this one!

So, if you are in a country whose traditional training methods involve training like this, you will need to question and think carefully about the methods you may encounter at your local training organisations or chapters — or sessions with 'pros'. You may already have decided not to go along with the punitive methods which occur when the dog is force-fetched or broke, maybe leaving the classes at that point. But you might not have realised that you also need to question the approach which precedes this — allowing the young dog to chase game, to run far and wide and out of contact with you, to become ever more independent. Keep in mind that all those other dogs you see around you at training seminars, will be broke at some point and forced to comply with their handlers. *Yours will not be.* Your ability to retain control over your dog will rely on natural biddability, desire to please, engagement, gradually increased 'distractions', successful prevention, the strength of your relationship, and a history of positive reinforcement.

Make your training choices with this awareness in mind. Because you may need to make very different choices to a traditional handler *from the start* — even before the use of aversives has entered the picture — and perhaps to model your training more on the approach which is taken in countries where e-collars are not routinely used.

This is not the place to do the hard-sell on why not to use an e-collar. But, I do want to make one point: When breeders are producing dogs for use in an e-collar training system, they can afford to breed ever harder-hunting dogs. Breeders have little need to select for biddability or handler focus, if dogs are to be trained using an e-collar. They can go all-out towards out-of-control dogs in a bid to achieve the widest-ranging, most independent dogs possible. Why? Because *any dog can be forced to comply*. She need not have much biddability or handler focus. She need not have much desire to cooperate or engage with the handler. To be successfully trained, she only needs to understand how to turn off pain ('pressure').

What's wrong with this? The e-collar becomes intrinsic to the training. The system becomes a self-perpetuating vicious circle, with e-collars considered necessary and justified, because 'these dogs can't be trained without one'. Forgetting that the very reason for this, is that they have been bred — for generations — only to be trained using one!

On the other hand, when dogs are bred for a system which does not use e-collars, then biddability, handler-focus and willingness-to-please *are* valued by breeders and *are* qualities which successful dogs will possess in buckets. They are things which *must* be brought-on and nurtured and selected for, in breeding programs — just as stylish hunting is.

In short: The training systems in place affect the breeding decisions that are made and the qualities which are selected for in dogs. This, in turn, affects the dogs that are produced and makes training methods seem inevitable — given those dogs. A vicious circle.

NEXT STEPS: THE REMOTE SIT WHILST QUARTERING

Once your basic quartering is going well, the next step is to import the remote sit into your hunting — ensuring you can stop the dog at any moment whilst hunting.

A hunting exercise — without any game present — when the judge requests a remote sit at any moment, is a very common exercise in working tests.

I cover the remote sit in the next section.

• • • • •

3.11

BEGINNING THE REMOTE SIT

The remote sit is the 'sit-at-a-distance' behaviour which all gundogs need. Here, you will cue your dog (with the 'sit' whistle cue) to stop and sit instantly, where she is. That means — whilst she is otherwise engaged and at a distance from you.

This behaviour is called for:

- on a retrieve, when stopping the dog to cast back, left or right
- for HPRs and spaniels, at the flush of game (it will become the sit-to-flush).

We can divide the remote sit into:

- stopping still (not chasing or moving)
- sitting.

It is useful to think of the remote sit in these two component parts, especially as the requirement (in UK trials) is that the dog is *steady* — not that the dog sits. Many experienced dogs abandon the sit and just stop still in a stand. However, we want to teach this with a sit to begin with — and to uphold that in training — since a sit is one step further away from running in.

If you live in North America and have a HPR breed (versatile dog or bird dog), you will need a remote stand instead of sit. This will become your 'whoa' cue for pointing and the position the dog remains in during the flush. I won't cover how to teach the stand as a position, here — but I would encourage you to explore competition obedience training, perhaps via the online Fenzi Dog Sports Academy — since the stand is a key obedience position. Once you have a reliable stand, you can follow the steps outlined here but with adjusting things for a stand instead of a sit. The following material is still relevant to your dog.

I'm going to show you two different methods for training the remote sit. I like both of them, and I use them alongside each other.

METHOD 1: REINFORCEMENT ZONE

Imagine someone throwing a tennis ball for a dog, over and over. When the owner raises her arm behind her head to throw the ball, the dog races out — to where she believes the ball is likely to come down. She doesn't hang out at the owner's feet when the owner raises her arm. Keep this idea in mind, as I explain the following.

The principle behind the reinforcement zone, is that the reinforcers always arrive at a distance from the handler. There is no need, then, for the dog to come back to you.

We're not going to use balls to begin with — we're going to use food.

PHASE 1

You need to train this exercise on a large area of tarmac or paving so that the dog can find the treat easily. If you throw treats into grass, the dog will spend a long time sniffing around to find treats (and sometimes never find them). You can start this indoors, to avoid the grass problem — but in order to achieve what you want to achieve (distance), you ideally will need more space.

You also need treats that can be thrown a good distance. This means that they have some weight to them. Cheddar cubes or frankfurter for example. Think about the colour of the ground and choose treats of a contrasting colour.

Before we get started, let's discuss where we are throwing the treats — and why. This is important: Treat delivery in clicker training often plays a part in the behaviours we are trying to train. Here, the treats are not thrown directly to the dog — they are thrown just *beyond* her. If the treats always appear just *behind her*, we will give the dog less of a reason to come closer to us — and more of a reason to stay at a distance. If we throw treats to the dog, she will often launch forwards and up in an attempt to catch the treat. She will end up closer to us than where she sat — which we don't want. We don't want the dog even thinking about coming closer to us during this exercise.

1. *With an exaggerated overarm hand-gesture*, throw a treat out as far as you reasonably and consistently can, in the space available. Imagine you are throwing the treat as you would throw a basketball, from your shoulder. (This is going to morph into your raised 'stop' hand signal.)

2. Let the dog run to get the treat. Keep doing 1) and 2) — over and over.

3. Try to get each successive treat out there *before* the dog has decided to return to you. She will be running out to get the treat but, as soon as she has eaten it, you are throwing the next treat — always with that exaggerated overarm hand gesture just *before* you throw.

4. The dog starts to recognise this picture: She eats the treat, turns around and immediately sees you there with your hand raised to throw the next treat — she knows a treat is coming.

5. Continue throwing treats in the same way, with the dog seeing you throw each one. Ideally, the dog is going to start to pause expectantly at this moment. But it can take many, many reps of purely and simply throwing treats out before you get that momentary pause from the dog. Try to throw the treats to roughly the same location — within a metre or two. This location is the reinforcement zone!

6. Every now and again, *pause* when you raise your exaggerated overarm hand-gesture — before throwing the treat. What does the dog do when you pause? Does she freeze, expectantly, waiting at a distance — where she believes the treat will fall? (Like the dog that waits at a distance for the tennis ball to be thrown?) If the dog instead returns to you, keep going with more treat-throwing, as above. All we are trying to achieve here is a dog which will freeze expectantly, in the area of fall, for a treat.

7. If you have paused with raised overarm hand-gesture — about to throw a treat — and the dog freezes at a distance, looking at you expectantly, click that moment of stillness. It will just be a split second. Throw the treat out to just *beyond* the dog. (If the treats always appear behind her, we will give her less of a reason to come closer to us — and more of a reason to stay at a distance.) At this point, our marker moment is the dog standing

still, for a split second — at a distance from us. Keep repeating this, for several more reps.

8. Keep repeating this for several more reps, pausing more and more frequently and clicking the stillness each time the dog is still. Continue until you pause each time and she is still each time. Click her stillness before throwing each treat. (If you have a pointing breed and live in North America, you can stop this exercise here because you don't need steps 9-12) — the sit — you have your remote stand. Attach the cue you will use ('whoa') by giving it just before the dog is still.)

9. Now we just need to get the sit in. This is the easiest part, since we already have the dog still and at a distance from us. Do as previously: Raise your arm as if to throw a treat. Wait for the dog to stop still, expecting you to throw the treat any moment.

10. Peep your 'sit' whistle.

11. Click when the dog sits.

12. Throw the treat *beyond* the dog to the reinforcement zone.

What you have there should look like the beginnings of a remote sit.

The only limitations with this method are that our distance is restricted to how far we can throw treats and we have to train on tarmac or paving so the dog can easily find them.

We address both those limitations, with Phase 2.

REMOTE SIT — The reinforcement zone

1 USING AN OVERARM THROW, TOSS A TREAT OUT AS FAR AS YOU CONSISTENTLY CAN. THE THROW IS THE SAME MOVE YOU'D USE TO THROW A BASKETBALL OR NETBALL FROM YOUR SHOULDER.

2 THE DOG WILL RUN TO EAT THE TREAT.

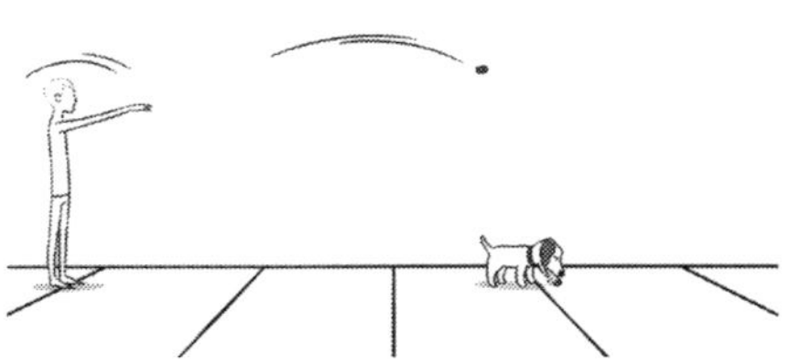

3 WHILST THE DOG IS EATING THE TREAT, THROW AN ADDITIONAL TREAT OUT TO ROUGHLY THE SAME LOCATION. YOU ARE NOT THROWING THEM TO THE DOG, BUT TO THE SAME ROUGH AREA ON THE GROUND AROUND THE DOG.

4 HE DOG WILL NEXT SPOT THAT TREAT, AND RUN TO EAT IT.

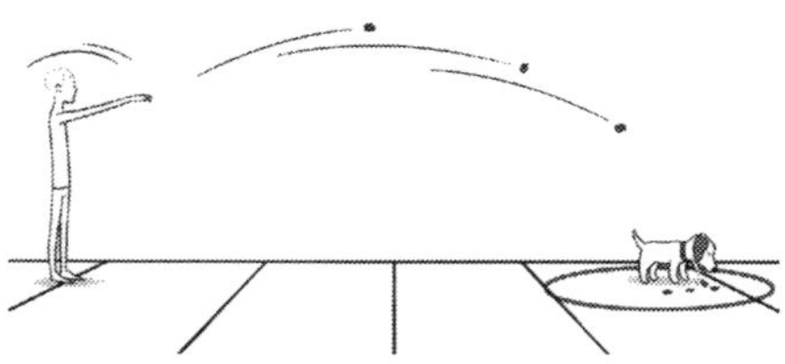

5 5CONTINUE TO THROW OUT TREATS, ONE AFTER ANOTHER, AS FAST AS NEEDED TO 'KEEP' THE DOG IN THE AREA OF FALL. USE THE SAME OVERARM GESTURE, EACH TIME. IF POSSIBLE, WAIT FOR THE DOG TO SEE YOU THROW EACH ONE.

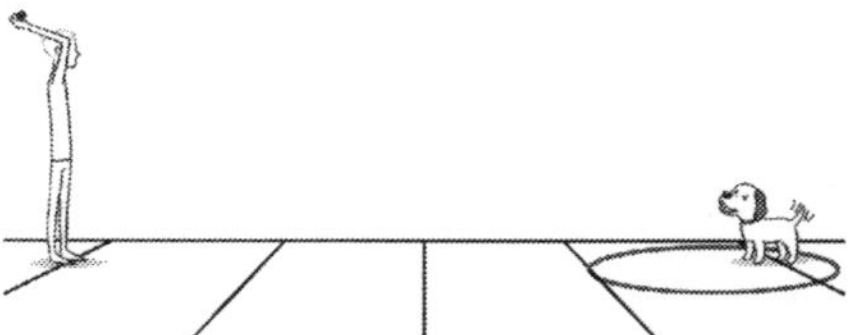

6 EVERY NOW AND THEN, RAISE YOUR HAND UP TO THROW THE NEXT TREAT - AND PAUSE. SEE WHAT THE DOG DOES. IF THE DOG RETURNS TO YOU, CONTINUE AS YOU HAVE BEEN FOR LONGER - KEEP THROWING TREATS. IF THE DOG STOPS STILL AT A DISTANCE, EXPECTING THE TREAT...

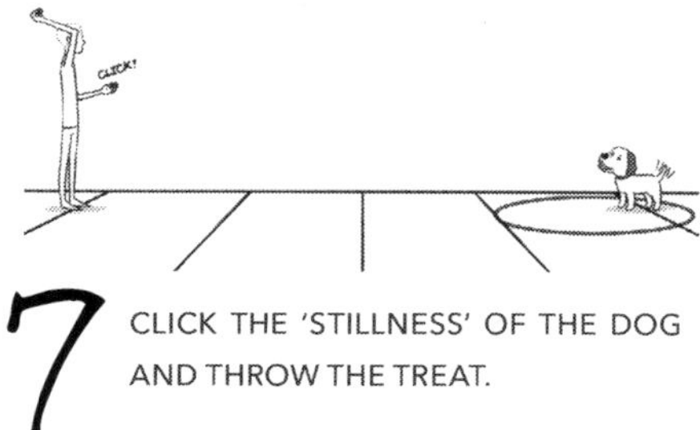

7 CLICK THE 'STILLNESS' OF THE DOG AND THROW THE TREAT.

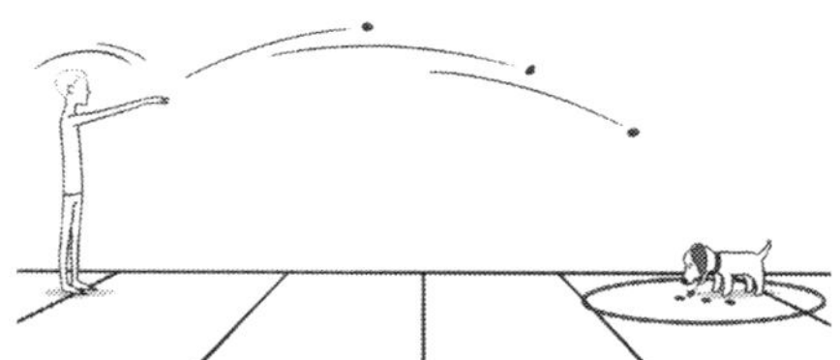

8 CONTINUE THROWING A FEW MORE TREATS AS BEFORE (WITHOUT PAUSING). EVERY 3-4 TREATS, PAUSE - AND CLICK THE STILLNESS. AS THE DOG IS ABLE TO BE SUCCESSFUL AT THIS, MOVE TO CLICKING THAT STILLNESS EVERY TIME, BEFORE YOU THROW.

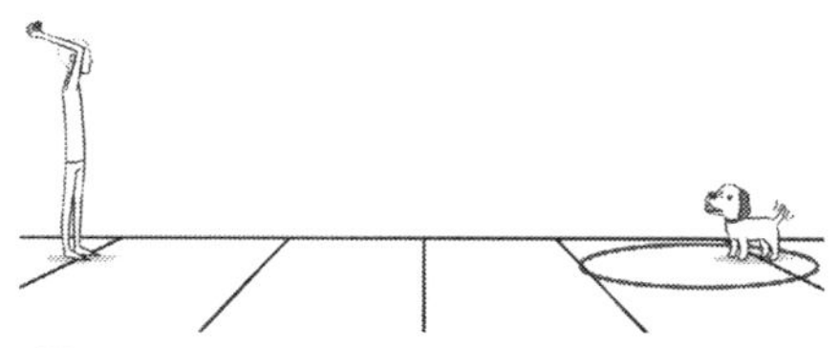

9 WHEN YOU ARE CONSISTENTLY GETTING A 'STILL' DOG - WHICH YOU ARE CLICKING BEFORE THROWING THE TREAT - THEN YOU CAN PUT THE SIT WHISTLE IN. TO DO THIS, RAISE YOUR HAND AS USUAL - YOUR DOG WILL BECOME STILL.

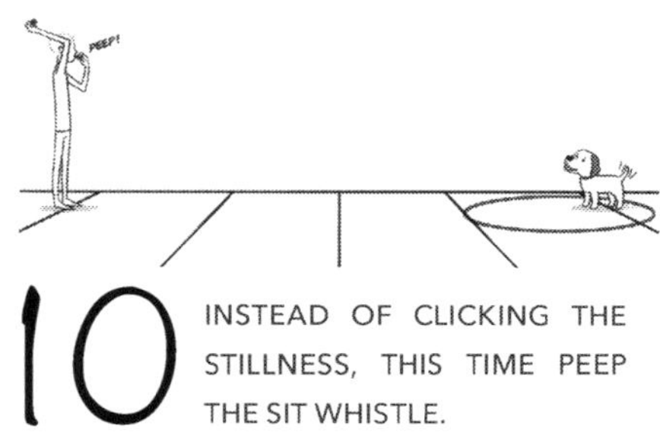

10 INSTEAD OF CLICKING THE STILLNESS, THIS TIME PEEP THE SIT WHISTLE.

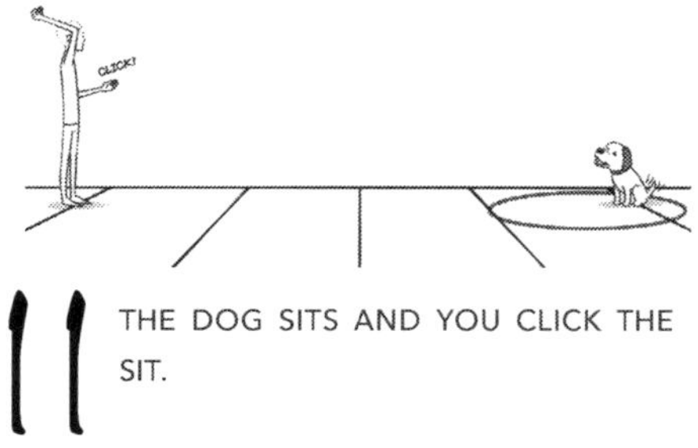

11 THE DOG SITS AND YOU CLICK THE SIT.

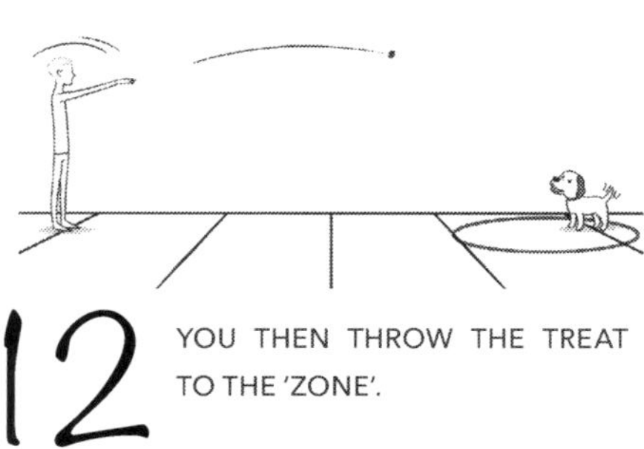

12 YOU THEN THROW THE TREAT TO THE 'ZONE'.

PHASE 2

This phase is only going to be possible if your dog finds balls reinforcing. If she doesn't find an ordinary tennis ball reinforcing, you can try a rabbit-fur-covered ball — which many dogs prefer. Some dogs don't find *any* balls that reinforcing. Don't worry if that's the case: These dogs can move on to the 'restrained dog' exercise, below.

For Phase 2, you will need a ball and a tennis ball thrower — one of those long plastic arms which will enable you to throw balls a good distance.

Since dogs can find tennis balls in grass, we can now start training in fields and away from tarmac and paving.

This exercise is the same as Phase 1, but we can throw the reinforcer much further than a treat and thereby achieve much greater distance.

1. Repeatedly throw freebies for your dog, raising the tennis ball thrower first into that overarm throwing position and pausing with your arm back — about to throw — before throwing the ball out as far as you can consistently throw it. The dog will race out and get the ball. (We are less interested in what happens after the dog gets the ball — since this exercise is all about the remote sit. But you should have a reliable clicker retrieve by this point — see Section 3.6 — so you can expect to get the ball delivered back to hand for the next rep.)

2. Raise the tennis ball thrower and pause to see if the dog runs out expectantly and then stops and looks at you. Click the stillness and throw the ball *beyond* where she stops (if possible). Repeat this many times. (If the dog does not run out expectantly, try some fake throws — moves of the thrower which will cause the dog to run out to a distance. Be aware that dogs get very clever at knowing when you are going to do a real throw and when a fake

The handler has blown the sit whistle and the dog has sat. The handler is clicking the clicker in her left hand. Note that the tennis ball thrower is hidden behind her back at this point. If the dog had not sat to the whistle, the handler would have raised the thrower and made some 'fake' throwing movements to cause the dog to stop still - before re-cuing the Sit.

After the click, the handler produces the tennis ball thrower and throws the ball just beyond where the dog sat. The dog can stand up at the click - since the click ends the behaviour.

one!) (Again, if you live in North America and have a pointing breed, you can stop here with a remote stand. Attach the cue you will use ('whoa') by giving it just before the dog is still.)

3. Add the sit. You have a dog running out to hang around in the reinforcement zone when you raise your thrower into the overarm throwing position and stopping still to wait for you to throw it, so it is now very easy to add the sit. Give your 'sit' whistle cue when she stops still. Click the sit, and again throw the ball out beyond where the dog sits. (If your dog does not sit to the whistle, give the verbal cue.)

If your dog likes balls, the tennis ball chucker enables you to get considerable distance and a very fast response!

PHASE 3

This phase is about becoming a sneaky tennis ball thrower!

So far, we have a great remote sit when we are having a formal training session. The dog prepares herself for what we are doing and knows which exercise we are working on.

But things aren't going to work like this in real life, when the dog needs to be stopped on a retrieve or when she has flushed game. To get things slightly more realistic, we need to get our remote sit working unexpectedly — at any moment of our choosing.

1. Wander around an enclosed field, ignoring your dog. Try to secrete the tennis ball thrower on your person — at least holding it behind your back. (You can purchase half-size tennis ball throwers if this makes hiding it easier — although they can't throw as far.)

2. When your dog is looking away from you or slightly distracted, peep your 'sit' whistle (or give your 'whoa' cue) and see if you get a response to the cue. If not, follow it up with the raised tennis ball thrower, since it is often *the sight of this raised behind you* which will really stop your dog at a distance at this stage of training. You can even do a few waggles of it in the air, faking a throw, if you need to help the dog stay out there. Click the sit (or stand, if training a 'whoa') and throw the ball *beyond the dog.*

3. If your dog won't leave you alone after the ball retrieve, put it in your bag or inside your coat, ignore the dog and keep walking. Get it out sneakily for the next rep when the dog is a bit distracted.

4. As your dog improves, give the cue whilst she is increasingly more distracted and even whilst she is running somewhere with intent — but not around game or on a retrieve just yet.

METHOD 2: RESTRAINED DOG

You can use this method alongside the reinforcement zone above, doing both simultaneously. Again, it's going to work best if the dog can easily find the treat on the ground — but since the dog is tied up and you will be throwing treats only within the length of the dog's leash, you can do this on short grass from the start.

PHASE 1

1. Tie the dog up to something secure — a fence post, a floodlight or a tree. (If your dog does not like being tied up to something, ask a helper to hold her on-leash. The helper should imagine that her feet are superglued to the ground and should resist being towed by the dog back towards you.)

2. Stand immediately in front of the dog.

3. Give your 'sit' whistle (or 'whoa' cue). Click the sit (or stand) and throw the treat just behind the dog, ensuring she can reach it within the length of her leash. (If you accidentally throw the treat out of reach of the dog, go and get it and throw it again.) That is the end of the first rep, which has you standing immediately in front of the dog.

4. If that was successful, take one step backwards away from the dog. Give your 'sit' whistle and repeat as above.

5. If that was successful, take another step back. Give your cue and repeat as above.

6. Continue, retreating further back from the dog each time you are successful. If you cannot throw the treat all the way back to the dog accurately when the distance is considerable, you should still give the cue from a distance, then click the behaviour when it occurs — and walk up to the dog to throw the treat whilst you are closer to her. Then walk back away to your original position again, for the next rep.The bit you need to practise is the dog hearing and responding to the cue *whilst you are at a distance*. If you have a helper holding the dog, they cannot give the dog the treat (alas!) — as convenient as that would be — or the dog will focus on the helper instead of focussing on the handler. If we are preparing the dog for the scenario of the handler being at a distance, we need the dog to remain focussed on the handler and the helper to do nothing more than hold the leash.

PHASE 2

Replace the regular leash with your long-line. If you were tying the dog up in Phase 1, you will now need a helper to hold the long-line because we need to get things mobile.

1. Ask your helper to hold the long-line at a couple of metres length but keep it slack and follow the dog around — until the cue. The helper should allow the long-line to flow through her hands to some degree, before the cue occurs — the idea is to give the dog the sense of being *free* and off-leash.

2. When the 'sit' whistle (or 'whoa') occurs, the helper should use the long-line to prevent the dog from moving off that spot — until she sits (or stands, if a 'whoa'). (The helper should look at the spot on the ground where the dog was when the cue occurred — her job is to ensure the dog does not leave that spot, through restraint.) The helper uses the long-line to immobilise the dog, so she cannot continue to sniff and reinforce herself for ignoring the handler. But it is not the helper's responsibility to ensure the dog responds — that's down to the handler. If the dog does not respond, the *handler* ap-

proaches closer and either gives a hand-signal or even uses a food lure to achieve the behaviour — then clicks and throws the treat *beyond the dog*. (The helper, again, should only deal with the long-line and should not interact with the dog in any way.)

3. When the dog responds, click and throw a treat *beyond the dog*. If you cannot throw that far, walk up closer to the dog to throw the treat — and then retreat back to your original position. Now the dog is not tied up, you don't need to worry about her not being able to reach the treat due to the leash — after the click, the helper should release the long-line to allow the dog to run and get the treat.

4. Between reps, if the dog tries to decrease the distance — by attempting to return to the handler — the helper should use the long-line to prevent that gently. (Otherwise the dog ends up back at the handler all the time and we don't get to practise the distance variable very much.) If the dog wants to sniff around and explore *away* from the handler, the helper will permit that and keep the line loose — until the cue occurs.

As you practise this, you will find that the helper needs to touch the long-line less and less frequently — until the dog is responding on the spot.

PHASE 3

Only move onto this stage when Phase 2 is working really well, with the dog responding immediately to the cue and the helper rarely needing to restrain the dog. There is no helper needed here.

1. Take a walk around an enclosed field with your dog trailing the long-line.

2. Peep your sit whistle (or give your 'whoa' cue), choosing easier moments at first — when the dog looks at you anyway, when she is not too far away

from you, when she is relatively still or not running fast, or when she is not too distracted.

3. Praise continuously when the dog responds — and walk towards her, still praising. The dog should remain in a stay. Reinforce with a jackpot (several treats, one after another) directly to the dog's mouth and release the dog with your release word ('ok'). (NB: If you are in North America with a pointing breed and you want to release your dog with a gentle touch to the head — as is conventional in some circles — this is where you would introduce that, along with your verbal 'ok'.)

4. If the dog does not respond to the cue, run up to her. This is *not* to intimidate her in any way (so keep that in mind as you run and watch her response). Instead, running to the dog is to prevent her from continuing to access environmental reinforcers (i.e. by sniffing) after your cue — thereby reinforcing herself for ignoring it. Your goal is to get to her as soon as you see that she is going to ignore the cue. Sprint! Use the long-line she is trailing to immobilise her as soon as it's within your reach — to prevent her from sniffing around. When you reach her, use a hand-signal or even food lure to achieve the position you want. Click, and throw a treat out behind her. Remember that to associate the cue (whether whistle or 'whoa' cue) with the behaviour, we need to pair these two things together: Cue and response. We don't want an age of sniffing around between the cue and the response. Hence you running to the dog!

This phase can take a while — because you are competing against environmental reinforcers and because the dog is at a distance from you. Keep going with it until the behaviour is reliable.

By this point, you should be able to give your cue and have the dog respond whilst she is free-running. This should be reliable even when it happens unexpectedly, and on the first rep of the session.

REMOTE SIT — The restrained dog exercise

1 YOU CAN BEGIN EVEN CLOSER THAN THIS - IMMEDIATELY IN FRONT OF THE DOG, FOR EXAMPLE. THE HANDLER GIVES THE SIT WHISTLE CUE AND THE DOG SITS. THE HANDLER CLICKS.

2 THE HANDLER APPROACHES THE DOG TO DELIVER THE TREAT. IF YOU ARE CLOSE ENOUGH AND CAN THROW ACCURATELY, YOU CAN ALTERNATIVELY THROW THE TREAT.

3 THE HANDLER PLACES THE TREAT ON THE FLOOR, WITHIN THE RANGE PERMITTED BY THE LEASH. THIS CAUSES THE DOG TO STAND UP AND SNIFF FOR THE TREAT(S).

4 WHILST THE DOG IS SNIFFING FOR THE TREATS, THE HANDLER MAKES A HASTY RETREAT TO THE DISTANCE REQUIRED FOR THE NEXT REP.

(CONT...)

5 THE HANDLER WAITS FOR THE DOG TO STOP EATING AND SNIFFING, THEN GIVES THE SIT WHISTLE AGAIN - THIS TIME FROM FURTHER AWAY. YOU SHOULD PROGRESS AWAY VERY GRADUALLY: WE HAVE SKIPPED MANY STEPS IN THIS PHOTO SERIES.

6 THE DOG SITS AND THE HANDLER CLICKS.

7 THE HANDLER APPROACHES AGAIN, TO DELIVER A TREAT.

8 THE HANDLER DELIVERS THE TREAT TO THE FLOOR, SO THE DOG STANDS UP TO EAT IT.

9 THE HANDLER RETREATS WHILST THE DOG IS EATING THE TREATS, TO THE DISTANCE REQUIRED FOR THE NEXT REP. AGAIN, YOU WILL NOT INCREASE DISTANCE THIS RAPIDLY.

THE END OF THE BEGINNING

The material we've covered to this point provides you with an essential set of basic skills you can take forwards to the next stage of training. The next stage of training is where we really start to teach the interesting material: Contact with game, flushing, steadiness, pointing for HPRs, sit-to-flush for HPRs and spaniels, heelwork under high distractions and blind retrieves with confidence. And lots of work on handling, casting and lining.

Let's recap on the skills we want a dog to have as we come to the end of 'basics'. All these skills should be pretty functional in an outdoors or rural environment:

- basic heelwork, on and off-leash

- recall cues, verbal and whistle
- sit-at-my-side behaviour, on verbal cue but also when you stop walking
- default sit
- basic retrieve to hand
- sit-stay, one to two minutes
- marked retrieves in light and medium cover, 50-80 yards for retrievers and HPRs and 30-40 yards for spaniels
- memory retrieves, with distance being ever-increased
- basic hunting/quartering away from game, with willingness to get out and explore yet under control (HPRs and spaniels)
- remote sit.

There is a lot you can do with these skills and many entry-level competitions and assessments you can now participate in — so get out there and enjoy training and working your dogs!

LIST OF ILLUSTRATIONS

ABOUT THE AUTHOR

Jo Laurens, MA, AdipCBM, PCBC-A, APDT(UK), CAP2, CBATI, is a trainer and behaviourist who specialises in force-free gundog training. She is a full assessor/instructor with The Gundog Club and enjoys helping owners retain a high degree of control over their dogs in 'realistic' rural environments. Jo has worked her dogs on various shoots, both picking up and beating. She has competed successfully in HPR working tests, run in field trials, and gained the KC Working Gundog Certificate. She now owns and trains Labradors.

Jo offers various online training courses for gundogs - including courses on the clicker retrieve, gundog heelwork and training a reliable recall. She also offers in-person classes for general training and gundog training in Jersey, Channel Islands. Jo hosts the popular force-free gundog training podcast 'Hold the Line'. In 2006, Jo founded School for Dogs in Brighton, UK. She ran School for Dogs for almost ten years, before moving back home to Jersey. On her return to Jersey, Jo established DogWorks. Through DogWorks she offers KC Good Citizen classes, co-operative care classes, behavioural consultations and BAT sessions.

Jo's interest in teaching others about force-free gundog training stems from her experiences with her own dogs when she began competing. These early efforts consisted largely of stumbling around in the dark, being quite confused, and trying to piece a lot of things together from diverse sources. She noticed a lack of any systematic training programme which is force-free.

Jo is also a published and produced playwright and a BACP accredited psychodynamic counsellor and group therapist. She originally studied French horn at the Guildhall School of Music and Drama in London.

For more information, see the websites dogworks.org.uk and galodygundogs.com

JOIN US ONLINE

SOCIAL MEDIA CHANNELS:

- **the author**
    - facebook.com/DogWorksOrg
    - facebook.com/galody/
    - twitter.com/DogWorksOrg
- **Positive Gundogs group**
    - facebook.com/groups/243522802504931/
- **The Gundog Trust** — Graded Training Scheme
    - facebook.com/groups/1104633892962840

WEBSITES:

- **to find training resources and online courses** — dogworks.org.uk
- **to find out more about Jo and her dogs** — galodygundogs.com
- **The Gundog Club** — thegundogclub.co.uk

PODCAST - HOLD THE LINE:

- **iTunes** — podcasts.apple.com/us/podcast/hold-the-line
- **Stitcher** — stitcher.com/podcast/jo-laurens/hold-the-line
- **Spotify** — spotify:show:4RoPIUk2zo1rNziDrkx1Np